ELITE ATTACK FORCES

TWO GREAT NAVAL BATTLES of WORLD WAR II

ELITE ATTACK FORCES

TWO GREAT NAVAL BATTLES of WORLD WAR II

Angus Konstam and
Chris Henry

CHARTWELL
BOOKS, INC.

This edition published by 2007 by

CHARTWELL BOOKS, INC.
A Division of
BOOK SALES, INC.
114 Northfield Avenue
Edison, New Jersey 08837

ISBN 10: 0-7858-2329-8
ISBN 13: 978-0-7858-2329-2

Previously published in the Spearhead series

Cataloging-in-Publication data is available from the Library of Congress

Printed in China through Printworks Int. Ltd

Acknowledgments

The photographs in the 'Hunt the *Bismarck*' section of this book are from the author's collection unless credited otherwise, while maps and colour material were provided by Jan Suermondt, as were those in 'Battle of the Coral Sea'. Photos in the latter were from the author's collection or the U.S. National Archives.

Note: Website information provided in the Reference section was correct when provided by the author. The publisher can accept no responsibility for this information becoming incorrect.

PREVIOUS PAGE: Captain Philip Vian, commander of the destroyer flotilla which harassed the *Bismarck* during the night of May 26-27, 1941. *IWM*

RIGHT: The *Bismarck* was both graceful and a stable gun platform

CONTENTS

HUNT THE
BISMARCK
Angus Konstam

Introduction

The hunting of the German battleship *Bismarck* was one of the most dramatic episodes of the Second World War, one that pitted the finest warship in the world against a hastily assembled naval force, in a pursuit that took the combatants halfway across the Atlantic and back. Few episodes in naval history have caught the public imagination in such a way, possibly because the stakes for both sides were so high. The pursuit of the *Bismarck* involved cunning, drama, tragedy, fortune and skill in equal measure, and saw the destruction of two of the most prestigious warships afloat.

The author C.S. Forester put it more colorfully in his book *Hunting the Bismarck*, which was later made into the movie *Sink the Bismarck*:

> This is a story of the most desperate chances, of the loftiest patriotism and of the highest professional skills, of a gamble for the domination of the world in which human lives are the stakes on the green gaming table of the ocean. At the heart was a pursuit without precedent in the history of navies; there were battles fought in which the defeated gained as much glory as the victors, and in which the most unpredictable bad luck was counterbalanced by miraculous good fortune. For six days that pursuit lasted, days of unrelenting storm, of tossing grey seas and lowering clouds, without a single ray of sunshine to lighten the setting of the backdrop of tragedy. Those actors in the tragedy who played their part at sea did so to the unceasing accompaniment of shrieking wind, leaping waves, flying spray, and bitter cold. (C.S. Forester, 1959)

The pursuit took place at a desperate time for Britain. She had been at war for over a year and a half, and her navy was stretched to the limit. For the past year she had fought on alone, following the surrender of France in the spring of 1940. The fall of France also gave the Germans access to the Channel ports, and to the substantial French naval ports and dockyards of Cherbourg, Brest and St. Nazaire. The French capitulation led to the destruction of the French fleet in the Mediterranean, as its commanders refused to agree to British demands to disarm or sail into internment. At sea, German raiders had broken out and played havoc on Allied shipping in the Atlantic and even as far afield as the Indian Ocean. The German pocket battleship *Graf Spee* had been cornered and forced to scuttle herself, but elsewhere, victories were scarce. The Italians had entered the war, pinning down British naval resources in the Mediterranean. Although Admiral Cunningham's Mediterranean Fleet had begun to win control of the Mediterranean, the German invasion of Greece and the relocation of the Luftwaffe's dive-bomber wings to the area threatened to tip the strategic balance in favor of the Axis powers. The whole strategic situation was gloom enough, without the disturbing reports that the German battleship *Bismarck* was being prepared for sea.

When she entered service in August 1940, she became a latent threat to British naval supremacy. During the nine months she spent conducting sea trials, training exercises and preparing for operational duties she became the focus of interest for British Naval Intelligence, who tried by every possible means to determine what the Germans planned to do with their new battleship. Spies were recruited in the *Bismarck*'s home port of Gotenhafen (now Gdansk in Poland) and reconnaissance flights were stepped up over the Baltic. Other German capital ships sortied into the Atlantic, and the U-boat threat increased, but the *Bismarck* remained the most serious threat to the British Home Fleet; what Forester described as "the largest, most dangerous, the most modern ship of war yet launched." No single battleship in the Royal Navy could

ABOVE: When the *Bismarck* was launched in Hamburg on February 14, 1939, she was regarded as the most powerful warship in the world. *IWM*

LEFT: *Bismarck* fitting out after launching. *Chris Ellis Collection*

engage her on equal terms. Hunting her down and destroying her would take all the available resources of the Home Fleet, and would test the resolve of its commander and his sailors to the limit. These seamen knew this, and viewed the coming clash with a mixture of foreboding and anticipation. In Scapa Flow, sailors hummed a reworking of a popular current ditty:

We'll all get promotion,
This side of the Ocean,
When we've sunk the old Bismarck and all.

The German battleship had become the new bogeyman for the sailors of the Royal Navy. For the most part the British fleet was committed to a battle for control of both the Atlantic and the Mediterranean, and its last strategic reserve was Admiral Tovey's Home Fleet at anchor in Scapa Flow. This small squadron of battleships and battlecruisers had already chased the *Scharnhorst* and *Gneisenau* during their own Atlantic sortie in January 1941. Tovey and his officers learned from their failure to bring the two battlecruisers to bay, and this time the Admiral was prepared to commit everything to the hunt. After all, the reputation of the Royal Navy was at stake. Should the *Bismarck* manage to cause havoc in the Atlantic, long-held assumptions about Britain's naval prowess would be called into question, and the loss of national prestige might have a grave impact on the course of the war. In port, the *Bismarck* was a moral and physical threat to British seapower. Loosed in the oceans, she became a mortal threat to a country whose continued survival depended on her control of the seas. The campaign that followed, codenamed Operation Rheinübung by the Kriegsmarine (the German Navy), would have a decisive impact on the war at sea. For all its drama, the real importance of the sortie of the *Bismarck* was that apart from the bitterly fought, drawn-out U-boat campaign, it represented the gravest naval threat the Royal Navy would face during six long years of war at sea.

ABOVE RIGHT: Admiral Lütjens inspecting the crew of the *Prinz Eugen* in Gotenhafen. Captain Brinkmann of the *Prinz Eugen* is on the Admiral's left-hand side. *MNF*

FAR RIGHT: *Prinz Eugen* photographed at anchor in Gotenhafen, shortly before she sailed in company with the *Bismarck*. *MNF*

RIGHT AND ABOVE RIGHT: The battlecruiser *Scharnhorst* was to rendezvous with the *Bismarck* in mid-Atlantic, but she was put out of action shortly before Operation Rheinübung was scheduled to start. The U-boat (RIGHT) is Günther Prien's *U-47* returning to Germany after sinking the *Royal Oak* at Scapa Flow, October 1940. *Chris Ellis Collection*

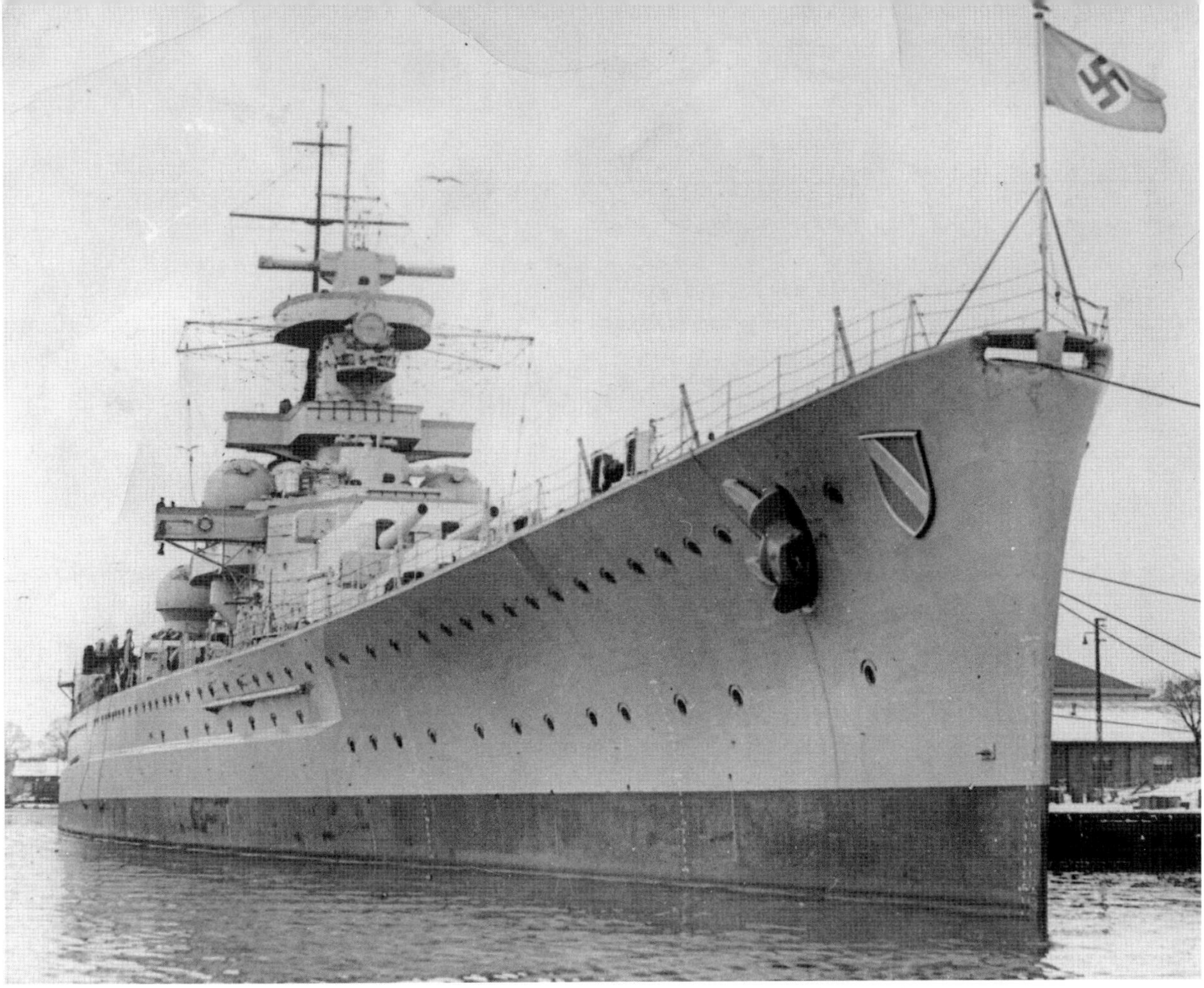

Context

For the British, the sortie of the *Bismarck* could hardly have come at a worse time. The Royal Navy was stretched to its limit, fighting a two-front naval war in the Mediterranean and in the Atlantic. Since the escort vessels ordered when the war began had still to enter service, valuable destroyers and cruisers had to guard Britain's vital transatlantic convoys from attack. The threat of attack from German surface raiders meant that battleships and even aircraft carriers were needed to provide additional protection for convoys. Britain's Royal Air Force had emerged victorious in the Battle of Britain, fought in the skies over southern England in the summer of 1940, and for the moment the threat of German invasion had receded. There was little respite, as the entrance of Italy into the war in June 1940 meant that the British Mediterranean fleet was immediately locked in a battle for naval supremacy. During the ten months that followed, the Royal Navy slowly gained the upper hand over the Italian "Supermarina", launching a dramatic carrier attack on the Italian fleet at Taranto in November 1940, and defeating the Italians at sea off Matapan in March 1941. This generally favorable situation changed in April, when the Germans invaded Yugoslavia and Greece. Greece was overrun within weeks, and the Royal Navy was forced to evacuate the army to the relative safety of Crete. Each day brought fresh losses and disasters in the Mediterranean, and German air superiority meant that Admiral Cunningham's fleet appeared on the brink of defeat.

In the Atlantic, the German capture of Norway in the spring of 1940 gave the Germans deep-water harbors and airbases within easy reach of the Atlantic. The collapse of France in May and June of 1940 was an even greater disaster, as the Germans could threaten Britain with invasion. Although this threat passed, the capture of France still gave the Germans a string of vital ports in Brittany. For the U-boats based in St. Nazaire and Brest, transit time to the hunting grounds in the mid-Atlantic was half that from Kiel or Wilhelmshaven. They also provided useful forward bases for the surface fleet.

German naval strategy was outlined by the Kriegsmarine's Operations Department (known as the Seekriegsleitung) as early as August 31, 1939. In its Directive Number 1, the Seekriegsleitung declared: "The Kriegsmarine is to carry out commerce warfare, and it will be aimed primarily against England". This meant destroying Britain's vital merchant shipping lifelines. Without fuel for her ships and aircraft, food for her population and armed forces or steel for her navy, Britain would be brought to her knees. If her maritime links overseas were severed, Britain would be unable to wage war, or defend her global possessions. In the First World War, German U-boats had almost succeeded in severing this maritime artery. The Kriegsmarine's commander-in-chief, Grand Admiral Raeder, was determined that this time Germany would succeed.

While the growing U-boat fleet of Admiral Karl Dönitz was to play a major part in this commerce warfare, the German surface fleet also had an important role. The first attempt to use a German capital ship to engage enemy merchant shipping came in September 1939, when the German pocket battleship *Graf Spee* sunk a British merchantman off the coast of Brazil. The *Graf Spee* continued her rampage in the Indian Ocean and the South Atlantic for ten weeks until a British cruiser force tracked her down. On January 22, 1941 Admiral Lütjens put to sea a force of two battlecruisers, *Scharnhorst* and *Gneisenau*. In an operation code-named Operation Berlin, Lütjens broke out into the Atlantic through the gap between Iceland and Greenland, then spent two months cruising the mid-Atlantic, sinking a total of 22 British ships, with a combined tonnage of 116,000 tons. His safe return to Brest on March 22 was seen as confirmation that the Kriegsmarine had the ability to roam the Atlantic at will, as her ships were faster than their British counterparts. Within ten days, plans for a fresh sortie had been sown. This time, the Germans would be able to use the *Bismarck*.

On April 2, 1941 Generaladmiral Otto Schniewind, Chief of Staff of the Seekriegsleitung, issued a directive with the approval of Grand Admiral Raeder. He stated the strategic importance of any capital ship sortie into the Atlantic, and outlined the possible nature of such a sortie and its objectives. This vital document is worth quoting in detail, as it contains the rationale behind Operation Rheinübung (Rhine Exercise), and lists the operational conditions in which the Fleet Commander could operate.

> During last winter the conduct of the war was fundamentally in accord with the directives of the Seekriegsleitung ... and closed with the first extended battleship operation in the open Atlantic. Besides achieving important tactical results, this battleship operation shows what important strategic effects similar sorties could have. They would reach beyond the immediate area of operations too of the theaters of war. The goal of the war at sea must be to maintain and increase these effects and repeating such operations as often as possible.
>
> We must not lose sight of the fact that the decisive objective in a struggle with England is to destroy her trade. This can be most effectively accomplished in the North Atlantic were all her supply lines converge, and where, even in the case of disruption in more distant areas, supplies can still get through by the direct route from North America.
>
> Gaining command of the sea in the North Atlantic is the best solution to this problem,

ABOVE LEFT: The *Bismarck* was a graceful warship, and her wide beam made her a particularly stable gun platform. *IWM*

LEFT: German troops in Norway. The successful invasion of Denmark and Norway provided the Germans with good harbors for their warships, which they made extensive use of; airfields, which improved the range of their offensive and defensive air assets; and control of the entrance and exit to the Baltic. *Chris Ellis Collection*

but this is not possible with the forces that at this moment we can commit it to this purpose, and given the constraint that we must preserve her numerically inferior forces. Nevertheless, we must strive for local and temporary command of the sea in this area and gradually, methodically, and systematically extend it.

During the first battleship operation in the Atlantic, the enemy was always able to deploy one battleship against us and protect both of its main supply routes. However, it became clear that providing this defence of his convoys brought him to the limit of the possibilities open to him, and the only way you could significantly strengthen his escort forces is by weakening areas important to him or by reducing convoy sailings.

As soon as the two battleships of the *Bismarck*-class are ready for deployment, we will be able to seek engagement with forces escorting enemy convoys and, when they have been eliminated, destroy the convoy itself. As of now, we cannot follow that course, but it would soon be possible, as an intermediate step, for us to use the battleship *Bismarck* to distract the hostile escorting forces, in order to enable the other units engaged to operate against the convoy itself. In the beginning, we will have the advantage of surprise because some other ships involved will be making their first appearance, and, based on his experience of the previous battleship operations, the enemy will assume that one battleship will be enough to defend a convoy.

At the earliest possible date, which it is hoped will be during the new moon period of April, the *Bismarck* and the *Prinz Eugen*, led by the fleet Commander, ought to be deployed as commerce raiders in the Atlantic. At a time that will depend on the completion of the repairs she is currently undergoing, *Gneisenau* will also be sent into the Atlantic.

The lessons learned in the last battleship operation indicate that the *Gneisenau* should join up with the *Bismarck* group, but a diversionary sweep by the *Gneisenau* in the area between Cape Verde and the Azores may be planned before that happens. The heavy cruiser *Prinz Eugen* is to spend most of her time oper-

ABOVE: During Rheinübung Lütjens was supposed to receive sighting reports from U-boats stationed in mid-Atlantic. Pictured here is the Type VII-B U-boat *U-48*, part of the 7th U-Boat Flotilla based at St. Nazaire. *Chris Ellis Collection*

ABOVE RIGHT: Admiral Günther Lütjens was an experienced senior commander, but he realized that the odds against him were probably too great to guarantee success. *IWM*

RIGHT: Generaladmiral Otto Schniewind's directive of April 2, 1941 outlined a plan that involved *Gneisenau* (seen here) joining forces with *Prinz Eugen* and *Bismarck*. *Chris Ellis Collection*

ating tactically with the *Bismarck* or with the *Bismarck* and *Gneisenau*. In contrast to previous directives to the *Gneisenau–Scharnhorst* task force, it is the mission of this task force to also attack escorted convoys. However, the objective of the battleship *Bismarck* should not be to defeat in an all-out engagement enemies of equal strength, but to tie them down in a delaying action, preserving her own combat capability as much as possible, so allowing other ships to attack the merchant vessels in the convoy. The primary mission of this operation also is the destruction of their enemy's merchant shipping; enemy warships will be engaged only when that objective makes it necessary and can be done without excessive risk.

The operational area will be defined as the entire North Atlantic north of the equator, with the exception of the territorial waters of neutral states. The Group Command has operational control and there are zones. The Fleet Commander has control at sea.

(Quoted from Müllenheim-Rechberg, 1980)

Admiral Lütjens was called to Berlin to discuss the operation, and detailed plans were developed over the next few weeks. The project was given the codename

Operation Rheinübung. Raeder and Lütjens thought they would have three capital ships and a heavy cruiser at their disposal; *Bismarck, Scharnhorst, Gneisenau* and the *Prinz Eugen.* The two battlecruisers were still in the French ports, while the battleship and heavy cruiser were in the Baltic. As proposed by the Seekriegsleitung the two forces would unite in mid-Atlantic, creating a powerful force. It was still an extremely risky undertaking, as it involved sending the bulk of the German surface fleet into hostile waters, where it would be unsupported by aircraft, U-boats or escort vessels. Regardless of the lofty aims of the Seekriegsleitung, any attempt to gain even temporary control of the Atlantic was pure fantasy. Any damage to a German capital ship in mid-Atlantic would invite her destruction. To this end Lütjens was ordered to preserve the combat capability of his ships, engaging enemy warships only when such an encounter was unavoidable in order to destroy a convoy. Raeder added; "It would be a mistake to risk a heavy engagement for limited and perhaps uncertain results." This strategy of limited risk was an ambiguous one, as it was unclear when Lütjens should press an advantage by seeking action, and when he should avoid a fight.

Then, on April 6, 1941, while in Brest, *Gneisenau* was attacked by a Royal Air Force Beaufort bomber. The plane was hit and her crew killed, but not before she had managed to drop her torpedo, which hit the *Gneisenau.* Four nights later she was hit during a second raid, this time by four bombs. The five hits meant the battlecruiser would be in dry dock until the end of the year. The *Scharnhorst* was already in refit, and it was estimated that the work would take until July. The German surface units available for Operation Rheinübung had been reduced to the *Bismarck* and the *Prinz Eugen.* Lütjens had originally planned to set sail on April 28, but when the Prinz Eugen was damaged by a magnetic mine the sortie was postponed. A faulty crane on the *Bismarck* caused another slight delay, so Lütjens selected a departure date in late-May, to take advantage of the new moon. He wanted to delay the sortie even longer, until the *Tirpitz* could sail with the *Bismarck.* The second German battleship was completing her shake-down trials in Gotenhafen, and would prove a valuable addition to Lütjens' squadron. However, Raeder refused to consider any further delay. The *Bismarck* would sail as planned, escorted by the *Prinz Eugen.*

On May 1, Adolf Hitler arrived in Gotenhafen to inspect the two ships. He was fascinated by the gunnery systems of the *Bismarck,* and talked knowledgeably about ballistics with the battleship's officers. He was less at home with naval strategy. Treated to a presentation by Lütjens, his only question concerned the numerical superiority of the British Home Fleet. Hitler had once said, "On land I am a hero, at sea I am a coward," an open criticism of the Kriegsmarine's policy of avoiding unnecessary engagements. Faced with the bare facts,

LEFT: When Adolf Hitler inspected the two warships at Gotenhafen on May 1, 1941, he expressed concerns about the risks involved in the forthcoming operation. *MNF*

TOP RIGHT: Lütjens ensured that German journalists and cameramen were carried on board both warships in order to record events for posterity. *MNF*

ABOVE RIGHT AND RIGHT: Lütjens wanted to postpone the operation until the *Tirpitz* (ABOVE RIGHT) had finished her working up period or the *Scharnhorst* (RIGHT) had been repaired, but Raeder ruled against any further postponement of Operation Rheinübung. *MNF*

he appeared hesitant, as if unwilling to commit his country's greatest battleship to action. Fearing Hitler might cancel the sortie, Raeder ordered Lütjens to avoid giving a date for the beginning of Operation Rheinübung. Once the Führer was safely out of the way, the two warships completed taking on stores, and prepared for sea. Lütjens set the date of departure, May 19, then supervised the departure of the auxiliary fleet that would support the German warships while they were at sea. Despite all the delays and problems, Operation Rheinübung would go ahead as planned.

The Commanders

The Kriegsmarine

The architect of Operation Rheinübung was Grossadmiral (Grand Admiral) Erich Raeder (1876–1960), the Oberbefehlshaber der Kriegsmarine (Ob.d.M.), or Supreme Commander of the Kriegsmarine from September 24, 1928 until January 30, 1943. The son of a language teacher from Wandsbek in Schleswig-Holstein, Raeder joined the navy in 1894, and after serving as Navigating Officer of the Kaiser's yacht *Hohenzollern* (1911) he was appointed as Chief of Staff to Admiral Hipper, the commander of Germany's battlecruiser force. He saw action at Jutland (1916), and remained in the navy after the war, becoming its head in 1928, some five years before Hitler came to power. As Oberbefehlshaber he oversaw the development of a large and secretive U-boat building program, and the creation of a powerful surface fleet of three pocket battleships, two battlecruisers and two battleships. Plans for an even more ambitious naval shipbuilding program (codenamed Plan Z) were abandoned when Hitler invaded Poland in September 1939, plunging the Kriegsmarine into a war with Britain for which it was not fully prepared. While Hermann Göring won Hitler's support for the Luftwaffe, Raeder failed to convince Hitler of the need for a powerful navy, largely because the Führer failed to understand the concept of seapower. Hitler became increasingly disillusioned with both Raeder and his Kriegsmarine, and replaced him as Oberbefehlshaber in 1943. Imprisoned after the war, he was released in 1955, and died five years later.

To assist Raeder in the planning of Operation Rheinübung, the Oberbefehlshaber could draw on the support of various departments of the German Naval High Command. His own office, the Oberkommando der Kriegsmarine (OKM) based in Berlin, contained the Seekriegsleitung (SKL) department (the Office of Naval Operations), headed by Generaladmiral Otto Schniewind, Chef der Stabs der Seekriegsleitung, who was assisted by Admiral Kurt Fricke. Two other senior naval officers were involved in the planning of the operation. Vizeadmiral Hubert Schmundt, the Befehlshaber der Kreuzer (BdK), or Commander-in-Chief of Cruisers, was the titular head of the surface fleet. Admiral Karl Dönitz, the Befehlshaber der Unterseeboote (BdU), or head of the U-boat arm, was also consulted.

Finally two operational departments provided the direct link between Admiral Lütjens on the *Bismarck* and the German Naval High Command in Berlin. While Lütjens' squadron was east of Greenland and Iceland, it came under the operational command of Kriegsmarine Gruppe Nord (Navy Group North), based in Wilhelmshaven: Generaladmiral Rolf Carls was the senior officer in charge of the department. Once the *Bismarck* broke out into the Atlantic, Carls handed over operational responsibility of the Operation Rheinübung force to Generaladmiral Alfred Saalwächter, head of Kriegsmarine Gruppe West (Navy Group West), based in Berlin.

The operational command of Operation Rheinübung was placed in the hands of Admiral Günther Lütjens (1889–1941), one of the most able senior officers in the Kriegsmarine. Born in Weissbaden, Lütjens entered the navy in 1907, and served in torpedo boats during the First World War. He received command of the light cruiser *Karlsrühe* in 1934, and the following year he was appointed to the staff of Gruppe Nord. He then served a spell as Chief of the Officer Personnel Section at Naval Headquarters in Berlin. In 1937 he was promoted to Konteradmiral, becoming Führer der Torpedoboote (Flag Officer in charge of the Torpedo Boat and Destroyer Fleet). Following the outbreak of war he was promoted to Befehlshaber der Aufklärungsstreitkräfte (BdA), or Commander of Reconnaissance Forces, in which role he gained vital operational experience as a fleet commander. A similar opportunity presented itself in April 1940, during the Norwegian Campaign, when Lütjens temporarily deputized for the Fleet Commander, Admiral Marschall, hoisting his flag in the battlecruiser *Gneisenau*. He also saw action when his force briefly engaged the British battlecruiser *Renown*. He was awarded the Knight's Cross (Ritterkreuz) for his performance.

Above: Admiral Günther Lütjens had reservations about Operation Rheinübung, but came within hours of making the operation a triumphant success. *MNF*

Above Left: Grand-Admiral Erich Raeder created the *Bismarck*, then conceived the operation which would result in her destruction. *MNF*

By September 1940 Lütjens had been promoted to Admiral, and had earned the trust of Admiral Raeder, who gave him operational command of Germany's first long-range raiding squadron. During the winter of 1940 he led the battlecruisers *Scharnhorst* and *Gneisenau* on an Atlantic sortie codenamed Operation Berlino, and his ships sank or captured 22 British vessels before returning safely to Brest. It was Lütjens who proved the effectiveness of German capital ships as Atlantic raiders, and his success sowed the seeds which would result in Operation Rheinübung.

He was a reserved, taciturn man, and a stickler for naval tradition. He demonstrated this by giving Hitler the naval salute rather than the Nazi one when the Führer inspected the *Bismarck* shortly before he sailed. He carried the responsibility for Operation Rheinübung on his own shoulders—and perished along with his flagship when the *Bismarck* was sunk.

Captain Ernst Lindemann (1894–1941) commanded the German battleship. The 45-year-old gunnery expert from Altenkirchen in the Rhineland was an ardent coffee drinker, chain smoker and man of energy. He entered the navy in 1913, and after receiving his commission two years later he served at sea until the end of the First World War. He rose quickly through the ranks during the interwar years, and was appointed as Chief Gunnery Officer of the pocket battleship *Admiral Scheer* in 1937, a post at which he excelled. The following year he was promoted to Kapitän zur See, becoming Kommandant (Commander) of the *Bismarck* two years later. He was

highly regarded in the service, and although he pushed his crew hard during their working up period, he was equally well respected by his men. He was last seen standing in the bow of his command, saluting its ensign as the *Bismarck* sank. He was posthumously awarded the Knight's Cross for his actions.

Kapitän zur See Helmuth Brinkmann (1895–1983), the Kommandant of the *Prinz Eugen*, was a former classmate of Lindemann. A native of Lübeck, he entered the navy and served aboard the naval training ship *Vineta* before receiving his commission in 1915. During the First World War he served as a Lieutenant zur See in armed merchant cruisers, the light cruiser *Regensburg* and in torpedo boats. He remained in the navy after the war, and was given his first command in the 1920s. In the early 1930s he was promoted to Korvetten-Kapitän and became advisor to the Defense Ministry, beginning a series of staff appointments which lasted until August 1940, when he was given command of the *Prinz Eugen*. A rotund, engaging officer, Brinkmann proved himself a skilled commander, and performed with distinction during the *Bismarck* sortie, earning the German Cross in gold for his efforts. He ended the war as a vice-admiral, having commanded naval operations in the Black Sea and the Baltic.

The Royal Navy

The man who was ultimately responsible for British naval strategy in May 1941 was the First Lord of the Admiralty, Admiral Sir Dudley Pound (1877–1943). In the First World War, Admiral Jellicoe was described as "the only man who could lose the war in an afternoon." Pound was in the same position, having complete operational, administrative and political control of the wartime Royal Navy. It was an incredible responsibility, and his task was not made any easier by interference from other members of the War Cabinet, and from Churchill. Fortunately Pound was usually willing to stand up to the Prime Minister, and held off ministerial interference in the everyday running of the Admiralty, and in its development of naval strategy. He had a distinguished career, serving as flag captain of the battleship *Colossus* at Jutland (1916), and commanding the Mediterranean fleet during the interwar years. By 1941 he was dying, suffering from the growing brain tumor that killed him two years later. Although suffering from constant pain and insomnia, he remained in office, making crucial decisions and maintaining a tight grip on all aspects of naval affairs.

The Admiralty as an institution was responsible for the command and administration of the navy, by means of a committee chaired by Pound as First Sea Lord and Chief of Naval Staff. He was answerable directly to Churchill through the War Cabinet, and played a major part in shaping British strategy. He was assisted by a staff of capable senior officers: Rear-Admiral Clayton in charge of Naval Intelligence; Captain Edwards (Director of Operations); Captain Daniel (Director of Plans); and his deputy, Vice-Admiral Sir Tom Phillips, Vice-Chief of Naval Staff and Second Sea Lord. Pound had a telephone line installed connecting his office in Whitehall with Admiral Tovey's flagship in Scapa Fow (at least while it was at anchor): he could thus communicate directly with the commander of the Home Fleet. Despite his controlling influence, Pound had faith in Tovey, and protected him from Churchill, who considered him too cautious and wanted him replaced. During the *Bismarck* operation, Pound simply passed on intelligence to Tovey, and allowed his deputy to formulate the strategy which would result in the destruction of the German battleship.

Admiral Lord John Cronyn Tovey (1885-1971) entered the navy at the age of 15, and commanded the destroyer *Onslow* at the Battle of Jutland (1916), an action in which his ship helped sink the German light cruiser *Wiesbaden*. A deeply religious man, he was a gifted commander, exuding confidence and encouraging his subordinates to follow his example of hard work. He was also stubborn, a trait that earned him the dislike of Churchill, who wanted to replace him; but this tenacity was also reflected in his approach to naval operations. Although he had a name for being a cautious commander, his high-speed pursuit of the *Bismarck* ran contrary to this, showing he was willing to take chances when the need arose. When off-duty he was a gracious host, a lover of good wine and a skilled golfer, civilized traits that underlined his gentlemanly qualities. He became commander of the Home Fleet in 1940, inheriting a force that was considered of secondary importance to the Mediterranean Fleet, as its main purpose was to thwart

ABOVE: Admiral Sir Dudley Pound allowed his fleet commander the freedom to conduct the hunt for the *Bismarck* as he saw fit, but at its climax he allowed Churchill to involve himself in Tovey's handling of the operation. *RNM*

ABOVE LEFT: After sinking the *Hood*, Captain Ernst Lindemann wanted to destroy the *Prince of Wales*, but was overruled by his superior. *MNF*

BELOW LEFT: Captain Brinkmann steered the *Prinz Eugen* to the safety of Brest after parting with the *Bismarck* in mid-Atlantic and then harassing British convoys. *MNF*

German attempts to break out into the Atlantic. He supervised operations against the *Scharnhorst* and *Gneisenau*, but the sortie of the *Bismarck* presented him with his greatest challenge.

Tovey's second-in-command and titular commander of the Home Fleet's Battlecruiser Squadron was Vice-Admiral Ernest Holland (1887–1941), who had only hoisted his flag in the *Hood* ten days before she sank. An intelligent, well-read and humorous man, he served in the navy during the First World War as a gunnery officer, and was promoted to Captain in 1926. He reached flag rank 12 years later, then served in the Admiralty as Assistant Chief of Naval Staff and the Air Ministry before being selected for operational command in 1940. He commanded British battleship and cruiser forces during the Norwegian Campaign and in the Mediterranean before he was sent to act as Tovey's deputy in May 1941.

Admiral Sir James Somerville (1882–1949) was the commander of "Force H", based in Gibraltar. Formed to provide a fast-reaction force for service in the Mediterranean or the Atlantic, the battlegroup consisted of the aircraft carrier *Ark Royal*, and a varying number of battleships, cruisers and destroyers. Somerville saw service in the First World War, and held both seagoing and staff appointments until the outbreak of war in 1939, when he was given command of Force H. During the next 18 months he and his force participated in the naval battle for control of the Mediterranean, where both the force and its commanders distinguished themselves. Somerville was seen as one of the navy's true characters; energetic, fun-loving and straightforward, with a dominating personality. Although not an incisive strategist like Tovey, Somerville made up for his simplistic approach to naval operations with his vitality and aggressiveness. He might have irritated his superiors and peers, but he could be relied upon to fight, and to inspire his men.

Admiral Sir William Frederic Wake-Walker (1888–1945) was a torpedo specialist, and one of the most able cruiser commanders in the fleet. He entered the navy in 1908, and after wartime service in cruisers and destroyers he was sent to Dartmouth, where he taught torpedo tactics. After holding several posts afloat and ashore, including command of the battleship *Revenge*, he was made a flag officer in 1939, just before the outbreak of war. He helped supervise the Dunkirk evacuation, then held the post of Commander of the Home Fleet's Cruiser Squadron from late-1940 onwards. A good friend of Tovey, he was a humorless officer, but extremely proficient at his job. He relaxed by shooting, either on the moors of Orkney or in Iceland while his flagship *Norfolk* was in port. It was his quick reaction that avoided the loss of his cruiser force in the Denmark Strait, then he masterminded the close pursuit of the German squadron in the hours that followed.

LEFT: Admiral Sir James Somerville (right), commander of Force H, and Captain Loeben Maund of the *Ark Royal*. *IWM*

BELOW: Rear-Admiral Wake-Walker shadowed the *Bismarck* during her passage through the Denmark Strait. *MNF*

OPPOSITE, LEFT: Admiral John Tovey masterminded the hunt for the *Bismarck* with considerable skill, despite subsequent criticisms levelled against him by Churchill. *RNM*

OPPOSITE RIGHT: During the Battle of the Denmark Strait Vice-Admiral Ernest Holland was well aware of the vulnerability of his flagship. *MNF*

The Opposing Forces

The Kriegsmarine

For various reasons, Operation Rheinübung had been scaled down in the weeks before the sortie, so that in the end only two warships were available to Admiral Lütjens; the battleship *Bismarck* and the heavy cruiser *Prinz Eugen*. The *Bismarck's* sister ship *Tirpitz* was also in Gotenhafen, but she still needed time to complete her sea trials and crew training. Even without the addition of this second battleship, or even one of the two German battlecruisers, Lütjens' small squadron was an extremely potent force.

Design work on the *Bismarck* had begun as early as 1932, reworking German battleship designs produced towards the end of the First World War. In theory Germany was still bound by the restrictions imposed by the Treaty of Versailles, but Admiral Raeder and the German Naval High Command flouted the rules wherever possible. In the case of the *Bismarck*, the size restriction of 35,000 tons was simply ignored, as designers added more armor, larger guns and a better propulsion system to their initial design. The result was a warship that displaced over 41,000 tons, a fact of some concern as her increased draught made her difficult to handle in the shallow estuarine waters of the German coast, and barely narrow enough to pass through the Kiel Canal. It was the development of Germany's own Krupp 15in. (380mm) gun in 1934 that gave the designers the greatest headache, as the original design called for the use of 13.7in. (350mm) guns in four twin turrets. When Hitler abrogated the Treaty of Versailles in March 1935, Raeder demanded that the larger guns be fitted, forcing a major redesign of the vessel, which included a small reduction in the thickness of her armor. Redesign work continued after the vessel was ordered, and during the first year of her construction. The result was well worth it, and by the time the *Bismarck* was launched on St. Valentine's Day 1939, she was regarded as the best-designed and most powerful battleship in the world.

The *Bismarck* was built to carry eight 15in. guns, housed in four twin turrets; two forward and two aft. Each weighed over 1,000 tons. Unlike the British, who labeled their turrets "A", "B", "X" and "Y", the Germans designated them sequentially from fore to aft "Anton", "Bruno", "Caesar" and "Dora". Also unlike their British counterparts, German designers were able to use the very latest in gunnery fire-control equipment, increasing the effectiveness of these guns. They could therefore fire their 1,764-pound projectile to a maximum range of 38,800 yards with a relatively high degree of accuracy compared to contemporary British battleships mounting guns of a similar size. Her secondary armament was designed for low-angle use against surface targets, and had a limited high-angle anti-aircraft capability. The secondary guns were the same as those fitted to the German battlecruisers *Scharnhorst* and *Gneisenau*, and shared the same fire-control system as the main armament.

Equally important, her hull was protected by 13 inches (325mm) of specially hardened Wotan steel; probably the best armored plate in the world at the time. However, weight and displacement restrictions meant that the *Bismarck's* protection against long-range plunging fire directed down onto her deck was less formidable than on some other contemporary battleships. In addition, her main armored belt was placed low-down in her hull, and its upper band was lighter than the lower portion, which protected her vitals. Also, her superstructure was only lightly protected, leaving many important spaces such as her communications and gunnery direction centers and sensors exposed to enemy fire. What was exceptional was her superb watertight sub-division, greatly increasing

ABOVE: The *Bismarck* was repainted in overall mid-gray for operations in the Atlantic while she was in Grimstadfjord, and her Baltic "splinter" camouflage shown here was painted over. *IWM*

her ability to cope with a penetrating hit by isolating any fire or flooding damage that resulted. In addition, her exceptionally broad beam made her a stable gun platform, and provided the space for improved underwater protection, making her largely impervious to torpedo hits.

Such raw statistics fail to sum up the *Bismarck* though. When she was launched with great pomp by *Bismarck*'s granddaughter in February 1939, the ceremony was treated as a full state occasion, and was witnessed by Hitler, Göbbels and most of his leading officials. After all, the *Bismarck* symbolized a rebirth, both of the German Navy and the nation. By the time she left Hamburg bound for her sea trials in the Baltic, she had been turned into a vessel that combined grace and menace in equal proportions, a beautiful ship which had become the pride of the German Navy. Her commander, Ernst Lindemann, was one of the best senior officers in the Kriegsmarine, a stern but intelligent seaman who was highly respected by both his superiors and his crew. Lindemann was assisted by a group of extremely able officers, although the *Bismarck*'s crew were for the most part very young and inexperienced. Their commander embarked on an extensive training program, turning this raw material into an efficient fighting force. They would be fighting the Royal Navy, whose seamen were imbued with centuries of tradition, and whose ships and crew had almost 18 months of wartime service, helping to bring both ships and men to the peak of efficiency. After a year of working up, the *Bismarck* was considered ready for operational use, and it was merely a matter of time before she would be unleashed against the warships of the Royal Navy.

The *Bismarck*'s consort was the *Prinz Eugen*, named after Eugene of Savoy, the Imperialist commander of the early-18th century who had fought alongside the Duke of Marlborough at Blenheim, and who had fought the Turks outside the gates of Vienna. Like the *Bismarck*, the heavy cruiser was built in violation of the restrictions imposed in the Treaty of Versailles. Along with the other four vessels in her group (known as the *Admiral Hipper* Class), she was designed for long-range operations in the Atlantic Ocean, a capability denied to the Germans under the terms of the Treaty. When Hitler tore up the Treaty of Versailles in 1935, German naval designers working on the cruiser were free to ignore its restrictions, as was the case with the *Bismarck*. The Washington Naval Treaty also limited the effectiveness of heavy cruisers, and although Germany was not a signatory, Admiral Raeder and his staff consistently played down the size and effectiveness of the cruisers they were building, in order to avoid international interference in Germany's program of naval expansion. The *Prinz Eugen* was the third vessel of her class to be commissioned, and varied slightly from her predecessors, the main difference being the incorporation of an improved propulsion system. She was launched at Krupp's Germania Yard in Kiel on August 22, 1938 and was commissioned just under a year later, on August 1, 1940.

The *Prinz Eugen* displaced over 14,000 tons, and her appearance was similar to that of the *Bismarck*, making her effectively a smaller version of the battleship. Her main armament consisted of eight 8in. (205mm) guns in four twin turrets, while her secondary guns were dual-purpose 4.1in. (105mm) weapons, capable of engaging both surface and air targets. Like the *Bismarck*, both main and secondary guns were linked into the same fire-control system for surface gunnery, while the secondary guns could be directed as part of an integrated high-angle direction system, which made the cruiser's anti-aircraft protection particularly effective. In July 1940, while nearing the end of her fitting-out period, the *Prinz Eugen* was hit by bombs during an air raid on Kiel. The damage was minor, and she entered service just over five weeks later. She was then sent into the Baltic to join the *Bismarck* at Gotenhafen, where the two warships worked up together. The cruiser's commander was Captain Helmuth Brinkmann, Lindemann's able former classmate. Like the battleship's commander, Brinkmann used his working-up period to increase the efficiency of his well-trained but largely inexperienced crew. The vessel almost missed the opportunity of participating in Operation Rheinübung, as on April 24 she set off a magnetic mine dropped just outside the harbor. Again the damage was minor, and she was repaired in a record time of two weeks, but it led to a temporary postponement of the operation until late-May, the next new-moon period and when the chances of surface detection by British patrols at night were reduced. Despite these setbacks, both Lindemann and Brinkmann had faith in their ships, and their crews. While the *Bismarck* was considered powerful enough to take on any British battleship she might encounter, the *Prinz Eugen* was superior to the heavy cruisers of the Royal Navy. Also, with a top speed of 32 knots she could outrun larger enemy warships, and run rings around any convoy escorts she might encounter. The two German warships were the most modern vessels of their type, and much was expected of them.

Apart from his two warships, Admiral Lütjens could also draw upon the support of several auxiliary vessels. Shortly before the squadron sailed, several support vessels slipped out of German ports and moved towards their assigned positions in the Arctic Sea and the Atlantic Ocean. The tankers *Heide* and *Weissenburg* were sent into the waters of the Arctic in case Lütjens needed to replenish his fuel stocks. A third tanker, the *Wollin*, was sent to Bergen in Norway, where she was in a position to supply the fuel tanks of both the *Bismarck*

LEFT AND BELOW LEFT: *Bismarck*'s superstructure and bridge. Note the domes covering the radars. *Bismarck* had three search and fire-control radars, plus radar detection. *Chris Ellis Collection*

and the *Prinz Eugen* after the warships reached Norwegian waters. Two more fleet tankers (*Belchen* and *Lothringen*) were deployed in the northern Atlantic to the south of Greenland, and a further two (*Esso Hamburg* and *Friedrich Breme*) were deployed in mid-Atlantic, around the latitude of the Azores. In addition the store ship *Egerland* was sent to the same area. Two additional ships, the auxiliary scouting vessels *Gonzenheim* and *Kota Penang*, were ordered to patrol the convoy route between Newfoundland and the southern tip of Greenland, where they could locate British convoys and radio news of their progress to the German Naval High Command. Finally, four weather ships (all converted trawlers) were scattered throughout the likely area of operations, and they sent back a constant stream of valuable meteorological information. In addition to fuel, the tankers also carried extra provisions, ammunition and water, and if used effectively they could extend the range and endurance of the *Bismarck*, giving her the ability to remain at sea for up to eight weeks. Like the two previous German sorties into the Atlantic, Operation Rheinübung was a well-planned operation, and considerable effort was made to provide Lütjens with the support he needed to make his mission a success.

Lütjens' final lines of support were the U-boat arm of the Kriegsmarine, and the Luftwaffe. On April 8, Lütjens flew to Paris to confer with Admiral Dönitz, the commander of the U-boat fleet. While Raeder would co-ordinate fleet movements, Dönitz would order his boats to act as an extra scouting force for Lütjens, and if need be, they could help cover any German withdrawal in the face

Bismarck

Laid down:	July 1, 1936
Launched:	February 14, 1939
Commissioned:	August 24, 1940
Displacement:	41,673 tons (standard), 49,136 tons (fully laden)
Dimensions:	823' 6" (251 m.) long, 118' 1" (36 m.) beam, 33' 6" (10.2 m.) draught
Propulsion:	Blohm & Voss steam turbines, 12 boilers, three propeller shafts, producing 136,112 s.h.p.
Maximum speed:	29 knots
Armament:	Eight 15in. (380mm) guns (4 x 2), Twelve 5.9in. (150 mm) guns (6 x 2), Sixteen 4.1in. (105mm) guns (8 x 2), Sixteen 37mm AA guns (8 x 2), Sixteen 20mm AA guns (16 x 1), Four Arado float planes
Armor:	Main belt—12.6"; upper belt—5.7"; upper deck—2"; main deck—3.7" turrets—14.2" (front), 12.8" (rear), 8.7" (sides), 7.1" (roof); conning tower—13.8" (front and sides), 8.7" (roof)
Radar:	Three search and fire-control radars, plus radar detection and passive sonar equipment
Complement:	2,065

Prinz Eugen

Laid down:	April 23, 1936
Launched:	August 22, 1938
Commissioned:	August 1, 1940
Displacement:	16,974 tons (standard), 19,042 tons (fully laden)
Dimensions:	681' 3" (201.7 m.) long, 71' 9" (21.9 m.) beam, 20' 9" (6.4 m.) draught
Propulsion:	La Mont Steam Turbines, 12 boilers, four propeller shafts, producing 133,631 s.h.p.
Maximum speed:	32.5 knots
Armament:	Eight 8in. (205mm) guns (4 x2), Twelve 4.1in. (105mm) guns (6 x 2), Twelve 37mm AA guns (6 x 2), Eight 20mm AA guns (8 x 1), Twelve 21in. (520mm torpedo tubes (4 x 3), Three Arado float planes
Armor:	Main belt—3.25"; upper belt—1.5"; upper deck—0.5"; main deck—1.25" turrets—6.25" (front), 4.5" (rear) 4.5" (sides), 2.25" (roof); conning tower—6" (front and sides), 2" (roof)
Radar:	Three search & fire-control radars, plus extensive passive sonar and hydrophone equipment
Complement:	1,600

of a superior British naval force. Similarly, the Luftwaffe was ordered to step up the frequency of its reconnaissance flights over the Atlantic, and if the need arose it was ready to provide long-range air cover for the battleship in the Western Approaches or in the Norwegian Sea. When the *Bismarck* sailed, Lütjens' staff duly included a U-boat liaison officer and a Luftwaffe staff officer. With his forces in place and his crews ready, all Lütjens needed was the order to begin the operation.

BELOW: With her eight 8in. guns and modern fire-control systems the *Prinz Eugen* was more than a match for any British cruiser of comparable size. *Chris Ellis Collection*

RIGHT: Scenes of the Channel Dash, that saw *Prinz Eugen*, *Scharnhorst* and *Gneisenau* run the gauntlet from Brest to Kiel and Wilhelmshaven. Protected by destroyers and the Luftwaffe (under the direction of Adolf Galland), the three capital ships reached German waters relatively unscathed, with only damage from mines to *Scharnhorst* and *Gneisenau*. *Chris Ellis Collection*

Location of Royal Navy ships

In Scapa Flow

Battleships (2):	*King George V* (flagship of Admiral Tovey), *Prince of Wales*
Battlecruisers (1):	*Hood* (flagship of Vice-Admiral Holland)
Aircraft carriers (1):	*Victorious*
Light cruisers (4):	*Galatea* (flagship of Rear-Admiral Curteis), *Aurora, Kenya, Neptune*
Destroyers (9):	*Active, Antelope, Achates, Anthony, Electra, Echo, Punjabi, Icarus, Nestor*

At sea

Battlecruiser:	*Repulse*
Heavy cruisers (2):	*Norfolk* (flagship of Rear-Admiral Wake-Walker), *Suffolk*
Light cruisers (4):	*Birmingham, Manchester, Arethusa, Hermione*
Destroyers (2):	*Inglefield, Intrepid*

RIGH: The flight crews embarked on the *Victorious* were inexperienced, but Tovey had no option but to throw them into action against the *Bismarck*. *RNM*

BELOW: The *Prince of Wales* was still experiencing technical problems and was not fully ready to assume operational duties. *MNF*

The Royal Navy

When the report that the *Bismarck* had left Gotenhafen reached Admiral Tovey in Scapa Flow on May 21, he took stock of the forces available to him to prevent the German battleship from breaking out into the Atlantic. In Scapa Flow he had three capital ships available for instant use, plus the aircraft carrier *Victorious*. In addition, several cruisers and destroyers were available, while others were either on station in the North Atlantic, or could be ordered to reach the area within a day or two. He also had the use of the battlecruiser *Repulse*, currently in the Firth of Clyde, where it was preparing to escort an important convoy to North Africa. Two other battleships (*Rodney* and *Ramillies*) were on convoy escort duty in the North Atlantic, and could also be expected to join in the operation if required. The *Victorious* was also preparing to take part in the same convoy, and her hangars were filled with crated Hurricanes destined for the Mediterranean Theater. The Admiralty also informed him that he could rely on the support of Rear Admiral Somerville's Force H, based at Gibraltar, comprising the battlecruiser *Renown*, the aircraft carrier *Ark Royal* and the light cruiser *Sheffield*. (See the box on page 28 for further details of the location of warships in Tovey's Home Fleet.)

Although this force looked impressive on paper, Tovey was well aware of its limitations. His most valuable asset was his own flagship, the modern battleship *King George V.* Commissioned six months before in December 1940, she was the first new British battleship to enter service for over a decade, and she was fitted with the latest in gunnery and fire-control systems. Her ten 14in. guns gave her a slight advantage over the *Bismarck* in terms of firepower, and she was well protected, with a 15in. waterline belt, which was considered proof against hits from the *Bismarck's* 15in. guns. This was actually less than her designers had wished, as concerns over her relatively low speed led to a reduction in armament from twelve to ten 14in. barrels, and a general reduction in armor thickness. Overall, she was a well-designed modern battleship, and her fire-control systems were on par with those found in the German fleet. By May 1941 her crew were also well trained, and had been made efficient through constant exercises and the occasional sortie. The month before she had participated in a raid on the Lofoten Islands in Norway, and had also provided long-range support for Atlantic convoys, so her crew were experienced in their duties.

By contrast the flagship's sister, the battleship *Prince of Wales*, had only just entered service: in an ideal world, she would not have been expected to take part in any operations against the *Bismarck.* Although officially she was completed on March 31, 1941 she was still plagued by some quite serious and persistent teething problems, and civilian contractors were still working on her, trying to fix various faults with the mechanical operation of her turrets and main armament. Her crew was also inexperienced. Although some had been drafted from other ships to form an experienced core, the majority of the ship's company was fresh out of training school, and lacked any experience of naval life, let alone experience of naval action. That day, Captain Leach of the *Prince of Wales* had reported to Tovey that his ship was ready for operational duties, but the Admiral was well aware of the technical problems plaguing the new battleship. He was also extremely reluctant to risk her new crew without giving them time to gain experience. Although the shortage of capital warships in the Home Fleet might force her use, the *Prince of Wales* could not be expected to engage the *Bismarck* alone.

In addition Tovey had two battlecruisers at his disposal, the *Hood* and the *Repulse.* They were the legacy of a flawed notion in naval design, which resulted in capital ships that had the armament but lacked the armored protection needed to engage enemy battleships on equal terms. The design of the *Repulse* (one of two *Renown*-class battlecruisers) predated the Battle of Jutland: the *Repulse* and her sister-ship the *Renown* entered service

While the battlecruiser *Hood* (Above) lacked the armor and fire-control systems to take on the *Bismarck* unaided, the battleship *Rodney* (Above Left and Left) was a far more effective warship, carrying nine 16in. guns. *All MNF*

Hood

Laid down:	May 31, 1916
Launched:	August 22, 1918
Commissioned:	May 15, 1920
Displacement:	42,462 tons (standard), 48,360 tons (fully laden)
Dimensions:	860' 6" long, 104' 2" beam, 28' 9" draught
Propulsion:	Brown-Curtis steam turbines, 32 boilers, four propeller shafts, producing 144,000 s.h.p.
Maximum speed:	29.5 knots
Armament:	Eight 15in. guns (4 x 2), Eight 4in. guns (4 x 2), Twenty-four (3 x 8) 2-pdr pom-poms, Sixteen 0.5in. machine guns (4 x 4), Four 21in. torpedoes in fixed hull-launched mounts
Armor:	Main belt—12"; belt periphery (fore and aft)—5"–6"; forecastle deck—1.25"-2"; upper deck—0.75"-2"; turrets—15" (front), 11" (rear), 12" (sides), 5" (roof); conning tower—11" (front and sides), 5" (roof)
Radar:	Main gunnery direction radar
Complement:	1,397

just months after the 1916 battle. The loss of three battlecruisers in the engagement had brought the whole notion of the battlecruiser into question, and Admiral Jellicoe viewed his two new capital ships with suspicion. Within months he had sent them back to the shipbuilders, where additional armor was provided. So began almost two decades of intermittent rebuilding, earning the *Repulse* and the *Renown* the nicknames of "Refit" and "Repair." Although the result was relatively satisfactory, they *Renown* was fully modernized, while the *Repulse* still carried outdated anti-aircraft protection, and was still considered inferior to most modern battleships. The real weakness of these two warships was that they were only fitted with six 15in. guns in three twin turrets. This meant they had only 75 percent of the firepower available to the *Bismarck*, and would therefore need to be supported by another capital ship if they were to be risked in battle against their German adversary.

The crew of both of the *Repulse*-class battlecruisers were well-trained, and had served together since the outbreak of the war. The *Renown* had even fought a brief engagement against the German battlecruisers *Scharnhorst* and *Gneisenau* off Norway the year before, and her crew had performed well. While the *Repulse* was available for immediate attachment to the Home Fleet, the *Renown* was still at Gibraltar, where she formed part of Force H.

If any single warship came to symbolize the prewar might of the Royal Navy it was the battlecruiser *Hood*. Laid down in 1916, her design was improved in light of the performance of the battlecruiser fleet at Jutland. By the time she entered service in 1920 she carried armor which was suitable for protection against most older battleships, but she was still vulnerable to penetration by the high-velocity 15in. shells fired by modern battleships such as the *Bismarck*. Even more importantly, her deck armor was far too light to protect her against plunging fire at long range, making her particularly vulnerable at ranges over 20,000 yards (12 miles). Under that range, shells tended to strike warships horizontally: at longer ranges, their flight followed a parabolic curve, and it was more likely that they would drop down onto their target, striking the deck rather than the belt. This poor "vertical protection" proved the Achilles heel of the *Hood*. During the interwar years the battlecruiser had been used to "show the flag", touring the world as a floating representative of the Royal Navy, and as an ambassador of the British Empire. She was ideally suited to this role, as her sleek lines and elegant profile were impressive. She became the best-known warship in the Royal Navy, and was dubbed "the Mighty *Hood*" by the press. Unlike the other two battlecruisers, she was never properly modernized, and therefore the old lady sailed into battle against the *Bismarck* with the armor and armament of a warship of the 1920s rather than the 1940s. Both her commander (Captain Kerr) and her embarked Admiral (Vice-Admiral Holland) were well aware that in any forthcoming action they would have to close the range with the enemy as quickly as possible, to reduce the risk of plunging fire. Despite the shortcomings of the *Hood*'s design, her ship's company was experienced, having served as a unit since the outbreak of the war. The *Hood* had already engaged the Vichy French fleet at Mers-el-Kebir in July 1940, and participated in several sorties and convoys in both the Atlantic and the Mediterranean. She was an asset to the fleet, but like the rest of Tovey's major warships (apart from his flagship), she would need to be supported by another capital ship when she encountered the *Bismarck*.

Tovey also had the aircraft carrier *Victorious* at his disposal. In theory she could carry 36 aircraft, but as noted earlier, at the time the *Bismarck* sortied her hangars were full of aircraft in crates—a consignment of Hurricane fighters en route to North Africa. Although she

RIGHT AND BELOW RIGHT: The effectiveness of the battlecruisers *Repulse* and *Renown* (nicknamed "Repair" and "Refit" because of the amount of time they had spent under modification) was limited by their armament of only six 15in. guns in three turrets. *MNF*

King George V* and *Prince of Wales

King George V

Laid down:	January 1, 1937
Launched:	February 21, 1939
Commissioned:	September 30, 1940

Prince of Wales

Laid down:	January 1, 1937
Launched:	May 3, 1939
Commissioned:	March 31, 1941

Displacement:	38,031 tons (standard), 42,237 tons (*King George V* fully-laden), 43,786 (*Prince of Wales* fully laden)
Dimensions:	745' long, 103' beam, 29' draught
Propulsion:	Parsons steam turbines, 8 boilers, four propeller shafts, producing 100,000 s.h.p.
Maximum speed:	28 knots
Armament:	Ten 14in. guns (2 x 4, 2 x 2), Sixteen 5.25in. guns (8 x 2), Thirty-two (4 x 8) 2-pounder pom-poms, Two Walrus float planes
Armor:	Main belt: 15"; upper deck: 2"; main deck: 6"; turrets: 12.75" (front), 6.75" (rear), 8.75" (sides), 6" (roof); conning tower: 4" (front and sides), 3" (roof)
Radar:	Air-warning and surface search radar, main gunnery direction radar, secondary gunnery direction radar
Complement:	1,543 (*King George V*)

RIGHT: The aircraft carrier *Victorious* accompanied Admiral Tovey's flagship when he steamed to intercept the *Bismarck* after the Battle of the Denmark Strait. *RNM*

FAR RIGHT: The aircraft carrier *Ark Royal* formed the main striking force of Admiral Somerville's "Force H", based at Gibraltar. *MNF*

BELOW RIGHT: The heavy cruiser *Norfolk* shadowed the *Bismarck* during her run south into the Atlantic. *MNF*

still had a squadron of the antiquated Swordfish torpedo bombers embarked, she could not be considered fully combat ready, her planes having only just made their first collective carrier landing two days before, when they embarked. Still, she was an asset that Tovey had to use, as however inexperienced her pilots might be, her Swordfish torpedo bombers represented a powerful offensive tool.

Technically, both *Repulse* and *Victorious* were not part of the Home Fleet, but as they were currently in the probable area of operations, control of the two ships was given to Tovey. In addition to his capital ships the British admiral also had several cruisers and dozens of destroyers under his command. While these vessels were too lightly protected to risk in conventional engagement against the German force, they might prove useful if the *Bismarck* was damaged, and they could scout ahead of the battleships and battlecruisers, acting as the eyes and ears of the fleet.

In addition to the Home Fleet, Tovey could call upon the support of other naval groups, including Force H. The most potent warship in Somerville's Force H was the aircraft carrier *Ark Royal*. Commissioned in 1938, she was a modern carrier, the first British fleet carrier to be designed from scratch. With a top speed of 30 knots and the capacity to hold 60 aircraft of various types she was classed as a fast fleet carrier, and although her Skua

fighter and Swordfish torpedo-bombers were relatively obsolete aircraft, she could still launch a decisive air strike when called upon. She had already seen extensive service off Norway and in the Mediterranean, and she was considered fully operational. She was supported by the battlecruiser *Renown* and the light cruiser *Sheffield*.

In the mid-Atlantic, the battleship *Rodney* and the old battleship *Ramillies* could be pulled away from their convoys and used in the hunt. The former was an ugly but impressive warship of the *Nelson* class, fitted with nine 16in. guns in three triple turrets, and protected by a 13in. main belt. Her crew were well trained, and had seen action during the Norwegian campaign the previous year. Although in need of modernization she was more than capable of meeting the *Bismarck* on her own terms. The *Ramillies* was a battleship of First World War vintage, one of five warships of the *Royal Sovereign* class. Her armor was considered inadequate by modern standards, but she carried eight 15in. guns, and although not fully modernized, her fire-control systems were reasonably effective: like all British battleships, she was fitted with radar. Although her crew were considered proficient, it was considered inadvisable to risk her in battle alone.

Finally Tovey could draw on the extensive resources of the Royal Air Force and Coastal Command. Bombers were put on standby for operations against the *Bismarck*, while Coastal Command and RAF reconnaissance flights were stepped up during the campaign. Although the bomber pilots lacked experience of naval operations, they had the capacity to launch a devastating air attack on the *Bismarck* if she was caught at anchor or came within range of the air bases of Northern Scotland or Northern Ireland. Admiral Tovey, therefore, had all the resources he needed. His problem was how best to use them to sink the *Bismarck* without risking significant losses.

RIGHT: While Wake-Walker's flagship, the *Norfolk*, lacked a modern radar set, the *Suffolk* (pictured here) was equipped with a powerful search radar, allowing her to track the *Bismarck* during May 22 and 23. *RNM*

BELOW RIGHT: The light cruiser HMS *Sheffield* formed part of "Force H", although with her twelve 6in. guns she was of limited use against a modern battleship. *RNM*

BELOW: HMS *Cossack* was Captain Vian's flagship, and led his night-time torpedo attack on the *Bismarck*. *RNM*

Logistics

The ultimate failure of the *Bismarck* to complete her mission, and the reason for her final destruction, were largely the result of logistics. While ammunition supplies and ship's provisions are important, the greatest limiting factor in any deep-water naval campaign is the supply of fuel. The range of a warship, and thus the time she can spend in an operational area, was and still is limited by the quantity of fuel she can carry. Also crucial is the correlation between a ship's speed and its fuel consumption. Like an automobile, the faster the speed, the greater the fuel consumption. During this period warships tended to steam at about half speed (usually under 20 knots) in order to make their fuel last as long as possible. During pursuit operations, speed became more important, hence so did fuel stocks.

The *Bismarck* had a fuel capacity of about 8,000 tons. At full speed (29 knots) she consumed this at a rate of approximately 1,000 tons (or 270,000 gallons) per day. This equates to 11,250 gallons every hour. At that speed, her operational radius was about 2,800 nautical miles, which was nothing in the vastness of the North Atlantic, and only allowed her a brief foray beyond the Greenland–Iceland–Faeroes line before having to return to a friendly port, such as Bergen or Kiel. At 20 knots her fuel consumption dropped dramatically to 600 tons per day, or 162,000 gallons. At this speed her range increased to 3,200 miles, giving her sufficient fuel to reach the convoy routes, operate for about 48 hours, then return to either a French port such as Brest or St. Nazaire, or a Norwegian one (Bergen or Trondheim). At 20 knots she also covered a respectable 500 nautical miles per day. Incidentally, at 16 knots, her fuel consumption dropped to just under 160 tons per day, or 4,320 gallons, giving her an operational radius of 9,600 miles. At the same speed, the *Prinz Eugen* had a range of 5,000 nautical miles. It was therefore imperative that the

Loading stores on board the *Bismarck* at Gotenhafen before the start of Operation 'Rheinübung'. RNM

two German warships should conserve their fuel during the operation, and restrict their speed to an economical 16 to 20 knots.

The *Bismarck* used up nearly 1,500 tons of fuel by the time she reached Bergen, leaving her with only 6,500 tons in her fuel tanks. During the planning phase of Operation Rheinübung, Lütjens had arranged for German tankers to precede the sortie by the *Bismarck* and *Prinz Eugen*, and these vessels were assigned to stations in the likely areas of operation. One tanker (the *Wollin*) was sent to Bergen, while two more were assigned to holding areas in the Arctic Sea. Two more took station to the south of Greenland, and another two were sent into the mid-Atlantic.

While the *Bismarck* was in Grimstadfjord, she should have refueled from the *Wollin*. Inexplicably, Lütjens opted not to do so, although he ordered the *Prinz Eugen* to refuel. Standard operating procedure in the Kriegsmarine (as in the Royal Navy) dictated that warships should refuel as soon as practicable after entering a friendly port. Lütjens' decision would have a decisive effect on the outcome of the campaign.

At a conservative estimate, the *Bismarck* will have consumed another 1,500 tons of fuel during her transit through the Arctic Sea and the Denmark Strait. Again, Lütjens had the opportunity of refueling at sea from the tanker *Weissenburg*, whose station was only slightly to the north of the *Bismarck*'s course from the latitude of Trondheim to the northern entrance of the Denmark Strait. Once more he elected not to waste time refueling. One can only suppose that he was staking everything on a speed transit through the gap, before the British could discover that the *Bismarck* had sailed. This meant affecting a rendezvous with the German tankers *Belchen* or *Lothringen* stationed south–south–west off the southern tip of Greenland. A successful replenishment of her tanks would have altered the whole picture, and would have given the *Bismarck* the opportunity to cruise the convoy routes for several days without needing to refuel again.

The damage inflicted on the *Bismarck* by the *Prince of Wales* during the Battle of the Denmark Strait meant that she lost about 1,000 tons of fuel, either through leakage from her forward tanks, or through contamination with sea water. This meant that by noon on May 24, the *Bismarck* had less than 4,000 tons of fuel in her tanks. Although it left her enough to reach St. Nazaire, she needed to refuel in order to continue operations in the Atlantic.

The speed with which Admiral Tovey reacted to the German sortie meant that Lütjens had no real chance to refuel at sea south of Greenland. This meant he had no option but to head at an economical speed towards the French coast. Even after the battleship was relocated by a Catalina on May 26, she could still have reached the limit of Luftwaffe air protection if she had enough fuel to steam at 20 knots. Instead her speed was reduced in order to make her fuel last, and she was duly located and attacked by Swordfish aircraft from the *Ark Royal*. Fuel therefore proved a decisive factor in the ultimate fate of the *Bismarck*.

The actions of the Royal Navy during the campaign were equally dictated by fuel consumption. Although this never proved critical, as friendly ports were never further than a day away for most of the campaign, there were several instances were logistical factors almost allowed the *Bismarck* to evade pursuit or destruction. For example, the *Suffolk* almost missed the *Bismarck*, as she needed to refuel in Iceland immediately before the *Bismarck* left the Norwegian coast. She returned to her station just in time. When Tovey sailed from Scapa Flow, he knew his warships had a limited fuel capacity, and yet he was prepared to gamble everything on a high-speed pursuit of the *Bismarck* into the North Atlantic. The *Victorious* had to turn back for lack of fuel, then the *Repulse*. The *Rodney* was diverted from her duties as a convoy escort, and by the time she joined Tovey's flagship *King George V* on May 26, both battleships were critically short of fuel. The *Prince of Wales* had already returned to port due to lack of fuel. The damage to the *Bismarck* which sealed her fate guaranteed that a final engagement would be fought early on the morning of April 27, so Tovey kept control of his battleships, reducing their speed to conserve fuel, and to come upon the enemy at dawn. Even with this fuel conservation, the two battleships had to disengage and retire towards their home bases before the *Bismarck* was finally sunk. The usually cautious Tovey had taken a gamble in his rapid response to the *Bismarck*'s sortie, and his luck held. When the *Bismarck* was finally tracked down, his battleships still had a couple of hours of fuel reserves left, giving them just enough time to pulverize their enemy before withdrawing. There was little margin for error, and although the *Bismarck* was destroyed, events could easily have turned out differently: Tovey's battleships might easily have been unable to engage their quarry before being forced to retire from the fight. In the end, while logistics proved crucial to the outcome of the campaign, luck was the final arbiter of victory or defeat.

RIGHT: Embarking dry provisions on board the *Prinz Eugen* in Gotenhafen, May 1941. *RNM*

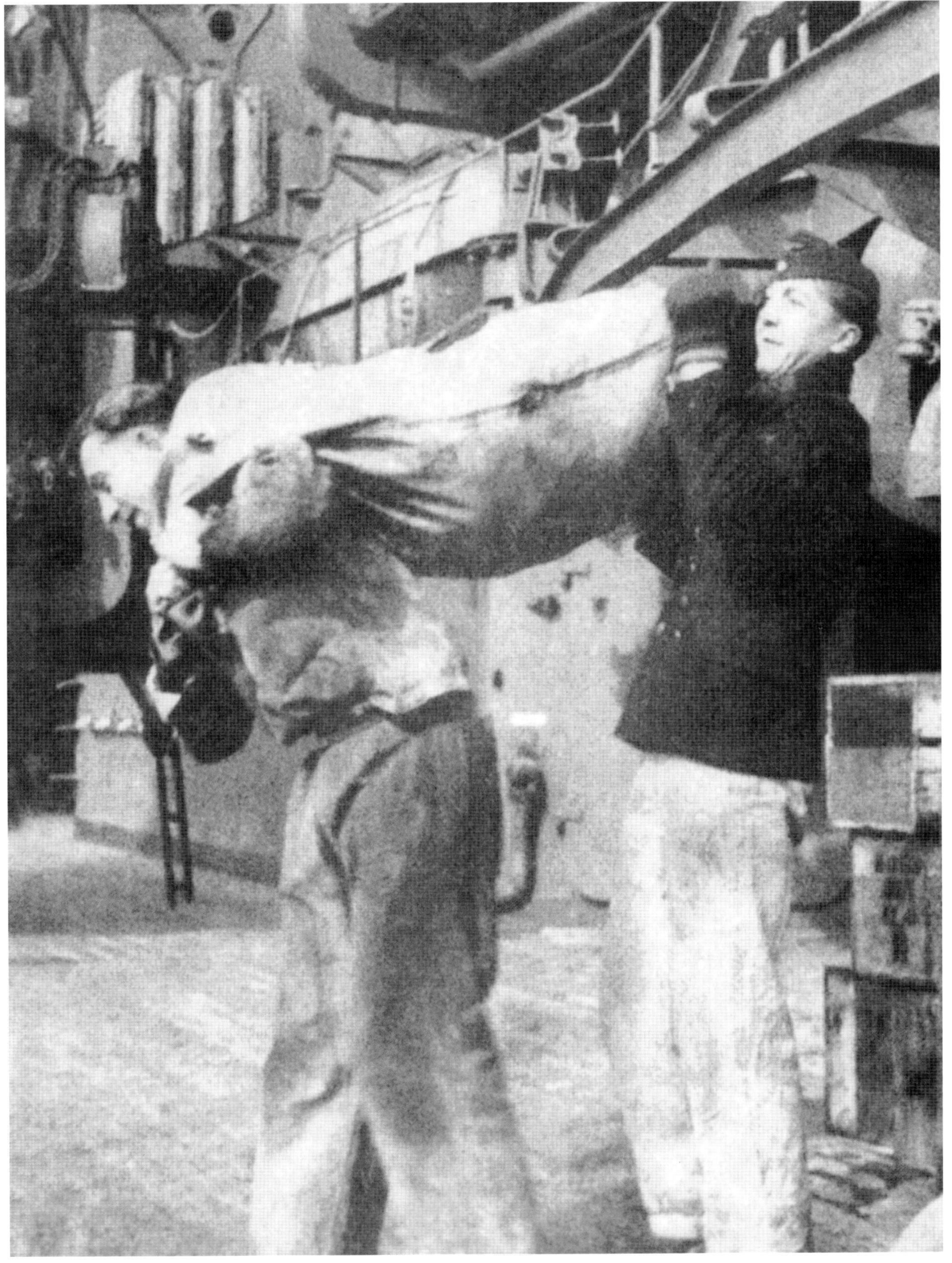

The Battle Arena

For a campaign fought in the virtually limitless waters of the North Atlantic, the geographical limits of the theater of operations proved surprisingly cramped. First, the *Bismarck* had to transit the Baltic to reach the Norwegian coast near Bergen. This meant a passage through narrow coastal waters, or else a transit through the Kiel Canal. Then, in order to reach the Atlantic, Lütjens had to pass through one of a limited number of gaps, each of them guarded by warships of the Royal Navy, and patrolled by British aircraft. Once safely through this barrier the Atlantic lay open to him; but although the *Bismarck* had physical sea room, her options were still limited by geography. These limitations included the proximity of British airbases, the location of convoy routes, and the distance between her and the safety of France, or at least of Luftwaffe air cover. Together, these geographical factors constituted the battle arena where the week-long campaign would be fought. Of almost equal importance was the weather, and Lütjens made full use of both the lunar cycle (to decrease the chances of detection) and the protection of bad weather fronts (to hamper British aerial reconnaissance.)

The first decision facing Lütjens was how to make the passage from Gotenhafen to Bergen. He had two options: use the Kiel Canal, or make the passage through the Sound between Denmark and Sweden before entering the Kattegat. He opted for the latter, which was faster and less restrictive, but increased the chance of a sighting by enemy agents. In retrospect this seems a strange decision, as Lütjens was well aware that the narrow channel was patrolled by neutral Swedish warships and frequented by fishing craft, and the *Bismarck* would also pass within range of watchers on the shore. The selection of this channel was his first operational mistake, which meant that the British were aware of the *Bismarck*'s departure from Gotenhafen within hours rather than days. His selection of the Grimstadfjord for his Norwegian anchorage was not particularly risky, although the area was part of two general areas targeted by the RAF for special attention by photographic reconnaissance aircraft. The critically important fusion of geography and strategic planning came next, when Lütjens had to choose which route to take to reach the North Atlantic.

Lütjens had two main options. The Denmark Strait between Greenland and Iceland was constricted by pack ice from a potential 300-mile gap to one half that or even less, depending on the season. At the time the *Bismarck* passed through the Strait, the gap was less than 100 miles wide at its narrowest point, at the top end. From that point the line of pack ice fringing the Greenland coast ran southwest, while the Icelandic coast ran south, meaning the gap widened from northeast to southwest. The narrowest point was even further restricted by British minefields, extending west–north–west from the northwestern corner of the Icelandic coast. On the other side of Iceland the gap between the southeastern corner of the island and the Faeroe Islands was approximately 200 miles, and was known to be heavily patrolled by units of the Royal Navy.

Lütjens had chosen the period of the new moon for his breakout, when night visibility would be poor due to the lack of moonlight. Also, it was the most direct route between the Norwegian Sea and the Atlantic Ocean, and the route favored by the German Naval High Command. Other routes existed, such as the gap between the Faeroes and Shetland, and the passage between Orkney and Shetland, neither of which was considered practical due to their proximity to the British base at Scapa Flow, and RAF and Fleet Air Arm airfields on both Orkney and Shetland. The final passage, between Orkney and the Scottish mainland, was considered suicidal for a U-boat, let alone a German surface squadron.

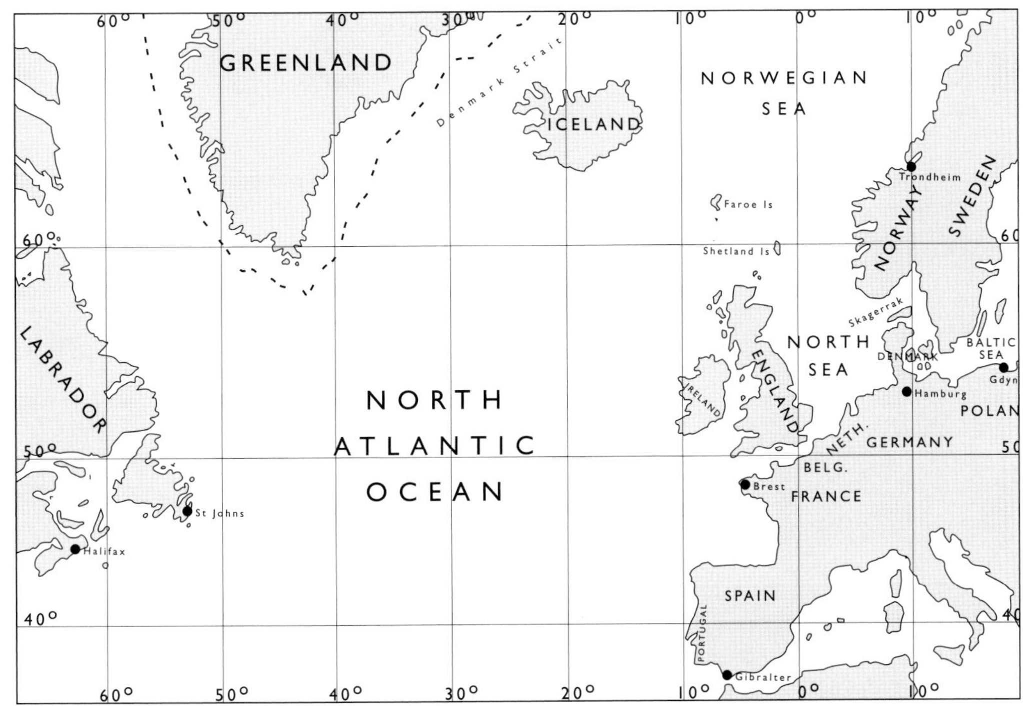

LEFT: The battle arena: once clear of enemy ships, the the North Atlantic was a hunting ground of great potential for *Bismarck* and *Prinz Eugen*. The key to the British strategy was blocking the gaps from the North Sea—and making sure they kept in touch with the German ships when they did break free.

Once in the Atlantic, the horizons broadened. Below the southern tip of Greenland lay two German replenishment tankers, and below them was a patrol line of four U-boats, lying astride the main convoy route between Newfoundland and Britain. It was unlikely Lütjens planned to sail any further west than this, as it brought him within aerial reconnaissance range of Canadian bases in Newfoundland. A similar consideration reduced his operational area to the east, as he needed to keep as far away from British air bases in Scotland and Northern Ireland as possible. This left a 500-mile stretch of the mid-Atlantic, an area of operations which covered several major convoy routes. Further south towards the Azores, the *Bismarck* would enter the area transited by convoys bound for and coming from Africa or the Mediterranean.

While his area of operations was somewhat restricted, Lütjens still had a lot of ocean to hunt in. Any attempt to reach the safety of the French ports involved coming within reach of British long-range aerial reconnaissance, but it also placed Lütjens in a region of U-boat activity to the south of Ireland, and within air range of the Luftwaffe's French bases.

Lütjens' other great ally was the weather. Apart from the lack of moonlight, the weather was poor, with fog banks off the coast of Iceland, occasional snow flurries, and low, threatening clouds to hinder aerial reconnaissance. A low pressure area centered to the south of Newfoundland and Nova Scotia was slowly moving eastwards across the Atlantic, pushing bands of rain squalls ahead of it.

The relatively stable weather conditions the *Bismarck* encountered in the Norwegian Sea and Arctic Ocean changed when she entered the Denmark Strait. The visibility was clear along the fringe of the pack ice along the Greenland coast, but fog banks lay in the northern part of the Denmark Strait. Further to the south sleet and snow squalls made visibility patchy, and assisted the British cruisers as they shadowed the German squadron.

By dawn on May 24, visibility had improved, and the snow squalls had given way to more occasional squalls of rain. The sea was moderately rough, but as the *Bismarck* passed into the Atlantic the bad weather moving in from the west brought low clouds ahead of it: this poor weather continued until the end of the campaign. While conditions improved as the *Bismarck* ran to the southeast, cloud cover continued to hamper air operations.

In general terms the weather was typical of the Northern Atlantic in May, and while not playing a major part in events, the poor visibility helped the *Bismarck* evade the British for 24 crucial hours. With even more overcast skies, the *Bismarck* might have evaded the British completely. Only the lucky sighting of the German battleship by search aircraft on May 26 altered the course of events in favor of the Royal Navy.

The hunt for the *Bismarck*

The German sortie

By the start of May 1941, the *Bismarck* was ready to undertake an active part in the naval war. Her crew had been highly trained, and both the ship and its equipment had been brought to a peak of efficiency. On May 16, 1941 Fleet Admiral Lütjens informed German Naval High Command that the training period was over, and he was ready to carry out Operation Rheinübung. He was immediately given the order to carry on with his mission, and two days later he briefed his senior officers. On the afternoon of Sunday May 18, 1941 the battleship *Bismarck* and the heavy cruiser *Prinz Eugen* sailed from Gotenhafen, their departure celebrated by a military band. They hove to just outside the harbor for the rest of the evening, taking on additional stores and provisions from waiting supply vessels. They finally got under way shortly after midnight, during the early hours of May 19. Once in the Baltic they headed almost due west, escorted by two destroyers. By 0400 on the morning of May 20 they had entered the narrow waters of the Kattegat, and the German squadron passed between German-occupied Denmark and Sweden. Although Sweden was officially a neutral country, the Swedish government was decidedly pro-Allied, so any sighting would certainly have been passed on to the British. A small fleet of Danish and Swedish fishing boats was in the Kattegat as the German force swept by, and Lütjens was concerned that his presence would be reported. During the early afternoon of May 20, the Swedish cruiser *Gotland* sighted the German ships during her regular patrol of the waters between the Kattegat and the Skaggerak. She immediately radioed a sighting report to the Swedish naval headquarters in Stockholm. Within hours, news of the sighting was leaked to the naval attaché in the British embassy, and an urgent message was sent to London during the night.

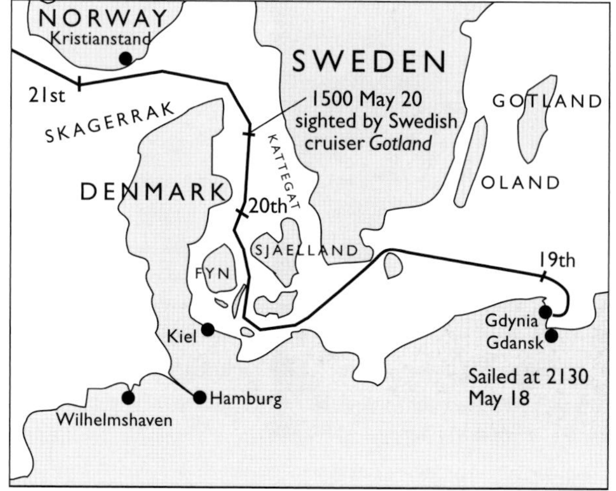

A spy in Gotenhafen also reported the departure of the German force the day after the squadron sailed. While all these signals were being sent, *Bismarck* and her consort rounded the northern tip of Denmark, and headed west–north–west through the Skaggerak into the North Sea.

At some time during the night of May 20 the *Bismarck* and *Prinz Eugen* steamed around the southern tip of Norway, and headed northwest, reaching the latitude of Stavanger by dawn the following morning (May 21). By noon they entered the confines of the Korsfjord, the sea approach to the Norwegian port of Bergen. The *Bismarck* then turned into Grimstadfjord, dropping anchor in the eastern end of the narrow inlet. The *Prinz Eugen* and her accompanying destroyers continued north past Bergen, finally anchoring in the Hjeltefjord, close to the island of Fjell. That afternoon, painting parties were sent over the side to repaint both ships in a dark gray color, deemed more suitable for operations in the North Atlantic than their lighter Baltic color scheme with its

OPPOSITE: The wolf leaves its lair: The *Bismarck* and *Prinz Eugen* leave Gotenhafen and thread their way through the Kattegat and the Skagerrak.

ABOVE: The *Prinz Eugen* leaving Gotenhafen harbor. She anchored outside the harbor to take on extra provisions before sailing into the Baltic. *MNF*

LEFT: The *Bismarck* in the Baltic the day after leaving Gotenhafen, photographed from the *Prinz Eugen*. A messenger line is being stretched between the two ships by the watch on deck.

characteristic dazzle stripe amidships. Further supplies were taken on board; but while the Kommandant of the *Prinz Eugen* took advantage of the day-long pause to top up his cruiser's fuel tanks, the *Bismarck* did not, a minor event which would have grave repercussions as the campaign progressed.

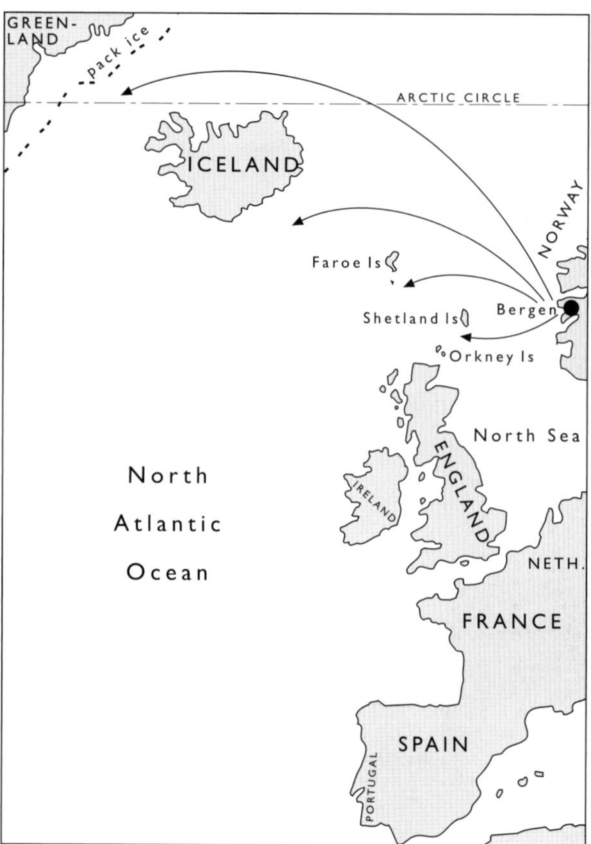

Admiral Lütjens spent the time weighing up his options. First, he surveyed the most recent intelligence available to him. Aerial reconnaissance of the British anchorage at Scapa Flow suggested that most capital ships were still in port, so it appeared that his presence in Norwegian waters had so far gone undetected. To break out to the North Atlantic, he would need to pass through one of four passages. The most northerly was the gap between Greenland and Iceland known as the Denmark Strait. This had the advantage of being furthest away from the British naval base at Scapa Flow, although the Strait itself was narrower than charted due to the presence of both British mines off Iceland and pack ice off the Greenland coast. The second route lay between Iceland and the Faeroe Islands, and although British cruisers would probably guard the passage, it was considered the most direct route available. This was the route suggested by the Seekriegsleitung. A third passage between the Faeroes and Shetland was also a possibility, although its proximity to the British naval base made it its passage an extremely hazardous undertaking. Similarly, the fourth gap, between Shetland and Orkney was so close to Scapa Flow and the RAF bases on Orkney and in the north of Scotland that any attempt was considered suicidal. For the same reason, a passage through the Pentland Firth between Orkney and the Scottish mainland was out of the question. Effectively, Lütjens' only two options were the Denmark Strait, and Iceland–Faeroes gap.

While the Seekriegsleitung might have favored the latter passage, Lütjens remained unconvinced, largely due to his concern that his presence might have been reported, and that the British had already left Scapa Flow and were steaming north to intercept him. As the Fleet Commander, the decision was his; so Lütjens opted for the most distant passage through the Denmark Strait. The aerial reconnaissance of Scapa Flow was probably a factor in his decision, as it appeared that the *Bismarck* might be able to pass through the Denmark Strait before the British fleet could sail to intercept her.

Late in the evening of May 21, the *Bismarck* weighed anchor and steamed north up the Hjeltefjord, picking up the *Prinz Eugen* and her two destroyers on the way, before turning west into the Norwegian Sea. By midnight

OPPOSITE: Berthed in Grimstadfjord the ships had four sailing options, each further from the British mainland.

BELOW: The *Prinz Eugen* in Norwegian waters, immediately to the west of Bergen. During her short stay in the fjords she took on fuel and tested her gunnery systems. In this photograph her main guns are being traversed.

she was heading north towards the Arctic Ocean. Around 0300 on May 22, the two accompanying destroyers were detached, and ordered to put in to the German naval base at Trondheim. Around noon that day, the *Bismarck* and the *Prinz Eugen* altered course to the west, bound for the Denmark Strait. Although the German tanker *Weissenburg* was stationed in the area, Lütjens made no attempt to rendezvous with her. This was the *Bismarck*'s last chance to take on additional fuel.

As for the British, they were not as unprepared as Lütjens thought. Once word that the *Bismarck* had passed through the Kattegat reached London, the Admiralty asked the Royal Air Force to search for the battleship along the Norwegian coast. Around noon on May 21, a Spitfire flying a high-altitude aerial reconnaissance mission near Bergen took photographs of vessels in Grimstadfjord and Hjeltefjord. That afternoon the film was developed and analyzed by a team of photographic interpreters. The images showed a large ship in Grimstadfjord, surrounded by smaller tenders. Another slightly smaller capital ship in Hjeltefjord was also surrounded by attendant craft. It appeared that the larger ship was a battleship, and the secondary vessel was an *Admiral Hipper*-class heavy cruiser. There was little doubt as to the identity of the battleship. Unknown to Lütjens, the *Bismarck* had been discovered. The photographs were flown to London for the attention of the First Sea Lord, while Tovey was informed of the sighting by his RAF liaison officer.

Also unknown to the German admiral, a British cruiser force was already patrolling the Denmark Strait. Rear-Admiral William F. Wake-Walker, commanding the 1st

RIGHT: The location of the waiting British ships, spread out to cover the entrances to the Atlantic.

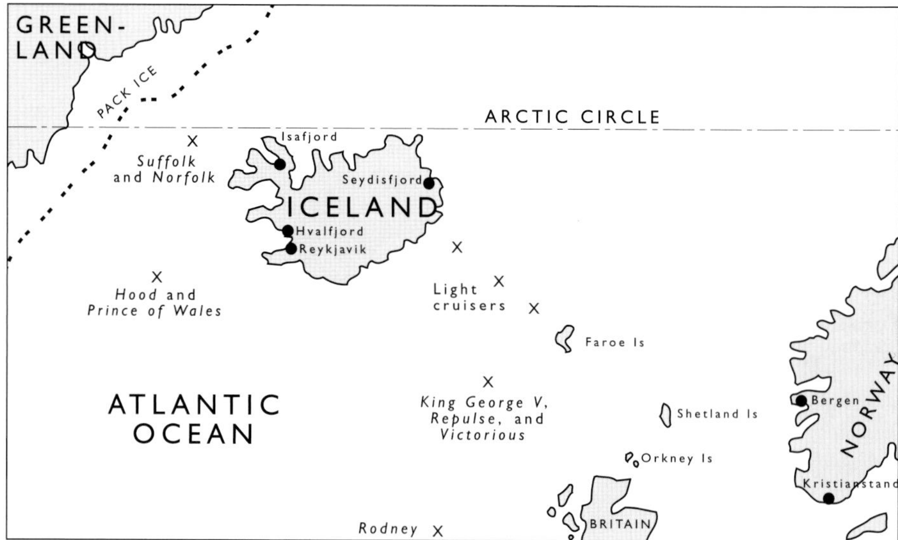

Cruiser Squadron, was in charge of two British cruisers: his flagship the *Norfolk*, and another heavy cruiser, the *Suffolk*. On May 19 the *Suffolk* had been on station for several days, and was running low on fuel. Consequently, Wake-Walker ordered her to put into the Icelandic port of Hvalfjord to refuel, and then to rejoin the *Norfolk* on station. Both vessels were *County*-class heavy cruisers, built during the 1920s, and armed with eight 8in. guns. With a displacement of 10,000 tons apiece and a top speed of 31 knots, they were comparable in size to the *Prinz Eugen*, although they were not so modern, and lacked the German cruiser's armor and up-to-date gunnery direction systems.

When the Germans invaded Denmark in 1940, Iceland was a quasi-independent Danish possession, and was duly occupied by British troops to prevent her capture by the enemy. The island was also well placed to act as a useful base for operations in the North Atlantic, the Arctic Sea and the Norwegian Sea. The Royal Navy soon established small naval bases around the island to serve as refueling and resupply depots, the largest of which was Hvalfjord, just north of the Icelandic capital of Reykjavik. The small base at Isafjord lay on the Denmark Strait, while two other small bases were sited on the eastern side of the island. The British were well aware that the sea passages on either side of Iceland would serve as avenues into the Atlantic for German surface raiders, U-boats and supply ships. For this reason the two cruisers were patrolling the inhospitable waters of the Denmark Strait, where pack ice off the Greenland coast reduced the width of the navigable channel dramatically. To further limit German access to the Atlantic the British laid minefields on the northern end of

LEFT: The passage through the Kattegat, with the *Bismarck* leading the *Prinz Eugen*, and the capital ships flanked by a screen of destroyers.

BELOW LEFT: The *Bismarck* entering Grimstadfjord.

BELOW: The Norwegian pilot embarking the *Prinz Eugen* in Korsfjord, prior to her entrance into the fjords.

the Denmark Strait, close to the Icelandic coast. The Germans knew the British had left a narrow channel close to the pack ice, and it was into this restrictive waterway that the two German ships were heading. It was also where Wake-Walker's cruisers were patrolling; the *Norfolk* on station at the edge of the minefield, and the *Suffolk* steaming north to join her, after her refueling visit to Hvalfjord. The Admiralty had already signaled Wake-Walker to inform him that the *Bismarck* and another large warship were on the move, so the British lookouts and radar operators were alert.

The man whose task it was to co-ordinate the British response to the German sortie was Admiral Sir John C. Tovey, the Commander-in-Chief of the British Home Fleet, based in Scapa Flow. Collectively, the naval units he had at his disposal were powerful enough to destroy the *Bismarck*, but ship for ship the Germans had a distinct advantage: his best battleship and also his flagship, the modern *King George V*, was the most capable of engaging the German battleship on something like equal terms. Her sister ship *Prince of Wales* still had problems with her main armament, and although ready for sea, she was not fully operational. Tovey's battlecruisers were poorly armored, although the *Repulse* was better protected than the *Hood*. At least the *Hood* had a well-trained crew, and was already in Scapa Flow, while the *Repulse* was several hours steaming to the south, in the Firth of Clyde. The aircraft carrier *Victorious* was also in Scapa Flow, along with four light cruisers and nine fleet destroyers. Two more destroyers were en route to Scapa from Iceland, while two more light cruisers were on passage through the northeastern Atlantic. Finally, he could draw on the two heavy cruisers in the Denmark Strait, and two more light cruisers guarding the Iceland-Faeroes gap. Tovey's task was to deploy these assets so that all possible German approaches to the Atlantic were covered.

The British admiral was still unsure as to the identity of the *Bismarck*'s consort, although he was fairly certain she was an *Admiral Hipper*-class heavy cruiser. Although the cruiser would be unable to engage a battleship on her own, she could lend the weight of her guns to the *Bismarck* in a naval engagement fought at less than 10 miles, giving the German battlecruiser a slight edge in a straight fight. Tovey therefore made the decision to operate his capital ships in pairs, teaming the battlecruiser *Hood* up with the *Prince of Wales*, and

LEFT: The *Bismarck* was spotted on May 21, 1941 by an RAF Spitfire piloted by Flying Officer Suckling during a photo-reconnaissance mission of the Bergen area. Suckling photographed the battleship at anchor in Grimstadfjord around 1315 from an altitude of 25,000ft, his presence undetected by the German crews below him. *IWM*

BELOW LEFT: During the afternoon of May 21 the crew of the *Bismarck* remained on alert in case of an enemy air attack. In this photograph, sailors survey the Norwegian scenery from their action stations.

FAR LEFT: Admiral Tovey (left) conferring with Captain Leach of the *Prince of Wales*. Despite his concern about the effectiveness of Leach's untried warship and raw crew, he had little choice but to commit her to action. *IWM*

his flagship *King George V* with the battlecruiser *Repulse* (when the *Repulse* reached him).

The *Hood* and her consort were commanded by Vice-Admiral Lancelot E. Holland, who flew his flag in the battlecruiser. Late in the evening of May 21, roughly at the same time that the *Bismarck* slipped out of Grimstadfjord, Holland led his force out of Scapa Flow, escorted by six destroyers. His orders were to head for the Icelandic coast off Hvalfjord, then await further orders. With Holland's force placed to cover either the Denmark Strait or the Iceland–Faeroes Gap, Tovey was making the best use of the ships he had. At the same time the *Suffolk* was ordered north from Hvalfjord at best possible speed to rejoin the *Norfolk*. The British light cruisers *Arethusa*, *Birmingham* and *Manchester* were ordered to refuel in Iceland, then patrol the Iceland–Faeroes gap. All three light cruisers carried 6in. guns, insufficiently powerful to do any damage to either of the German ships. Instead, like the heavy cruisers of Admiral Wake-Walker, they were there to locate the enemy if he passed through the gap, then report the sighting to Tovey. The cruisers would then evade the German battleship while shadowing her, sending in constant updates on her course and speed. This would allow Tovey and Holland to move their capital ships into place to bar the way.

During the night of May 21, the RAF bombed the Grimstadfjord, but poor visibility meant that it was the following afternoon before another reconnaissance flight could return to see what damage had been done. It found that the fjord was empty, as was neighboring Hjeltefjord. The *Bismarck* had escaped. In fact both German ships were hundreds of miles away to the north, steaming up the Norwegian coast. The problem for the British was that some 24 hours had passed since their last confirmed sighting of the German battleship. If the *Bismarck* had sailed soon after she was first spotted, she could be 600 miles away from the fjord, placing her anywhere from the Arctic Circle to the Baltic. At least by the evening of May 22, Admiral Tovey knew that the *Bismarck* was heading his way, as British intelligence passed on their spy's report that the Germans planned to sortie into the Atlantic. It was time for Tovey to guess where Lütjens was heading, and to make his dispositions accordingly.

Shortly before midnight on May 22, Tovey sailed from Scapa Flow in *King George V*, accompanied by the aircraft carrier *Victorious*, six light cruisers (*Aurora*, *Galatea*, *Hermione*, *Kenya* and *Neptune*), and six destroyers. The *Repulse*, in the Firth of Clyde, was ordered to steam north at full speed to join the flagship in the Iceland–Faeroes gap. Both capital ship groups were therefore concentrated to the south of Iceland, ready to strike at the Germans as soon as the cruiser screens sighted the enemy. In the Arctic Ocean, *Bismarck* and *Prinz* Eugen continued to steam west, unaware of the naval activity to the south. As far as Admiral Lütjens was aware, the British Home Fleet had still not left Scapa Flow. The same bad weather, which had hindered the British search aircraft over Norway, also plagued the German reconnaissance aircraft over Orkney. By the morning of May 23, as Tovey's units were reaching the Iceland–Faeroes gap, Lütjens was approaching the northern end of the Denmark Strait. By late-afternoon they had sighted the edge of the pack ice off Greenland, and had turned south-south-east in line astern, with the *Bismarck* in the lead. As Lütjens did not know exactly how

ABOVE: The heavy cruiser HMS *Norfolk*, flagship of Rear-Admiral Wake-Walker. The photograph was taken in Scapa Flow in 1940. *RNM*

TOP: The *Bismarck* leaving the Norwegian fjords, photographed from the forecastle of the *Prinz Eugen*. *MNF*

ABOVE LEFT: HMS *Hood* at anchor in Scapa Flow, photographed from the fleet flagship. The battlecruiser sailed from Orkney on the evening of May 21, 1941. *IWM*

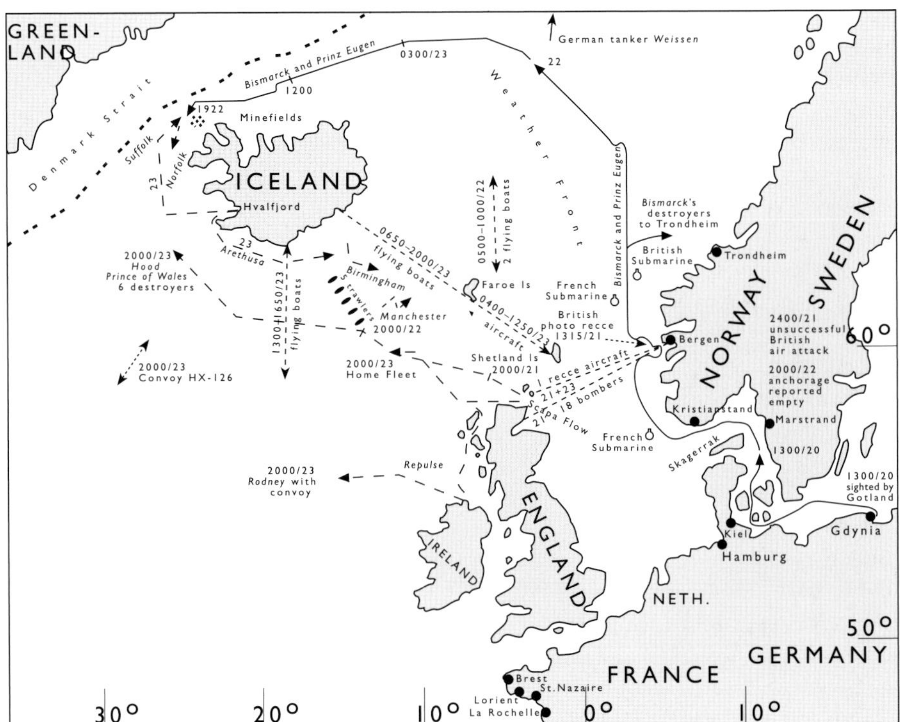

RIGHT: Major ship movements May 21–23.

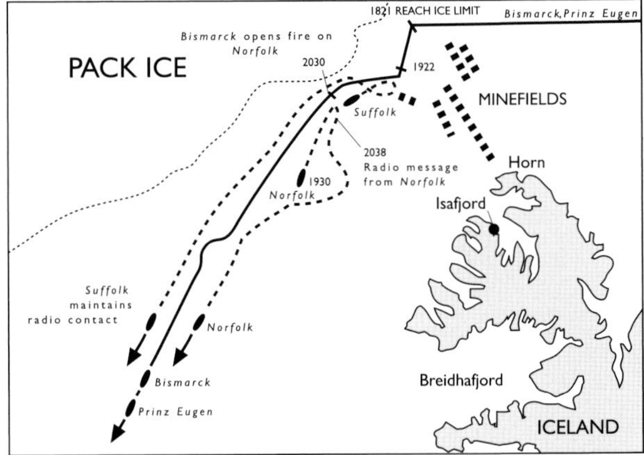

BELOW RIGHT: The Germans enter the Denmark Strait and get past *Norfolk* and *Suffolk*.

OPPOSITE, ABOVE: Although the *Suffolk* was equipped with an effective radar set, it was not completely reliable, and lookouts remained indispensable while the cruiser patrolled the Denmark Strait. *IWM*

OPPOSITE, BELOW: The *Suffolk* on patrol in the Denmark Strait. Her crew are manning an eight-barrelled machine-gun position. *MNF*

far the British minefield extended, he chose to play it safe and skirt the western edge of the Strait.

That afternoon, the German forced edged into the Strait: their progress was uneventful until 1920, when they were spotted by the British cruiser *Suffolk*. As soon as the *Bismarck* was sighted the *Suffolk* turned away and raced for the safety of a covering fog bank, then escaped any pursuit by skirting the minefields on the Iceland side of the Strait. She radioed the information to the Admiralty, and an hour later the cruiser was joined by her consort, the *Norfolk*, flagship of Vice-Admiral Wake-Walker. *Bismarck* opened fire, forcing the *Norfolk* to run for cover, prompting a game of cat and mouse amid the fog and rain squalls and the gathering darkness. Eventually the two British cruisers worked their way around astern of the German ships, maintaining contact and sending a stream of progress reports to both Admiral Tovey and the Admiralty. While Wake-Walker's flagship had only a fairly basic gunnery radar, the *Suffolk* carried a more sophisticated search set, enabling her to track the movements of the *Bismarck* and her consort from a safe distance. During the brief engagement between the *Bismarck* and the *Norfolk*, the blast from her guns knocked out the radar set on the German battleship. Lütjens therefore ordered the *Prinz Eugen* to take the lead and act as the eyes and ears of the German force.

This change of position went undetected by the radar operators on the British cruisers. Lütjens knew his position had been reported, but still thought it unlikely the Royal Navy would have capital ships in the area within the next 24 hours or so. The cruisers were most likely on a regular patrol, and their presence did not necessarily prove that the British were aware that the *Bismarck* had sailed.

On board the *Hood*, Admiral Holland was informed of the sighting report, and received orders to steam at high speed to the west to intercept. He was already due south of Hvalfjord in Iceland, and a quick calculation showed that the *Hood* and the *Prince of Wales* could be in a position to intercept the German ships by nightfall. His two ships should be able to take on the *Bismarck* on something approaching equal terms, while Wake-Walker's cruisers could occupy the *Prinz Eugen*. He ordered his squadron to come round onto a heading of 270°, and to increase speed. The weather conditions were bad, the seas rough, but given that the British cruisers could keep up their stream of sighting reports, Holland estimated that contact would be made around 0300. The six destroyers escorting the British capital ships were unable to keep up in the rough seas, so shortly after 2200 Holland detached them, ordering them to follow on at best possible speed. About the same time, the radar operators on *Suffolk* detected a change in the course of their target. The *Bismarck* had reversed course, in an attempt to attack or drive off the two cruisers that were following her. The radar gave the British ships ample warning, and they slipped away under cover of the fog. Unable to find a target, the *Bismarck* resumed her original course, and the British cruisers resumed their station astern of her. Around midnight a heavy snowstorm interfered with the *Suffolk's* radar reception, and the *Bismarck* and *Prinz*

Eugen increased speed, slipping away under cover of the weather. Contact was lost for two crucial hours, prompting Holland to turn northwest, in case the *Bismarck* had turned away to the south and was slipping past the British net. It was a tense period, and the relief felt when radar contact was resumed at 0300 was heartfelt. The Germans had continued on their original course of 220°, by which time Holland had ordered another course change to 240°, planning to intercept the *Bismarck* during the early hours of the morning. When the relative positions of the forces were plotted, Holland altered the speed of his ships in order to make contact with the Germans at dawn.

The Battle of the Denmark Strait

As Vice-Admiral Holland's small force steamed west to intercept the *Bismarck*, his crews prepared for action and remained at their posts. With contact expected at dawn, few would have managed to snatch any sleep. On the *Prince of Wales*, the handful of civilian contractors who had remained on board worked through the night to iron out the few remaining mechanical problems which still plagued the new battleship's main guns. Shortly before dawn, the crews were put on full alert, and lookouts peered to starboard in the direction the Germans were expected to appear from. Finally, at 0537, a lookout on the *Hood* spotted smoke and a possible ship on the horizon, directly on the starboard beam. The gunnery

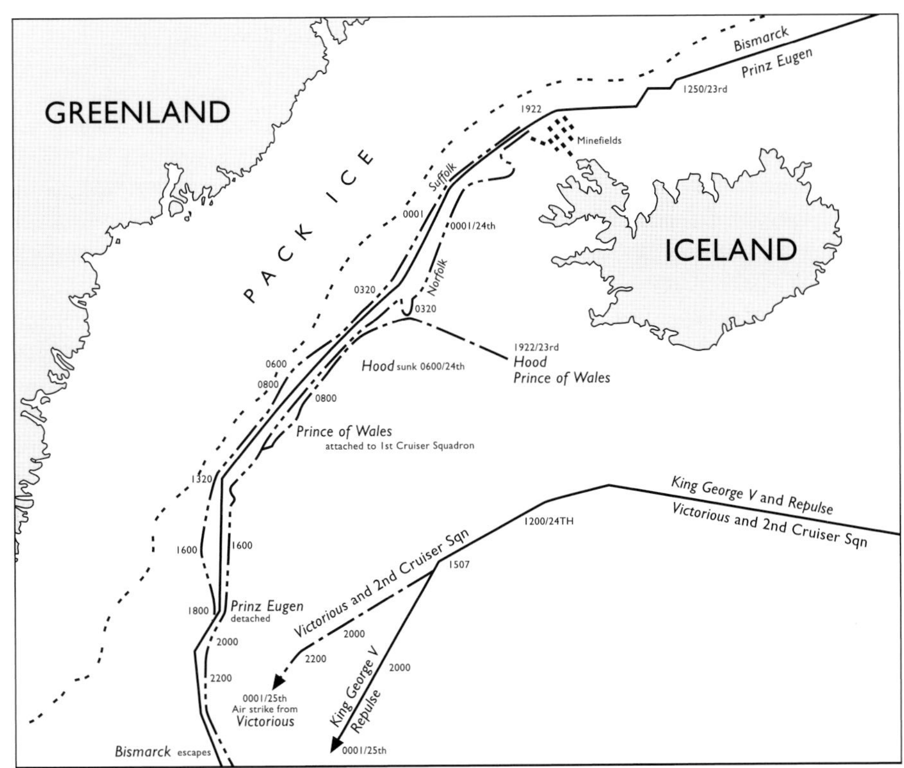

LEFT: The Battle of the Denmark Strait.

BELOW LEFT: The *Bismarck* in Arctic waters, viewed from the *Prinz Eugen*. *MNF*

directors turned towards the target, and computed the range to be 30,000 yards (or 17 miles); beyond the effective gunnery range of both British warships. The crews were already prepared for action, so it simply became a matter of waiting for the order to shoot.

A few miles to the north, Admiral Lütjens had also kept his crews at their battle stations during the night, as he had no idea what dawn might bring. German Naval Intelligence still insisted that the Home Fleet was at Scapa Flow, but the German Admiral was taking no chances. He knew the British cruisers that were shadowing him were keeping Admiral Tovey informed of the *Bismarck*'s progress, and that the British would undoubtedly send ships to bar his way. While he still thought it unlikely that any capital ship would reach him before he broke out into the Atlantic, he knew he was hemmed into a narrow channel, and was unable to run to the west due to the Greenland pack ice. Shortly before dawn, the underwater acoustic detectors fitted to the *Prinz Eugen* detected the sound of ships' engines, some 20 miles to the southeast. Fifteen minutes later, at 0535, lookouts on the *Prinz Eugen* spotted smoke on the horizon, in the same direction as the two acoustic contacts. Like his British counterpart, Lütjens did some quick calculations. The enemy ships were some 20° forward of the port beam, meaning they were slightly ahead of the Germans. Given the reports, Lütjens doubted the contacts were capital ships, thinking it more likely that they were two British cruisers sent to relieve the heavy cruisers that had shadowed him throughout the night. If the intelligence reports were wrong and the two ships were battleships, Lütjens hoped he could use the superior speed of his ships to avoid contact, and to circle round the enemy by heading west–south–west. After all, his mission was to destroy enemy convoys, not risk his ship in a major engagement against enemy capital ships. Only the British battlecruisers or the fast modern battleships of the *King George V*-class posed a serious threat, as they had the speed to force a battle on the Germans. The next few minutes would reveal what kind of opponent Lütjens faced.

Although the 15in. guns carried by the *Hood* could theoretically fire at a range of 30,000 yards, the gunnery direction systems only worked effectively at around 26,500 yards (or 15 miles), and even then the range was considered extreme. Current practice meant that it was necessary to close within 25,000 yards before opening fire, and even then the chance of a single hit on target from a full eight-gun salvo was considered to be no more than 25 percent. In the seconds after the sighting, Holland and his staff would have calculated the ranges, bearings and angles of fire, allowing the Admiral to come up with a plan. He knew he had a superiority of 2:1 in firepower, but that the gun crews on the *Prince of Wales* were inexperienced at fire control, and his own flagship was vulnerable at long range. As the range decreased, not only would the accuracy of gunnery improve, but also the *Hood* would become less vulnerable to plunging fire, from enemy shells dropping down at the end of their parabolic arc onto her poorly-armored upper deck. Her zone of vulnerability to plunging fire extended for 8,000 yards, meaning it was vital that the battlecruiser close to within 22,500 yards as quickly as possible.

When contact was made, the British ships were steaming in line astern (the *Prince of Wales* following 800 yards astern of the *Hood*), following a course of 240° (west-south-west), while the Germans were on a nearly parallel course of 220° (southwest). The German ships were also in line, with the *Bismarck* 1,000 yards astern of the *Prinz Eugen*. Although the range was closing, Holland wanted the range to decrease as fast as possible while still maintaining a position between the Germans and the open Atlantic to the south. Unfortunately, the engagement was still a race, as the *Bismarck* and her consort could still evade the British by turning to starboard. If Holland had arrived in the area just 30 minutes before, he would have been in a position to cross the "T" of the Germans, giving his ships an inestimable advantage in gunnery, as all their guns could bear on the enemy, while only the forward guns on his lead ship could fire back. Less than 30 seconds after the sighting was made, the Admiral duly ordered both ships to turn in succession to starboard, onto a new course of 280°. That meant the two forces would close at almost 780 yards per minute, bringing the leading German ship into range of the *Hood* within five minutes.

For his part, Admiral Lütjens opted to keep the range open, and at 0539 he ordered an alteration of course from 220° to 265°, heading almost due west. While the two forces were still closing, the rate had now dropped to 235 yards per minute, giving Lütjens more chance to evaluate the threat. It also meant giving up his maneuvering room to westward, as the new course brought his ships closer to the line of pack ice some 20 miles to the west. The British gunnery officers reported the course change to Holland. He realized that he needed to alter course to decrease the range, but any further turn would mean that the rear turrets of both the *Hood* and the *Prince of Wales* would be obscured (as they could only train as far as 45° forward from the beam). Still, it was the only way to reduce move the *Hood* out of her zone of vulnerability. At 0549 he ordered another course change, onto a new heading of 300°. Although this meant the

ABOVE: The *Hood*, photographed from the Prince of Wales during the afternoon of May 21, 1941. *RNM*

BELOW: The converging tracks of the vessels involved in the battle.

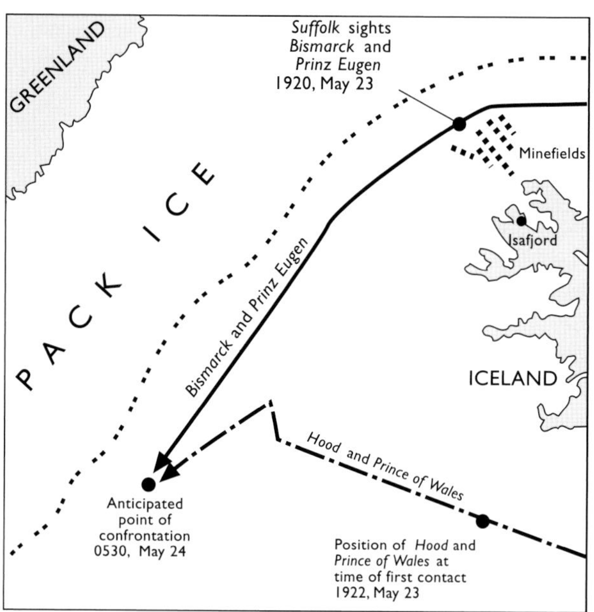

British ships had lost half of their firepower, and reduced the risk of a hit from each salvo, the rate of closure had now increased to 540 yards per minute. The *Hood* was also almost within range of the leading German ship, which her gunnery officer took to be the *Bismarck*. Within three minutes, the range would be down to 25,000 yards, at which point Holland would give the order to commence fire. The German ships were now 40° to starboard of the British flagship.

Fourteen miles to the north, Lütjens had realized that no British cruiser force would deliberately choose to close the range with an enemy battleship. The ships approaching him had to be capital ships. He also realized that from their speed, they were not old, slow battleships, but more probably the *Hood* or another battlecruiser, and a battleship of the *King George*-class. He was left with no option but to fight. He was also aware that as the British were now abaft the beam of his ships, his forward turrets were almost at their extreme angle of fire. Any move by the British to starboard would place his ships in the same position as his opponents, by making half his guns unable to bear on their target. He decided to alter course.

Just as he did so, at 0552, the *Hood* opened fire. The range had decreased to 25,000 yards, and Holland had given the order to fire. The four forward guns of the battlecruiser were elevated at the 22°-angle necessary for their shells to reach their target at that range, and the gunnery officer opened fire with a salvo. At that range it took almost 50 seconds for the shells to reach their target. Once the salvo landed, the gunnery officer would note where the shell splashes fell, then correct his aim onto the target. In 1941 gunnery was a process of gradual refinement as the range was corrected with every salvo until the enemy was straddled. Then it would be a matter of time before one-ton 15in. armor-piercing shells began ripping into the decks and armored sides of their target. The only problem was that the *Hood* was firing on the wrong ship. When Holland gave the order to open fire, he ordered that both ships should fire on the leading German ship, which he and his staff believed to be the *Bismarck*. The problem was, at that range and angle, the *Bismarck* and the *Prinz Eugen* had a similar silhouette, and the difference in size between the two ships could still not be clearly determined. Also, the last report from the cruiser Suffolk stated that the *Bismarck* was the leading German ship, followed in line astern by the *Prinz Eugen*. The damage to the *Bismarck*'s radar during her brief engagement with the shadowing British cruisers a few hours before meant that she had to rely on the *Prinz Eugen* to scout the way, so the cruiser had taken the lead. It was a costly mistake, as it would take precious minutes for the gunnery officer and his team to switch targets, calibrate range and distance, then engage a different target.

LEFT: Vice-Admiral Holland was committed to a race for the southern exit of the Denmark Strait in order to block the *Bismarck*'s route into the Atlantic.

On board the *Prince of Wales*, Captain Leach faced a dilemma. His experienced gunnery officer had identified the second German ship as the *Bismarck*, but Holland had ordered the battleship's guns to concentrate on the leading German ship, the *Prinz Eugen*. To disobey a senior officer's order in peacetime was a court-martial offense, but in battle, the stakes were higher, both for Leach and for his ship. The *Prince of Wales* had better optics than the flagship, and Leach had faith in his gunnery officer. Risking everything, he ordered his guns to be trained on the second German ship. Strangely, no attempt was made to pass on the change or the identification to Holland, but presumably Leach hoped the *Hood*'s gunners had already realized their mistake. Some 20 seconds after the *Hood* fired, the six forward 14in. guns of the *Prince of Wales* fired at the *Bismarck*. The slight delay was to avoid confusion, as shell splashes from two ships landing around a target at the same time made gunnery direction extremely difficult. In fact, as both British ships fired at different targets, no such confusion occurred. In less than a minute shell splashes rose up close to the *Prinz Eugen*, followed seconds later by a similar fall of shot near the *Bismarck*. The gunnery officers corrected their aim and fired again. Any lingering doubts that the Germans might have had about the size of their opponents vanished as huge columns of water rose from the sea beside their ships.

As the initial British salvos landed, Lütjens was giving the order to change course, and the *Prinz Eugen*

RIGHT: The last photograph of the *Hood*, taken during the early evening of May 22 from the *Prince of Wales*.

FAR RIGHT: The Achilles heel of the 'mighty *Hood*' was her poor protection against plunging fire onto her deck.

heeled 65° to port onto a new course of 200°, followed a minute or so later by the *Bismarck*, astern. The German admiral also gave the order to open fire with both ships as soon as the turn was completed, and the gunnery calculations could be recomputed. The time was now 0553, and the ships were 24,000 yards apart. The range was still decreasing at almost 1,000 yards per minute, but on the new course, the Germans were assured they could fire all their guns at either target, and if the British continued on course then the Germans would also cross their "T". Also, at that angle, because the British could only bear on their target with their forward guns, the Germans had nullified the numerical superiority of the British. In fact, the odds were now in the Germans' favor, as one of the forward 14in. guns of the *Prince of Wales* had ceased firing due to mechanical failure; the result of the problem which had caused her civilian contractors to work on the guns throughout the night. This meant that four British guns were firing at each German ship, while the *Bismarck*'s eight 15in. guns were concentrated on the *Hood*. In addition, the *Prinz Eugen* also added the weight of her 8in. guns to the equation, as she too concentrated on the British flagship. The cruiser was the first German ship to open fire, having completed her turn by 0554. The range was 23,000 yards. It took 40 seconds for the shells to reach their target, and a hit was scored with this first salvo. Although the 8in. shells of the cruiser were unable to penetrate the main armor of the battlecruiser, they might hit a lightly protected portion of the ship, or cause damage to her superstructure. One of her shells hit an ammunition locker on the *Hood*, located amidships on the starboard side of her upper deck. The 4in. shells in the locker "cooked off," causing concern to her crew but no real damage to the ship. The *Prinz Eugen* had found her range with her first salvo, and unlike the larger battleship guns, she could fire three rounds per minute. Seconds later the first salvo from the *Bismarck* made the sea erupt close by the *Hood*. While the initial British salvos had been well-aimed, the German opening shots were right on target. By this time it was clear that the *Hood* was firing at the wrong target, and Holland ordered her to switch targets to the *Bismarck*. He also ordered Leach to do likewise, relieving Leach of his problem of insubordination.

Holland was also aware that the German ships had altered course, and were now almost perpendicular to his own course. While he was still within the zone of vulnerability, the new angle increased the risk of plunging fire, as falling shells had the whole length of the *Hood*'s upper deck as a target. He needed to change course to port to reduce this risk, and to bring his aft guns into play. He also needed to continue to close the range. At 0555 he ordered the British ships to turn in succession 20° to port, onto a new course of 260°; the first of two

minor alterations of course he would order within four minutes. That way the gunnery control teams would have less problem keeping track of the target than if they made one major course change. The turn was made as the first salvos fell around her, and as the shell from the *Prinz Eugen* caused damage to her upper deck.

At that point Lütjens made two decisions. He had already identified the two British ships, although he remained convinced that the second warship was Admiral Tovey's flagship, *King George V*. German intelligence had assured him that her sister ship the *Prince of Wales* had still not entered service, so the battleship had to be Tovey's flagship. Too dangerous to leave unengaged, Lütjens ordered the *Prinz Eugen* to switch targets to the British battleship, in order to keep her occupied. He also ordered her to reduce speed, allowing the *Bismarck* to pass her to port and take the lead. With the *Prinz Eugen* astern of the *Bismarck*, it was better placed to engage the British battleship, and to counter any aggressive move made by the shadowing British cruisers.

By 0557, when the German cruiser swiveled her guns onto the *Prince of Wales*, the British ships had each fired at least four salvos, but had scored no hits. After the first two, both ships were targeting the *Bismarck*. The third salvo from the *Bismarck* landed a minute later, bracketing the Hood, but scoring no hits. The German gunners had found the range, meaning that any more salvoes would be right on target. At 0559 Holland gave the order to turn to port a second time, a 20° alteration which would put the *Hood* on a course of 260°. At that angle, with the enemy 35° forward of her beam, her aft turrets would be able to fire. She was also still closing the range to her opponent. As Holland was issuing the command, the gunnery officer on the *Bismarck* gave the order to fire to fire three salvos in quick succession, some 30 seconds apart. The range was 18,000 yards, just over 10 miles. The fourth salvo from the *Bismarck* landed at 0559 and 30 seconds, straddling the battlecruiser but scoring no hits. Thirty seconds later at 0600 the fifth salvo landed, just as the *Hood* was completing her turn. The German gunners had reduced the elevation slightly with each salvo, expecting the *Hood* to continue on her course of 280° and "walk" into her fall of shot. The *Hood*'s turn had almost taken her out of the beaten zone, but her stern was still within the target area. While most of the shells missed and landed where the *Hood* should have been if she had remained on course, one struck her in the stern, close to her after turrets. That one shell was all it took to end a legend.

Observers in the *Prince of Wales* saw a huge flame shoot up from abaft the *Hood*'s mainmast (the rearmost mast of the ship). This was followed by an incredible explosion from the stern of the battlecruiser. The

Bismarck's shell had penetrated the vulnerable deck armor of the *Hood*, plunging through her decks into the after magazines. The shells and propellants were ignited, causing a second cataclysmic explosion, which ripped the stern of the *Hood* apart. A huge yellowish cloud loomed over the stern of the battlecruiser, hiding the carnage beneath it.

Naval analysts have considered the cause of the catastrophe, and some cite the first explosion as being the precursor of the second, marking the detonation of the *Hood*'s small torpedo magazine towards the after end of her upper deck. The blast from this then ignited the ship's main magazine, beneath "X" turret. While it is not impossible that two shells hit the *Hood*, the two explosions were some two seconds apart, suggesting that one detonation caused the other. Whatever the cause, the effect was cataclysmic.

A survivor reported that on the *Hood*'s bridge, nobody realized the full extent of the damage for several seconds until the helmsman reported that the rudder refused to answer, and lookouts reported the stern was sinking. The shattered stern had indeed sheared off near the mainmast, and as both parts of the ship filled with water, the bow and stern slowly rose up out of the water, forming a huge "V". As the sixth salvo from the *Bismarck* slammed into the water astern of the *Hood*, the forward section of the ship continued sliding forward through the water, propelled only by her momentum. Within a minute the stern had gone, taking everyone in it down with it.

It took two more minutes for the forward section of the battlecruiser to slip under, sufficient only for a handful of men on lookout positions or on deck to jump for their lives. As she slipped under, the sea seemed to boil as air pockets broke to the surface and burst; then nothing was left but debris, oil and a pitiful handful of

LEFT: Like the *Bismarck*, the *Hood* carried eight 15in. guns, but lacked the modern fire-control systems and armored protection of her adversary. *RNM*

BELOW LEFT: According to one of the three survivors, Captain Kerr of the *Hood* elected to remain on the bridge and go down with his ship. *RNM*

survivors. Both Admiral and Captain went down with their ship. Of the 1,420 men who formed her crew, there were only three survivors.

Observers from all three combatants and the two shadowing British cruisers recall a moment of awe at the destruction and catastrophic loss of life they had just witnessed. The moment passed, and a somewhat stunned Lütjens ordered the *Bismarck* to turn her guns on the British battleship, which was swerving to starboard to avoid running through the wreckage of the *Hood*. As Rear-Admiral Wake-Walker ordered the news of the *Hood*'s loss to be radioed to the Admiralty, Captain Leach was left to take on Germany's most powerful battleship alone.

By 0602, the *Prince of Wales* had resumed her intended original course of 260°, allowing all her guns to bear on the *Bismarck*. She resumed her fire, straddling the German battleship with her salvos, but apparently not scoring any hits. The range was now just over 15,000 yards, and with the Germans still on a course of 200°, the distance between the combatants was decreasing steadily. A minute later a shell from the *Bismarck* struck the bridge of the *Prince of Wales*, killing several vital crewmen and officers, and momentarily stunning the battleship's captain. For a few minutes, control was passed to the After Control Position, and the ship fought on while Captain Leach recrewed the damaged bridge. Simultaneously, 8in. shells fired from the Prinz Eugen struck the fire control director for the British ship's secondary guns, while two more shells struck her below the waterline.

Fortunately for Leach it was at that moment that the *Bismarck* overhauled *the Prinz Eugen* to port, obscuring the cruiser's guns for two minutes while she passed. Once the battleship had passed ahead of the cruiser, the *Prinz Eugen* resumed her firing. In the meantime Leach had resumed control, and ordered a turn to port to 200°, putting both battleships on a parallel course, some 14,500 yards apart. At that range virtually every salvo could score multiple hits. Unfortunately for Leach, it was the German guns that proved the more accurate. Within the next two minutes the *Prince of Wales* was hit twice, once amidships by her hangar, causing a serious fire, and another amidships below the waterline, causing flooding. By 0605, Leach was forced to bow to the inevitable. His major guns were proving faulty, his secondary armament was made largely ineffective by the gunnery direction damage, and his ship was taking on water. Worse still, his rear turret had jammed. By contrast the *Bismarck* appeared to be undamaged, and the *Prinz Eugen* was about to resume fire. He decided to break off the action, radioing to Wake-Walker in the *Norfolk* for permission to disengage. Wake-Walker, now the senior officer in the area after the death of Holland was forced to agree that risking further damage or loss to the battleship was probably not going to achieve anything. Leach swung his ship away onto a new course of 150°, and covered his withdrawal by a smokescreen. For the

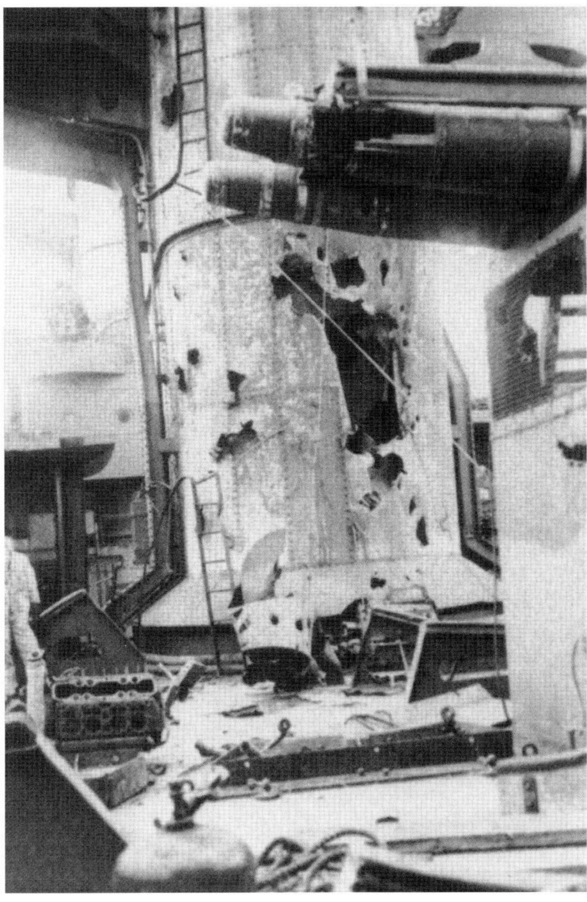

THIS PAGE AND OPPOSITE, BELOW: Damage to the *Prince of Wales* included hits to her superstructure and turrets, and minor damage below the waterline. *IWM*

OPPOSITE, ABOVE: The *Bismarck* firing her opening salvo against the *Hood*, photographed from the quarterdeck of the *Prinz Eugen*. *IWM*

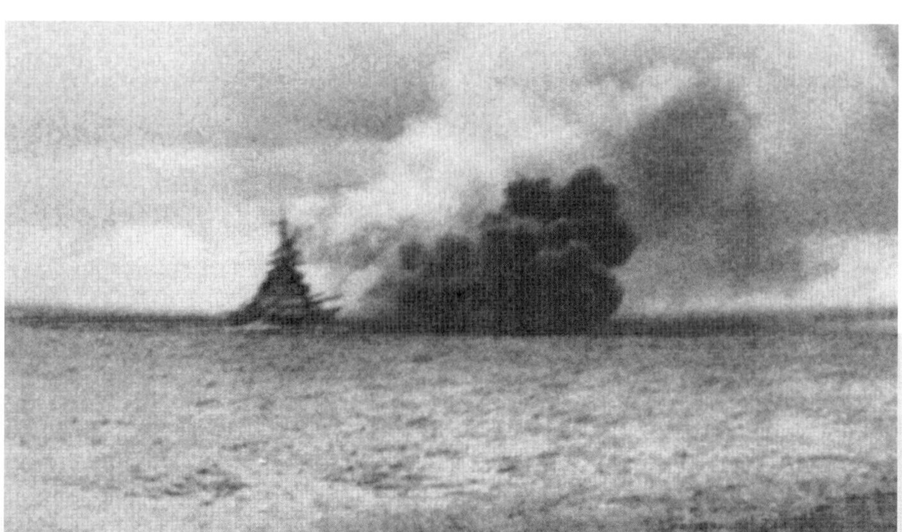

ABOVE: The *Hood* (right) and *Prince of Wales* on the horizon, photographed from the *Prinz Eugen*. *MNF*

RIGHT: The *Bismarck* firing on the *Hood*, photographed from the stern of the *Prinz Eugen*. *MNF*

BELOW: The *Bismarck* in action against the *Prince of Wales*, captured as she overhauled the *Prinz Eugen* on her port side. *MNF*

LEFT: The *Bismarck* firing on the *Norfolk* and *Suffolk* in an attempt to drive them off during the afternoon of May 23. *MNF*

BELOW LEFT: A near-miss from a salvo of 15in. shells from the *Hood* land on the port beam of the *Prinz Eugen* during the opening moments of the engagement. *IWM*

next four minutes the *Bismarck* and the static rear turret of the *Prince of Wales* exchanged salvos, but neither ship inflicted hits. Simultaneously at 0609, both Lütjens and Leach gave orders to cease-fire. The bloody engagement, which became known as the Battle of the Denmark Strait, had lasted less than 20 minutes, and claimed the lives of almost 1,500 British sailors.

On the German ships the order to cease-fire was met by widespread jubilation. The *Bismarck* and her consort had destroyed the pride of the Royal Navy, and had suffered no significant damage in return. Lütjens opted not to pursue the British battleship. His orders were to avoid action except to attack the escorts of a convoy, and any further fighting would endanger his ship. Also, unknown to Leach the *Prince of Wales* had also scored three hits on the *Bismarck*. While two caused insignificant structural damage, the third hit struck the *Bismarck* below the waterline, causing some flooding and the loss of precious fuel. Lütjens might have won a significant victory, but he still had cause for concern, and as the battleship's crew worked to repair the damage, the German Admiral pondered how this fuel loss might effect his plans.

The pursuit of the *Bismarck*

Despite the pleas of Captain Lindemann of the *Bismarck*, Lütjens opted not to chase the *Prince of Wales*. His orders were to avoid unnecessary engagements, and he was unwilling to risk his ships any further. The German squadron headed southwest, and once again the *Prinz Eugen* took the lead. The hit to her fuel tanks and waterline meant that the *Bismarck* was down slightly by the bows and the loss of fuel severely restricted her range of operations. In the circumstances Lütjens decided that the *Bismarck* needed to be repaired before she began prowling in the Atlantic. The nearest dry-dock was at St. Nazaire in Brittany, on the French Atlantic coast. St. Nazaire also offered other possibilities, as the battlecruisers *Scharnhorst* and *Gneisenau* were close by in Brest. The repairs would not take more than a week to complete, and Lütjens thought that a new sortie with all three capital ships would have a major impact on the war at sea. In other words, he saw the opportunity to relaunch Operation Rheinübung, using the ships which had originally been allocated to the battlegroup. He also decided to detach the *Prinz Eugen*, which could return to the Norwegian Sea, hunting for stray British ships as she returned home.

Meanwhile, Wake-Walker's cruisers had been joined by the *Prince of Wales*, and the British warships shadowed the German force as it steamed south. Damage control teams managed to repair the battleship's main guns, meaning that once again the *Prince of Wales* was ready for action. The Admiral had been unable to pick up any survivors from the *Hood*, as to do so would involve losing radar contact with the *Bismarck*. Instead he vectored the six destroyers detached by *Hood* during the night into the area of the sinking. The destroyer *Electra* reached the site of the disaster approximately one hour after the sinking, but by that stage only three survivors were found, clinging to rafts in the icy sea. The destroyers searched the area, but no other survivors were found, and the three were duly taken to Hvalfjord, the first stage of their sorrowful journey home.

For the rest of the day, the *Bismarck* and *Prinz Eugen* continued to steam in a southwesterly direction, followed at a distance by Wake-Walker's force. The weather was relatively clear, with occasional fog banks scattered across the North Atlantic, although the weather conditions worsened and the fog thickened as the day wore on. Lütjens made several attempts to shake off the pursuers, changing speed and direction, but the British maintained contact allowing Admiral Tovey and his superiors in the

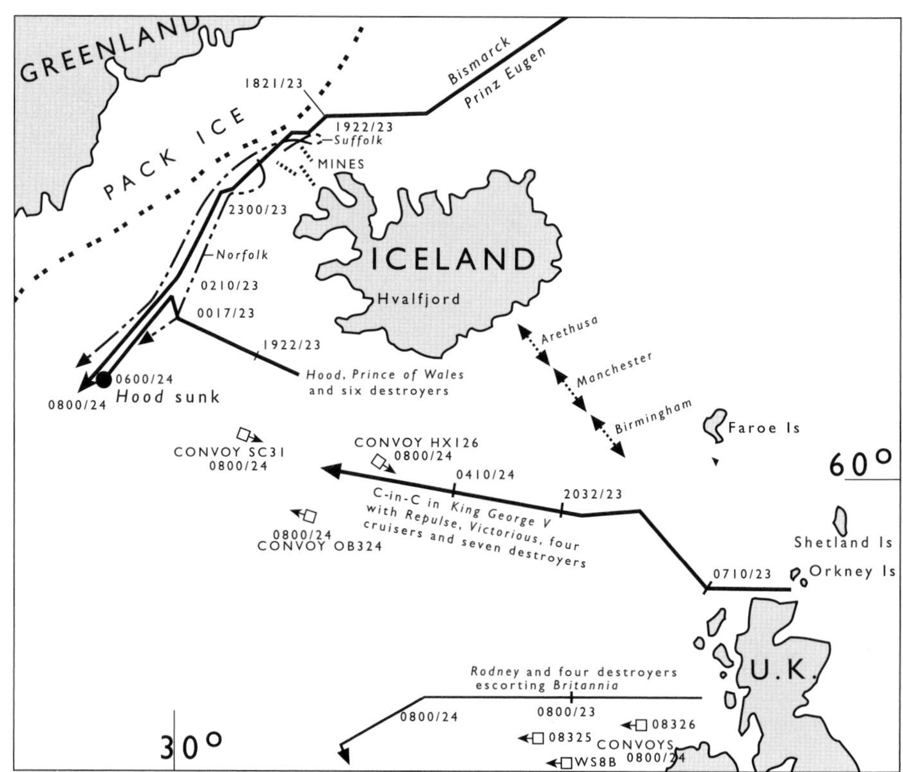

RIGHT: Position of the major vessels after the sinking of the *Hood*.

OPPOSITE, ABOVE: A hit from a 14in. shell fired by the *Prince of Wales* caused flooding in the bow of the *Bismarck*, and damaged her fuel tanks. In this photograph, taken shortly after the engagement ended, she is clearly down slightly by the bow. *IWM*

OPPOSITE, BELOW: The 8in. guns of the *Prinz Eugen* scored the first hit against the *Hood*, and then caused damage to the *Prince of Wales*. *MNF*

RIGHT: Captain Brinkmann and the *Prinz Eugen* were given orders to cruise independently of the *Bismarck*, and then to return to a port on the French coast. *RNM*

OPPOSITE, ABOVE: The British forces close in on *Bismarck*.

OPPOSITE, BELOW: Tovey steamed to intercept the *Bismarck* with everything he could. In this photograph taken from the quarterdeck of the *King George V* the battlecruiser *Repulse* and the aircraft carrier *Victorious* keep station astern of Tovey's flagship. *IWM*

Admiralty to co-ordinate the fleet movements which would bring every available British ship into the action. Tovey in *King George V* was steaming on a southwesterly course from Scapa Flow, accompanied by the *Victorious*, the *Repulse,* nine destroyers and the 2nd Cruiser Squadron (*Galatea, Aurora, Kenya* and *Neptune*, commanded by Rear-Admiral A.T.B. Curtis). By nightfall Tovey would be within 80 miles of Lütjens. In addition the battleships *Rodney, Ramillies,* and *Revenge* were detached from Atlantic convoy duties, and ordered to converge on the location the *Bismarck* was expected to be in by evening, as were two light cruisers (*Edinburgh* and *London*). Finally, Vice-Admiral Sir James Somerville's Force H based in Gibraltar was placed on stand-by for immediate operations in the mid-Atlantic. Somerville's group consisted of the aircraft carrier *Ark Royal*, the battlecruiser *Renown* (his flagship), and the light cruiser *Sheffield.*

If Lütjens was to successfully detach the *Prinz Eugen* and evade his pursuers, he needed to shake off Wake-Walker. Consequently, at 1839 the *Bismarck* made a rapid 180° turn, her movement covered by fog. She emerged from the fog and opened fire on the Suffolk at a range of 18,000 yards, forcing the cruiser to break off pursuit and turn northward. She returned fire with her 8in. guns, but scored no hits. Five miles beyond her, the *Norfolk* and *Prince of Wales* joined in the fighting, firing on the *Bismarck* with their main armament. Within minutes two of the 14in. guns on the *Prince of Wales* had malfunctioned, but fortunately the *Bismarck* failed to close any further and seemed to be concentrating her fire on the *Suffolk*, which Lütjens realized was the main radar picket of Wake-Walker's force. Meanwhile the *Prinz Eugen* raced on to the south until she was out of radar contact with the British, then she looped round to the north and escaped. With the *Prinz Eugen* safely out of the way, the *Bismarck* turned onto a southwesterly course, and the sporadic long-range gunfire petered out. Lütjens was steaming towards a patrol line of U-boats, strung out in mid-Atlantic to the southwest of Greenland, a threat which Wake-Walker was aware of through intelligence supplied by the Admiralty. As the pursuit resumed, the British ships began steaming in a zig-zag pattern,

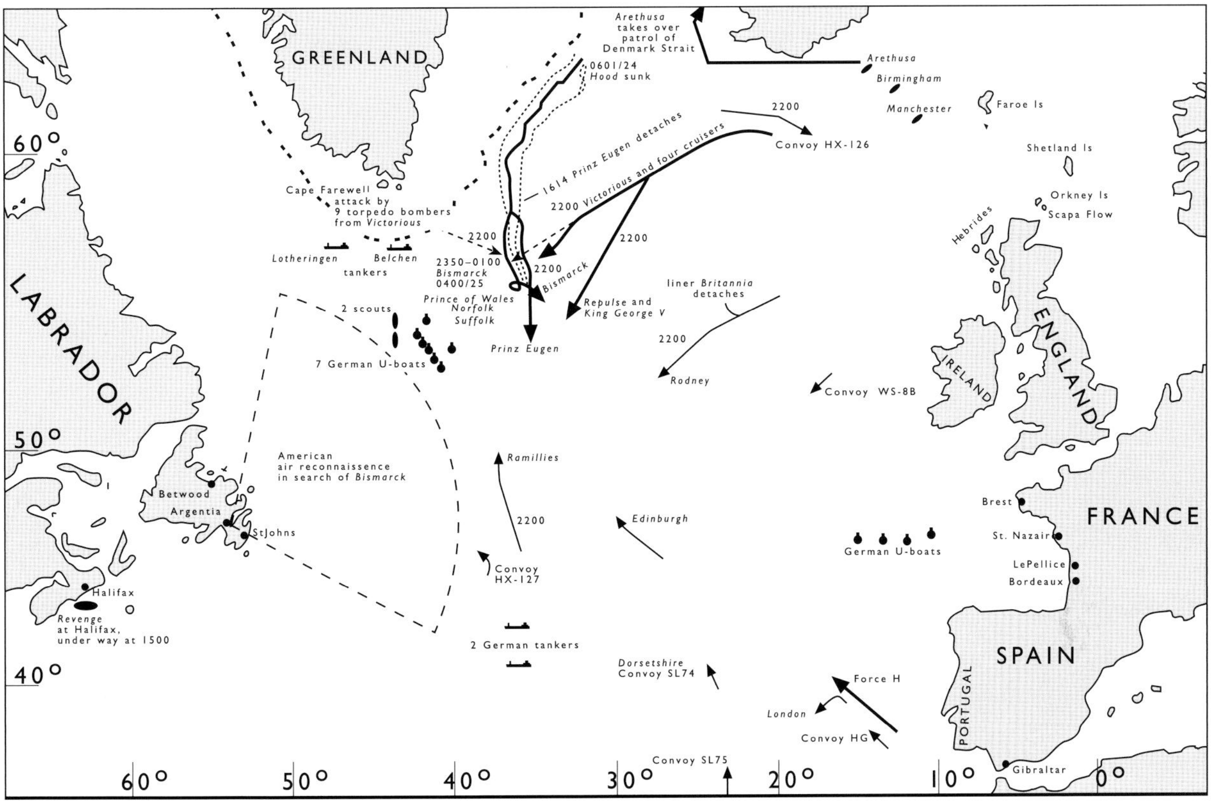
GREENLAND
LABRADOR
Arethusa takes over patrol of Denmark Strait
0601/24 Hood sunk
Arethusa
Birmingham
Manchester
Faroe Is
Shetland Is
Orkney Is
Scapa Flow
Hebrides
2200
Convoy HX-126
1614 Prinz Eugen detaches
2200 Victorious and four cruisers
Cape Farewell
attack by 9 torpedo bombers from Victorious
2200
Lotheringen
Belchen
tankers
2350–0100 Bismarck 0400/25
2200
Bismarck
Prince of Wales
Norfolk
Suffolk
Repulse and King George V
liner Britannia detaches
2200
2 scouts
7 German U-boats
Prinz Eugen
Rodney
Convoy WS-8B
IRELAND
ENGLAND
American air reconnaissence in search of Bismarck
Ramillies
Betwood
Argentia
StJohns
2200
Edinburgh
Brest
FRANCE
St. Nazair
German U-boats
LePellice
Bordeaux
Convoy HX-127
Halifax
Revenge at Halifax, under way at 1500
2 German tankers
SPAIN
PORTUGAL
Dorsetshire
Convoy SL74
Force H
London
Convoy HG
Convoy SL75
Gibraltar
60°
50°
40°
60°
50°
40°
30°
20°
10°
0°

THE BATTLE OF THE DENMARK STRAIT

When contact was made, the British ships were steaming in line astern (the *Prince of Wales* following 800 yards astern of the *Hood*), following a course of 240° (west-south-west), while the Germans were on a nearly parallel course of 220° (south-west). The German ships were also in line, with the *Bismarck* 1,000 yards astern of the *Prinz Eugen*. If Holland had arrived in the area just 30 minutes before, he would have been in a position to cross the "T" of the Germans, giving his ships an inestimable advantage in gunnery, as all their guns could bear on the enemy, while only the forward guns on his lead ship could fire back. Less than 30 seconds after the sighting was made, the Admiral duly ordered both ships to turn in succession to starboard, onto a new course of 280°. That meant the two forces would close at almost 780 yards per minute, bringing the leading German ship into range of the *Hood* within five minutes.

Observers in the *Prince of Wales* saw a huge flame shoot up from abaft the *Hood*'s mainmast (the rearmost mast of the ship). This was followed by an incredible explosion from the stern of the battlecruiser. The *Bismarck*'s shell had penetrated the vulnerable deck armor of the *Hood*, plunging through her decks into the after magazines. The shells and propellants ignited, causing that second explosion which literally ripped the stern of the *Hood* apart. A huge yellowish cloud loomed over the stern of the battlecruiser, hiding the carnage beneath it. Naval analysts have considered the cause of the catastrophe, and some cite the first explosion as being the precursor of the second, marking the detonation of the *Hood*'s small torpedo magazine toward the after end of her upper deck. The blast from this ignited the ship's main magazine, beneath "X" turret.

By 0557, when the German cruiser swiveled her guns onto the *Prince of Wales*, the British ships had each fired at least four salvos, but had scored no hits. The third salvo from the *Bismarck* landed a minute later, bracketing the *Hood*, but scoring no hits. The German gunners had found the range, meaning that any more salvoes would be right on target. At 0559 Holland gave the order to turn to port a second time, a 20° alteration which would put the Hood on a course of 260°. At that angle, with the enemy 35° forward of her beam, her after turrets would be able to fire. She was also still closing the range to her opponent. As Holland was issuing the command, the gunnery officer on the *Bismarck* gave the order to fire three salvos in quick succession, some 30 seconds apart. The range was 18,000 yards, just over 10 miles. The fourth salvo from the *Bismarck* landed at 0559 and 30 seconds, straddling the battlecruiser but scoring no hits. Thirty seconds later at 0600 the fifth salvo landed, just as the *Hood* was completing her turn. The German gunners had reduced the elevation slightly with each salvo, expecting the *Hood* to continue on her course of 280° and "walk into" her fall of shot. The *Hood* 's turn had almost taken her out of the "beaten zone," but her stern was still within the target area. While most of the shells missed and landed where the *Hood* should have been if she remained on course, one struck her in the stern, close to her after turrets. That shell was all it took to end a legend.

hoping to reduce the risk of being hit by an enemy torpedo in the gathering darkness.

While this drama was being played out to the west, Tovey's force was steaming at full speed in an effort to intercept the *Bismarck*. By 2200 the German battleship was within range of the aircraft embarked on the *Victorious*, and Tovey ordered a strike to be launched. Ten minutes later nine Swordfish torpedo-bombers took off from the carrier, commanded by Lt. Cdr. Esmonde. Heading west-south-west they sighted the *Bismarck* at 2330, then lost sight of her again in the fog. Aided by the British cruisers they relocated the German battleship, then dropped down to make their attack at 2350. It was difficult enough to hit a fast-moving, zig-zagging battleship with a plane-launched torpedo in the dark. It was especially difficult from a Swordfish, which had to make a seemingly suicidal run towards the target at under 100ft, and at less than 100 knots, making the oncoming plane a prime target for the battleship's anti-aircraft gunners. Miraculously all eight planes that made the run emerged unscathed, but only one of the torpedoes hit their target. It hit the *Bismarck* amidships, causing flooding to a boiler room, and causing more flooding through the gash in her damaged bows. This temporarily reduced the speed of the battleship to 16 knots. All aircraft returned to the *Victorious* without mishap. At midnight the Admiralty ordered Somerville to proceed to sea with Force H, hoping to trap the *Bismarck* between the pincers of the Home Fleet and Force H.

The pursuit continued, but this time there was a chance that Tovey's ships could actually catch the *Bismarck*. Lütjens made a turn to the south, wanting to

ABOVE: Swordfish torpedo bombers are prepared for action on the flight deck of the *Victorious* during the afternoon of May 23. *RNM*

OPPOSITE, RIGHT: Gun crews on the *Prinz Eugen* stood by their weapons during the tense hours before they managed to evade the pursuing British cruisers and break off into the wastes of the Atlantic. *MNF*

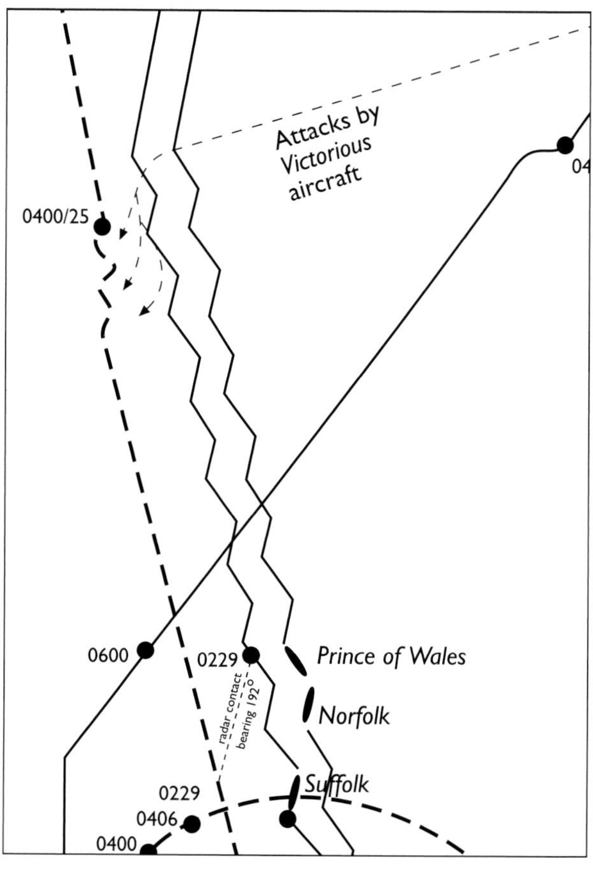

RIGHT: Lütjens slips his pursuers with a brilliant maneuver that left the British pursuers chasing ghosts. This could have been a decisive moment for the German commander, but in fact all it did was delay the inevitable for a little longer.

move closer to St. Nazaire. During the early hours of May 25, damage control teams worked hard to restore power to the *Bismarck*'s engines. At 0130, the *Prince of Wales* resumed her long-range sniping at the *Bismarck*, but the brief exchange of fire ended when both sides lost contact with each other in the darkness. The only effective means of tracking the German battleship was the radar on the *Suffolk*, and although the Wake-Walker's force maintained station about 25,000 yards on the port quarter of the *Bismarck*, the effective range of the *Suffolk*'s radar. They were also forced to continue their zig-zag pattern, for fear of attack by U-boats. On the extreme southeastern leg of each zig-zag, the *Suffolk* would lose radar contact for several minutes. Lütjens had already worked out the pattern, and saw his opportunity to evade his pursuers. With his speed partially restored by 0230, he was able to make a respectable 24 knots; not enough to outdistance the cruisers, but fast enough to lose the enemy in the darkness. At 0306, when the *Suffolk* was approaching the end of her zig-zag leg, Lütjens ordered the *Bismarck* to make a hard turn to starboard, then steered due west at full speed. When the *Suffolk* made her turn, she could not relocate the *Bismarck*. Wake-Walker ordered his ships to increase speed and steam to the southwest, hoping to regain contact. Instead, Lütjens swung the *Bismarck* in a wide loop to the north, skirting around the radar range of the *Suffolk*, then passing some 32,000 yards to the rear of the British ships. Once safely out of the way, he finished his circle by crossing his wake, then set a new course of 130°, the direction of St. Nazaire. By 0600 Tovey was informed that all contact with the *Bismarck* had been lost. The Germans now had the initiative, and as the British combed the Atlantic in search of their prey, the *Bismarck* slipped away to the southeast.

The search for the *Bismarck*

For more than 24 hours, the British had no idea where the *Bismarck* was. Contact had been lost at around 0315 in the early hours of May 25. It was an extremely tense period, as not only was the location of the *Bismarck* unknown, but Admiral Tovey and his superiors in the Admiralty also had to guess what the intentions of Admiral Lütjens might be. It was unknown whether she had been damaged in the fight with the *Hood* and the *Prince of Wales*, but if the damage was serious, the *Bismarck* might well turn back to Norway or Germany. Another possibility was that she might head towards the French coast for repairs. Then again, if she were undamaged, she could be almost anywhere, and could descend on any of the transatlantic convoys at any moment. Although the British could estimate the amount of fuel she carried, it was also possible that a rendezvous might have been arranged with the German tanker.

THE HIT THAT DOOMED THE *BISMARCK*

Two Swordfish (below) approached *Bismarck* from starboard. One of these fired its torpedo a textbook two ship-lengths ahead of the *Bismarck*, at a range of about 800 yards (main picture). Captain Lindemann immediately ordered the helmsman to alter course to port, in an attempt to avoid the torpedo. All this achieved was to move the point of impact astern. If *Bismarck* had not begun a 15° turn to port, she would have been struck amidships, where her armor was most effective, and the damage would probably have been negligible.

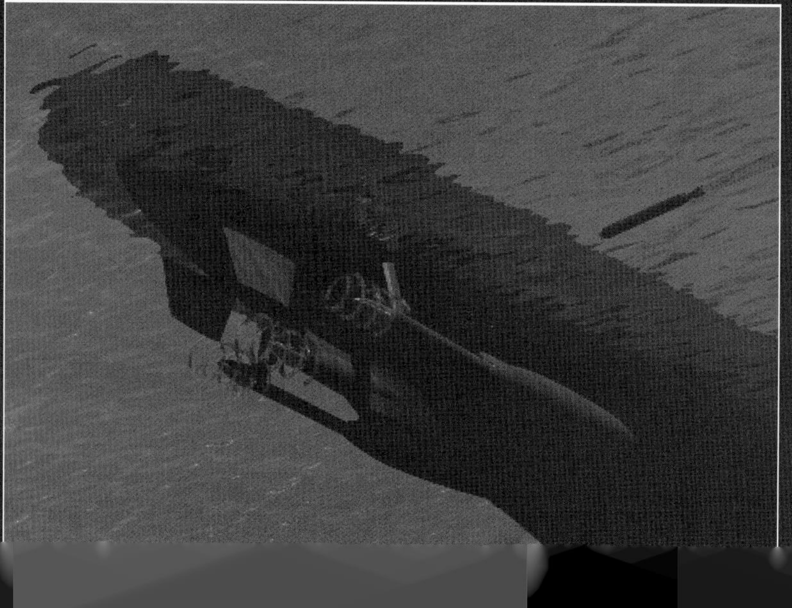

Instead the torpedo struck her in the stern (left), jamming her rudder and flooding her steering compartment. As the aircraft returned to their carrier in the gloom, Lütjens and Lindemann tried to assess the damage, and the *Bismarck* continued her slow turn to port. Damage control parties reported that there was little that could be done, even with divers or explosive charges. Lindemann tried to use the engines to counteract the effect of the jammed rudders, but this was only partially successful. That one hit had doomed the *Bismarck*.

GÖTTERDÄMMERUNG
At 08:48, *Rodney* (left) opened fire with her two forward 16in. turrets, and a minute later the *Bismarck* returned fire. *King George V (below left)* started firing two minutes after *Rodney*. The skill of the *Bismarck's* gunners was demonstrated when they straddled the *Rodney* with their third salvo. At 0854 the *Norfolk* joined in with her 8in. guns hitting the *Bismarck* at 0859 with her own third salvo. *King George V* altered course to starboard, opening the angle between herself and the *Rodney*. The course change meant that both British battleships could engage the enemy with all their main armament. At 0902 a 16in. shell from the *Rodney* knocked out the *Bismarck*'s "B" turret, and seriously damaged "A" turret. The *Bismarck* managed to fire four more salvoes with her after guns before her after control director was knocked out by a 14in. shell from *King George V*. *Bismarck* was finding it increasingly difficult to reply to her enemy's fire. Her after turrets were silenced by 0925. At 0927 the forward turret of the *Bismarck* opened fire again, and was promptly knocked out three minutes later. By 0930 all of her main guns were out of action. Reluctant to disengage while his enemy was left afloat, Tovey continued to pound her. By 0940 the *Bismarck* was a flaming hulk.

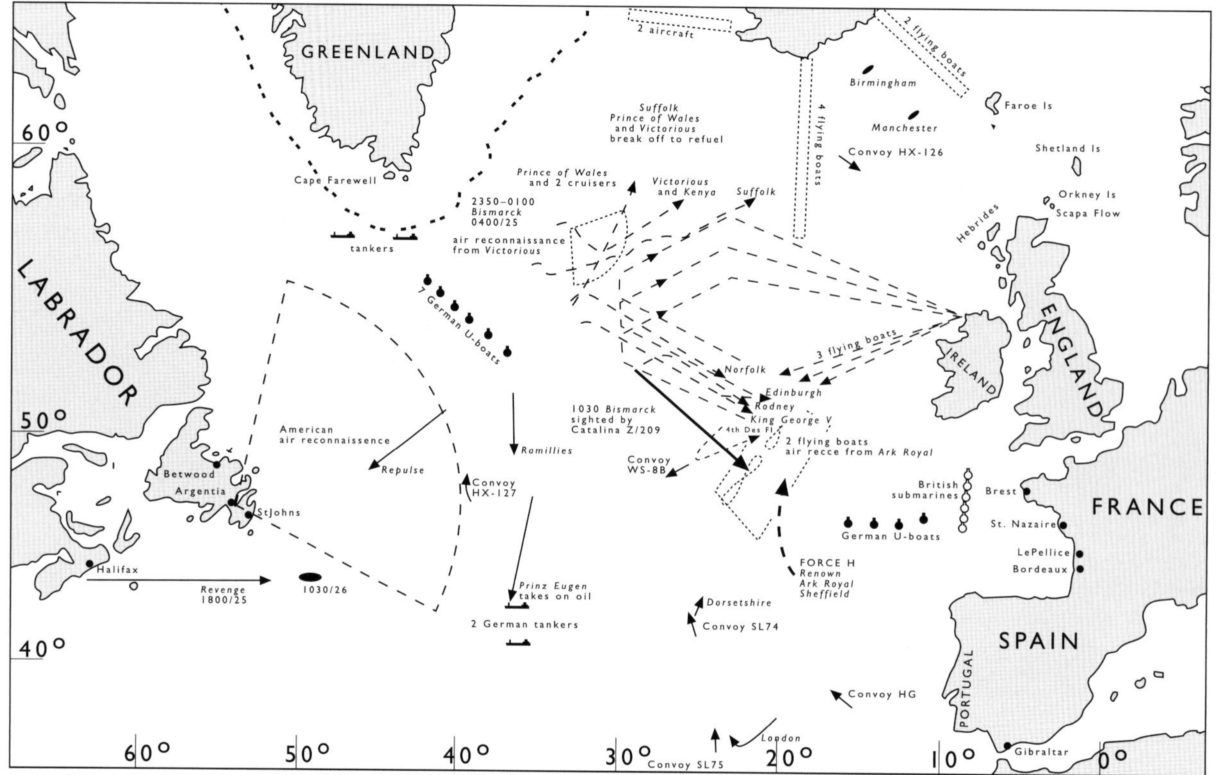

Lacking the resources to guard against every eventuality, Tovey decided to continue the search to the southwest, their area for the *Bismarck* would pose the greatest threat to British convoys. Although other units it including Force H were approaching the naval arena, there were simply too much ocean and too few ships to undertake a full-scale search of the mid-Atlantic.

Another growing problem was fuel. During May 25, Wake-Walker's two cruisers had to break off and returned to Iceland due to lack of fuel. While the *Suffolk* would resume her post on patrol in the Denmark Strait, Wake-Walker in the *Norfolk* was ordered to return to join the Home Fleet at best possible speed after refuelling his cruiser. During the day, air searches from the *Victorious* covered their area to the northwest of the carrier, but again, no enemy ship was sighted. She then returned to Scapa, as she was running low on fuel. The *Repulse* was also forced to return to Scapa Flow for the same reason, while the *Prince of Wales* was ordered to refuel in Iceland. Once there she landed her dead, then steamed south to Rosyth in the Firth of Forth where the damage inflicted on her could be repaired. This left Tovey with just his flagship, they *King George V* and a handful of cruisers to continue the search.

Fortunately, reinforcements were on the way. The battleship *Rodney* with her powerful armament of nine 16in. guns was due to join Tovey's flagship by dawn the following morning, after having been detached from convoy duties. In addition, the *County*-class cruiser *Dorsetshire* was ordered to leave a convoy and joined Tovey by the morning of May 26. Away to the southeast, Somerville's Force H was steaming north-north-west, and would reached the Western Approaches, some 350 miles westward of Brest, by the following morning. Although warships of the Royal Navy appeared to be converging from various directions, no sighting of the *Bismarck* had been made by nightfall on May 25. This did not mean that Tovey had no idea where the *Bismarck* was. During the morning of May 25, the British had intercepted a transmission from the *Bismarck* to the German Naval High Command. In the signal, Lütjens informed his superiors in Kiel that the *Hood* had been sunk, and that the *Bismarck* had suffered minor damage, and was losing fuel. It also informed German Naval High Command that the *Bismarck* was heading towards St. Nazaire. Although the British were unable to pinpoint exactly where the transmission was sent from, their radio direction finders did give them a general bearing. From this it was clear that Tovey was looking in the wrong area and that the *Bismarck* was heading towards the French coast. Tovey duly ordered all the ships to head southeast in pursuit at best possible speed. The hunt for the

LEFT AND ABOVE: Catalina flying boats combed the western approaches in an attempt to locate the *Bismarck* during May 24. She was finally located by a Catalina flown by Flying Officer Briggs (pictured above) at 0945 on the morning of May 25. *RNM*

FAR LEFT: Searching for the *Bismarck*.

BELOW LEFT: The position of the major vessels when the *Bismarck* was located.

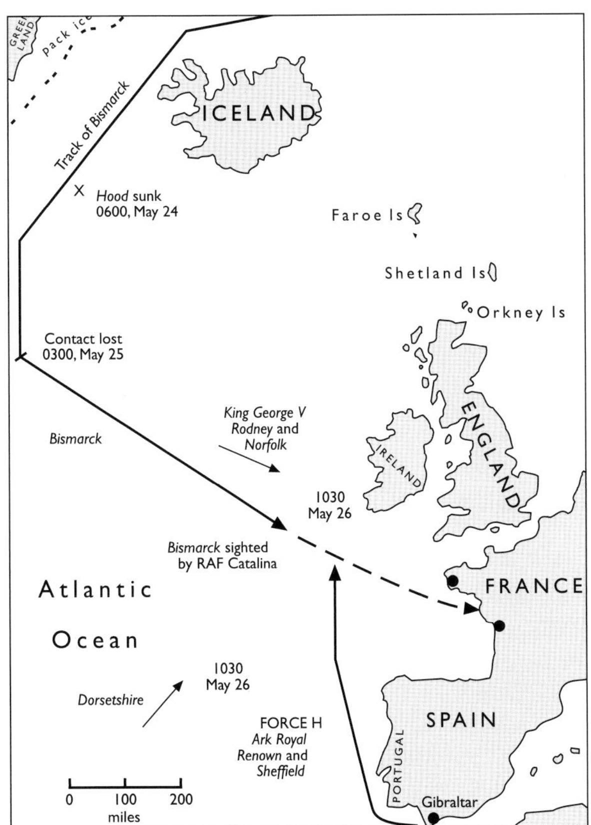

Bismarck had now become a chase, with both the Home Fleet and Force H now heading towards the same point, some 250 miles to the southwest of Ireland.

Early in the morning of May 26, two Catalina flying boats operated by Coastal Command took off from the base in Northern Ireland, and headed southwest. Just after 1000 one of the planes spotted a large solitary ship, and radioed its position back to Coastal Command. The information was passed on to the Admiralty, who quickly realized that they had no warships in the area, and the vessel could only be the *Bismarck*. When the Catalina dropped down for a closer look, the warship fired on the British plane with her anti-aircraft guns, removing any doubt as to the nationality of the vessel. An hour later, at around 1110, Swordfish from the aircraft carrier *Ark Royal* also spotted the ship, and provided a positive identification. The *Bismarck* had been found. She was heading on a southwesterly course at a leisurely speed of 20 knots, and soon this information was in the hands of both the Admiralty and Admiral Tovey. Shortly after noon, the light cruiser *Sheffield*, part of Force H, appeared from the south, and began shadowing the *Bismarck*. While Lütjens was largely unaware of British naval movements, the British knew exactly where there enemy was, and where she was heading.

Swordfish strike

A quick look at the chart told a senior British commanders that only Force H was close enough to intercept the *Bismarck*. At the time of the Catalina sighting, Force H was actually some 150 miles east of the *Bismarck*, between her and St. Nazaire. When confirmation of the *Bismarck*'s position reached Somerville, he ordered the *Ark Royal* and *Renown* to turn onto a course of 120°, parallel and approximately 120 miles to the north of the German battleship's track. As the battlecruiser *Renown* was too poorly armed and poorly armored to fight the *Bismarck*, it was up to the Swordfish torpedo bombers of the *Ark Royal* to attack the enemy. Their only hope of stopping the *Bismarck* was to damage her with torpedoes and slow her down, so that Tovey and his battleships could catch up with her.

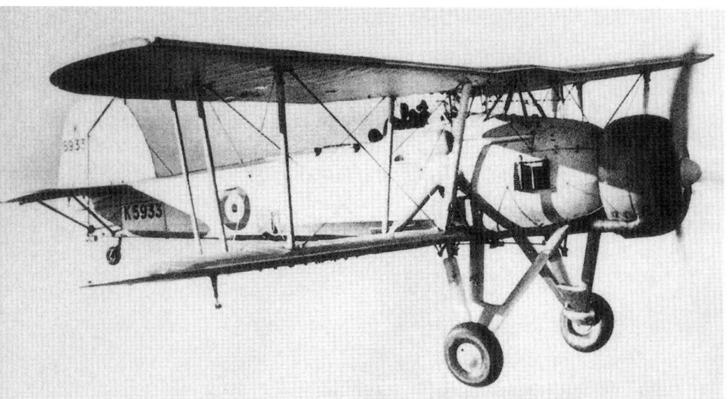

By noon, preparations were underway to launch an air strike and at 1500 on May 26, 15 Swordfish took off from the *Ark Royal*, and headed south-south-east. Unfortunately, during the briefing, the pilots were told that none of their ships were in the vicinity of the *Bismarck*. The briefing officer clearly forgot about the *Sheffield*, which was in the direct line of flight between the carrier and the German battleship, some 25,000 yards off the *Bismarck's* port quarter. At 1610, the torpedo bombers sighted their target, and launched their attack—but they were attacking the wrong ship. The captain of the *Sheffield* ordered his gun crews to hold their fire, and his ship took extreme action to avoid the oncoming torpedoes. Fortunately, many of the torpedoes exploded on contact with the water due to a problem with their magnetic detonators. Other pilots realized the mistake, and broke off the attack. The Swordfish pilots returned home, and the *Bismarck* continued unmolested on her course. The planes were immediately rearmed, but this time the magnetic detonators were removed, and simple contact detonators fitted in their place. All this took time, as the operation had lasted over three hours, meaning that it would be early evening before a second strike could be launched. While *the Ark Royal* informed Tovey and the Admiralty of the failure of the strike, they omitted the detail about the "friendly fire" incident. The

ABOVE: HMS *Sheffield* was mistaken for the *Bismarck* and was attacked by Swordfish from the *Ark Royal*. Fortunately she was not damaged in the "friendly fire" incident. *IWM*

LEFT: *Bismarck* and *Prinz Eugen*.

FAR LEFT: The Swordfish torpedo bomber carried a single torpedo. With a top speed of little more than 100mph she was considered obsolete by 1941; but since the Fleet Air Arm had no viable replacement, she remained in service. *Both MNF*

news was bleak, as everyone realized that the chances of damaging the *Bismarck* before nightfall were dwindling fast. Dusk was approaching, allowing no more than one more air strike before nightfall. Given the lack of success of the previous attacks by *Victorious* and *Ark Royal*, there was not much hope that a third attack against the *Bismarck* would meet with any more success.

On the *Bismarck*, Lütjens realized that they were within striking range of a British aircraft carrier (having seen the patrolling Swordfish), and an increase in enemy radio traffic suggested surface units were in the vicinity to port and astern of the battleship. The fuel shortage caused by the leak from the *Prince of Wales'* shell meant that if the *Bismarck* was to reach St. Nazaire, speed had to be reduced to an economical 20 knots. As dusk approached, it seemed that the expected air attack was not going to appear before night protected the battleship. By the following morning the *Bismarck* would be within air range of the French coast, and Lütjens knew the Luftwaffe were planning to cover his ship with enough aircraft to deter any British attack. It began to look as if the *Bismarck* might escape after all.

At 1910, a hundred miles to the north on the *Ark Royal*, a second strike was launched, comprising 15 Swordfish in three flights. Although the three groups lost each other in the low clouds, the leading group flew over the *Sheffield*, and vectored in the other flights. One after another they then headed southeast towards the *Bismarck*. The first attack went in at 2047, and the others followed over the space of the next 20 minutes, approaching their target from different directions. The *Bismarck* responded with an intense anti-aircraft barrage, but somehow all the Swordfish passed through the storm to drop their torpedoes. One hit was scored amidships on the port side by the first wave, and possibly a second hit was also achieved in the same location, according to survivors from the *Bismarck*. However many hits there were, no serious damage was done, as the *Bismarck*'s armored belt proved virtually impervious. Finally, two aircraft from the third flight approached the battleship from starboard. One of these aircraft fired its torpedo a textbook two ship lengths ahead of the *Bismarck*, at a range of about 800 yards. Captain Lindemann immediately ordered the helmsman to alter course to port, in an attempt to avoid the torpedo. All this achieved was to move the point of impact astern. If the battleship had not begun a 15° turn to port, she would have been struck amidships, and the damage would probably have been negligible. Instead the torpedo struck her in the stern, jamming her rudder and flooding her

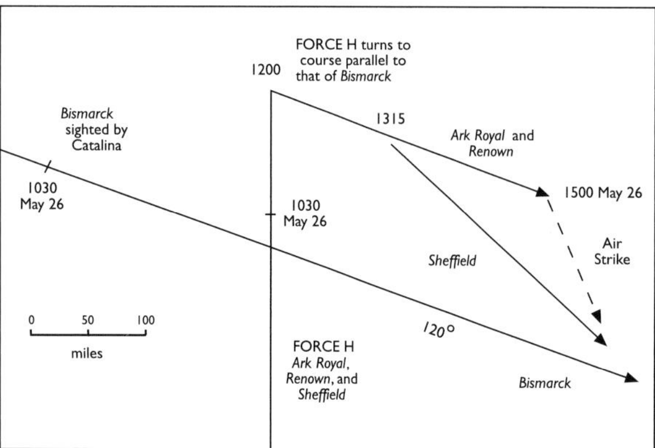

steering compartment. As the aircraft returned to their carrier in the gloom, Lütjens and Lindemann tried to assess the damage, and the *Bismarck* continued her slow turn to port. Damage control parties reported that there was little that could be done, even with divers or explosive charges. Lindemann tried to use the engines to counteract the effect of the jammed rudders, but this was only partially successful. That one hit had doomed the *Bismarck*.

Initial reports from the Swordfish pilots were not encouraging, as none of their hits appeared to have caused any damage. Then, a signal from the *Sheffield* reported that the *Bismarck* was steering erratically: she was no longer heading on a southeasterly course towards France but was circling around to the northwest, steaming away from safety. Then, when the last Swordfish pilot

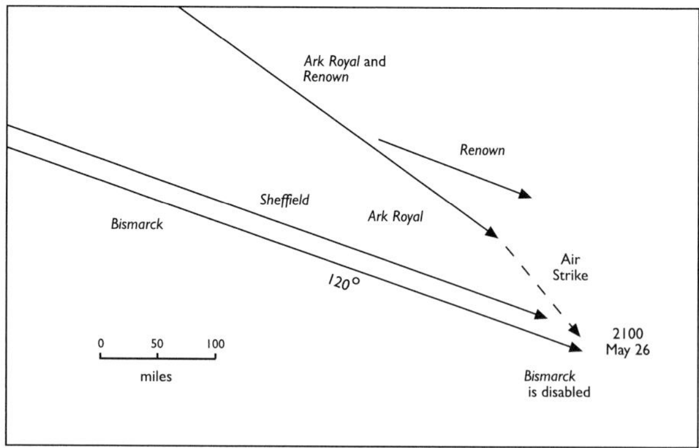

reported hitting the *Bismarck*'s stern during his debriefing, the pieces fell into place. The *Bismarck* was damaged, and unable to steer a proper course. Tovey's battleships would be able to reach her, and together with Force H, they could engage and destroy their opponent. While Tovey could forge ahead and fight a night action with the *Bismarck*, he decided against it. The problem was both the flagship *King George V* and the battleship *Rodney* were low on fuel, and would have to return to base by mid-morning the following day at the very latest. Not only was a night-time attack a gamble, it was also wasteful in fuel, as it meant increasing the speed of his ships above their best economical rate of 18 knots. A delay would also allow Tovey to move his forces into the most advantageous position possible. The *Bismarck* was actually helping the British, as its new course was taking it closer to the approaching battleships.

At 2238, five British destroyers approached the *Bismarck*, taking up positions with one ship on each of the port and starboard beams, and the port and starboard quarters. The fifth destroyer, the flotilla leader formed up astern of the German battleship. These warships were the 4th Destroyer Flotilla, commanded by the highly-experienced Captain Philip Vian, veteran of the *Altmark* action of February 1940. His force consisted of the modern *Tribal*-class destroyers *Cossack* (his flagship), *Maori*, *Sikh* and *Zulu*, and the Polish destroyer *Piorun*. The *Bismarck* opened fire on the *Piorun* and the *Maori*, forcing the latter to take evasive action and prompting the Polish vessel to launch an lone attack on the battleship. Vian quickly ordered all his destroyers to withdraw out of range, and to shadow the *Bismarck*, waiting for an opportunity to launch a co-ordinated attack. At 2324, Vian ordered all his vessels to close on the enemy and fire their torpedoes, but a combination of poor visibility, bad weather and German fire made him abandon the attempt. Instead he ordered individual attacks to be be made during the night, partly to keep

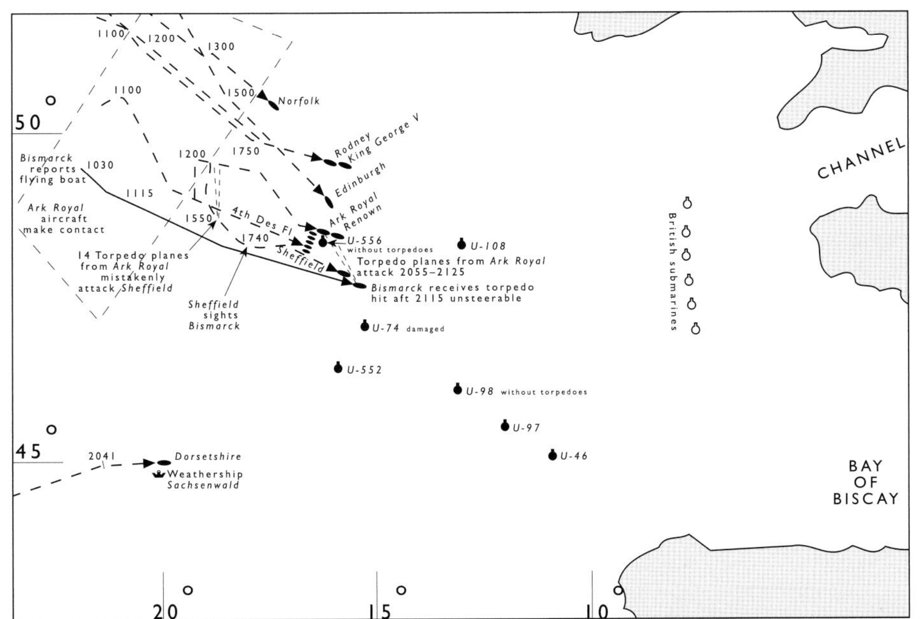

OPPOSITE: The two air strikes, at 1500 (LEFT) and 2100.

LEFT: The quarry is caught.

the Germans at action stations, and partly because the individual captains were better placed to determine when conditions were best suited for an attack. At 0120 the *Zulu* fired four torpedoes at the *Bismarck*, but scored no hits. While the Germans were distracted to port, the *Maori* attacked from starboard, firing two torpedoes of her own. Neither hit their target, and the destroyer was forced to withdraw under heavy fire from the *Bismarck*'s secondary armament. Next the *Cossack* attacked at 0140, firing three torpedoes, and claimed she scored a hit. The *Bismarck* slowed down then stopped, possibly due to the hit from Vian's torpedo, but more probably to allow damage control parties to examine her rudder. Next it was the turn of the *Sikh*, firing four torpedoes at 0218. She reported scoring one hit, but the effect if any was negligible, as the *Bismarck* was under way again by 0240. Forty minutes later the *Cossack* fired her last torpedo, but no hit was scored, and Vian was forced to withdraw under a hail of shells. Although 16 torpedoes were fired during the night, despite claims to the contrary it is unlikely that any hits were actually achieved by Vian's destroyers. What they did achieve was to harass the Germans, taunting them and forcing them to remain alert throughout that last night.

On the *Bismarck* morale was extremely low as the crew finally realized that their situation was hopeless. They were still 500 miles from the safety of St. Nazaire, and dawn would bring British battleships, not German aircraft. Although the armament of the battleship was undamaged and her fighting abilities unimpaired, the damage to her rudder meant that she could not avoid an engagement against an overwhelming opponent. Her luck had run out.

Just before midnight Admiral Lütjens signalled to the German Naval High Command, informing them of the fatal hit and the inability of his ship to steer towards France. He concluded with the message: "We fight to the last in our belief in you, my Führer, and in the firm faith of Germany's victory." Admiral Raeder in Kiel responded by saying that U-boats and tugs were on their way to assist the battleship, but everyone knew that any help would come too late to save the *Bismarck* and her crew. Even Hitler joined in the communications, sending the signal that, "What can still be done will be done." The signals continued throughout the night while Vian's destroyers conducted their attacks in the darkness. On the recommendation of Lütjens, Hitler radioed that he had awarded Adelbert Schneider, the *Bismarck*'s Chief Gunnery Officer, the Knight's Cross for his part in destroying the *Hood*. A final bizarre exchange involved the Ship's Log, which Lütjens believed would help the German Naval High Command plan future operations. He ordered the *Bismarck*'s Arado seaplane to prepare to fly the log and other papers to France, but it was found that damage to the catapult prevented the aircraft from being able to take off. Instead Lindemann ordered the seaplane and her fuel to be jettisoned, in order to reduce the risk of fire damage. Lütjens even ordered that a U-boat be sent to collect the documents, but by that stage daybreak was just a few short hours away, and the *Bismarck*'s last battle was fast approaching. Her young, exhausted crew could do little but await the inevitable.

Götterdämmerung

Dawn on May 27 ushered in the final stage of the drama. Rear-Admiral Wake-Walker in *Norfolk* had returned to the scene after his cruiser was refueled in Iceland. She joined Admiral Tovey's squadron the day before, and the heavy cruiser was sent to scout ahead of the flagship. At 0753 lookouts on the *Norfolk* sighted the *Bismarck*. She kept a distance, and passed on news of the contact to Tovey. Wake-Walker also sought Vian's destroyers on station around the battleship. Within ten minutes the flagship came into sight astern of the cruiser. Admiral Tovey was well aware that she was still a dangerous foe, although he also knew that the damage to her rudder meant that she could not escape, and her ability to counter any British moves would be extremely limited. In addition, the British could dictate when and where the battle would begin. Tovey therefore decided to keep his two battleships apart, and if the opportunity presented itself, the *King George V* and the *Rodney* would attack the enemy from different directions. By splitting the *Bismarck*'s fire, the chances of her inflicting a serious hit to one of the British battleships would be reduced. Also by approaching from the west at dawn, the German ship would be illuminated by the rising sun, making target acquisition a little easier. Although records indicate that part of Somerville's Force H was within 30,000 yards of *Bismarck*, Tovey ordered it to keep clear of the action. He had no wish to risk a second poorly-armored battlecruiser in an engagement with the *Bismarck*.

Morale was high as the British ships prepared for action. At 0843, the *Bismarck* was sighted to the southeast, about 25,000 yards from Tovey's flagship, steering an erratic northerly course. As soon as their enemy was sighted, the *Rodney* turned to port in accordance with Tovey's plans to split the enemy's fire. At 0848, she opened fire with her two forward 16in. turrets, and a minute later the *Bismarck* returned fire. Lütjens decided to concentrate his fire on the *Rodney*, rightly assuming but she was the more powerful of his two adversaries. By using her engines, she was able to turn slightly to starboard, allowing all her turrets to bear on the enemy. The *King George V* commenced firing two minutes after the *Rodney*. Like her consort, the after turret of the flagship was unable to bear on the target. All along, the crew of the *Bismarck* assumed that the *Prince of Wales* was actually *King George V*, and they were surprised that the battleship appeared to be undamaged. The skill of the *Bismarck*'s gunners was demonstrated when they straddled the *Rodney* with their third salvo. At 0854 the *Norfolk* joined in with her 8in. guns hitting the *Bismarck* at 0859 with her own third salvo, knocking out the *Bismarck*'s main fire-control director. This was a crucial hit, as it would take time for the *Bismarck* to bring her aft fire-control director into operation. At that point the *King George V* altered course to starboard, opening the angle between herself and the *Rodney*, which was now 3,000 yards away to the north. He also ordered the *Rodney* to turn onto the same heading as the flagship. The range to the *Bismarck* had now dropped to 21,000 yards. The *Bismarck* responded by altering course to the north as best she could, and switching targets to the *King George V*. This put the *Bismarck* and the British flagship on almost parallel and reciprocal courses. The course change did mean that both British battleships could engage the enemy with all their main armament. They were also beginning to hit their target. At 0902 a 16in. shell from the *Rodney* knocked out the *Bismarck*'s "B" turret, and seriously damaged "A" turret. The *Bismarck* managed to fire four more salvoes with her after guns before her aft fire-control director was also knocked out

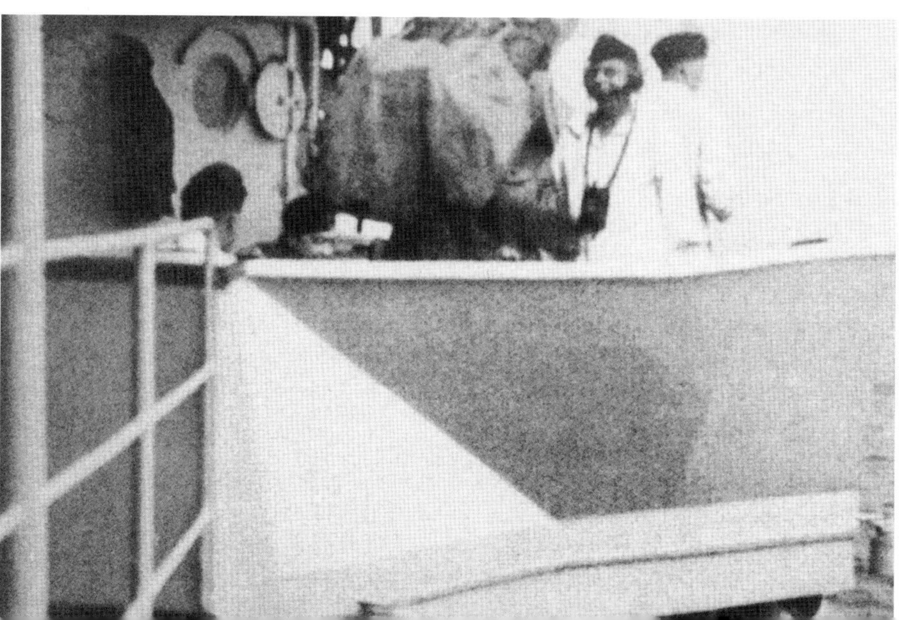

RIGHT: On watch aboard *Prinz Eugen*.

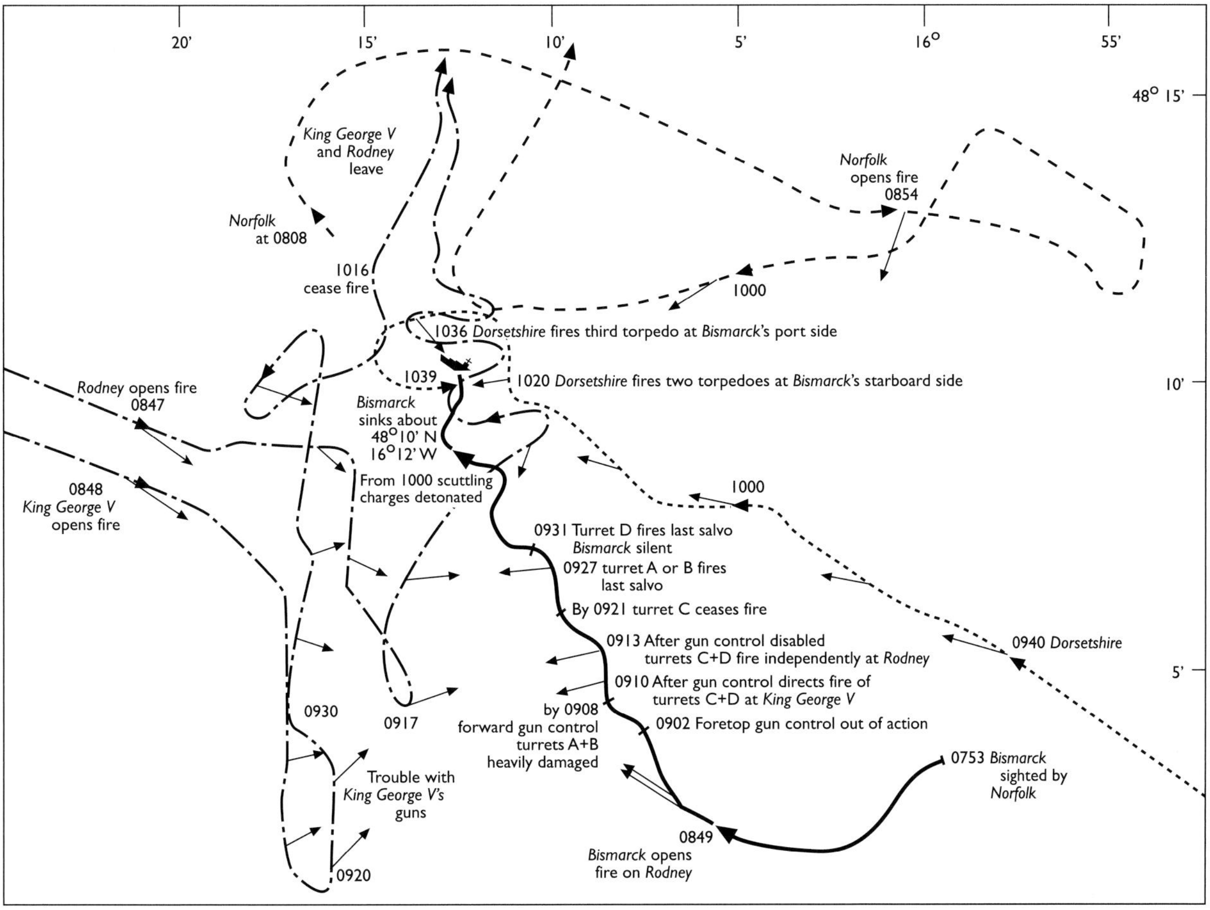

by her 14in. shell from *King George V*. Her guns could now only fire under local control (i.e. directed individually by the captain of each gun turret.) At 0915 Captain Dalrymple-Hamilton of the *Rodney* reversed his southerly course, turning to starboard to avoid crossing the line of fire of the flagship. For his part Tovey ordered another course change for his battleship, turning through 180° onto a northerly heading to follow the *Rodney* to the north, and to keep the *Bismarck* in clear line of arc of all her turrets. At this stage the *Bismarck* was just 15,000 yards northeast of *King George V*, and 10,000 yards due east of the *Rodney*. At that range it was almost

Above: The final battle.

Left: Once damaged by the torpedo strike from the *Ark Royal*'s swordfish, the *Bismarck* was doomed. Unable to maintain a course towards Brest she was forced to circle round towards the north, allowing Tovey's battleships to catch up with her. *IWM*

impossible to miss. By this stage the cruiser *Dorsetshire* had joined in from the east of the *Bismarck* with her 8in. guns. With her guns under local control and two of her four turrets knocked out, the *Bismarck* was finding it increasingly difficult to reply to the enemy's fire. Her aft turrets were silenced by 0925. At 0927 the forward turret of the *Bismarck* opened fire again, and was promptly knocked out three minutes later. By 0930 all of her main guns were out of action, and her secondary armament was rendered largely ineffective by damage to both gun turrets and her secondary fire control. Unable to fight back, the *Bismarck* was now little more than a hulk. By this stage she was receiving multiple hits, her superstructure was being reduced to a twisted shambles, and fire was spreading throughout the ship. Tovey continued to edge closer to the German battleship. He knew that both his capital ships were critically short of fuel, and had barely enough to return to port at half speed. Reluctant to disengage while his enemy was left afloat, Tovey continued to pound the *Bismarck* with his flagship while the *Rodney* closed to point-blank range. By 0940 the *Bismarck* was a flaming hulk. The flagship lay 12,000 yards to the southwest, while the *Rodney* had closed to within 4,000 yards, and was northwest of the *Bismarck*. The cruisers *Norfolk* and *Dorsetshire* had also closed to within 12,000 yards by that stage. Observers saw her hull glowing orange from multiple fires, and her tower mast and funnel were cut to pieces. The battleship had become an inferno, and although her armored belt still offered some protection to the men below decks, fires were raging unchecked, and she was flooding from numerous waterline hits. She was no longer under her own power, and she lay wallowing in the swell. The only sign of resistance left was her German naval ensign, flying above the carnage.

By 1000 the fuel situation in Tovey's battleships was becoming critical, and at 1015 he ordered them both to break off the action. The *Rodney* had just circled past the *Bismarck* at point-blank range, then turned to follow a reciprocal course. She fired one last salvo and her last torpedoes into the floating wreckage, then steamed away. The *Bismarck* was already slowly settling in the water, and at 1015 the order was given to abandon ship. Scuttling charges were rigged, and the order was given to open the sea valves on the underside of her hull to speed the sinking. Unaware that the enemy was abandoning ship, Tovey ordered the cruiser *Dorsetshire* to use her torpedoes against the *Bismarck,* as gunnery had apparently done little to pierce the hull. She was the only warship left in the area with the ability to finish off the stricken German battleship, as the battleships had left,

and the *Norfolk* and Vian's destroyers had already fired off all their torpedoes. This left *Dorsetshire* to administer the coup de grace. She took up position on the starboard beam of the *Bismarck* and at 1030 fired two torpedoes, which struck the battleship amidships. She then circled around the wreck to fire two more into her port beam six minutes later, one of which hit the wallowing hull of the battleship.

It was the last shot of the engagement. The *Bismarck*'s crew were already abandoning ship, and hundreds were in the freezing water, watching their ship slip under. The *Bismarck* settled by the stern, taking on a list to port as she did so. The list increased until she rolled over onto her side. Then pieces of her superstructure started to break away, and her four turrets fell out of their barbettes—only gravity had been holding them in place. After a brief pause she continued to roll over, as men scrambled onto her upturned hull, or tried to jump clear. She finally sank from view just after 1040, leaving an ocean filled with debris, men and oil.

The *Dorsetshire* edged through the wreckage to pick up survivors, throwing ropes and nets over her side to assist in the recovery. The destroyer *Maori* was also on the scene within minutes. The *Dorsetshire* and the *Maori* had taken on board just 119 survivors when a lookout spotted what it thought was a U-boat periscope. Captain Martin of the *Dorsetshire* had no choice but to get under way, and to abandon the men in the water. Certainly U-boats were in the vicinity, and although the decision was an unenviable one, Martin had to consider the safety of his own men first. The following day, *U-75* and the German weather ship *Sachsenwald* recovered five

LEFT: The *Rodney* (on the right of the photograph) viewed from the *King George V*. In the background a pall of smoke marks the location of the damaged *Bismarck*. *IWM*

FAR LEFT: The *Rodney* carried nine 16in. guns in three triple turrets, all mounted forward of her bridge. Their shells pounded the *Bismarck* during the morning of May 27. *MNF*

BELOW: The final moments of the *Bismarck* were captured by a photographer on board the cruiser *Dorsetshire*.

more survivors. This meant that all of 2,000 German sailors were lost, including both Captain Lindemann and Admiral Lütjens.

As for the *Prinz Eugen*, after she left the *Bismarck* during the evening of May 24, she steamed south towards the main British convoy routes, to rendezvous two days later with the German tanker *Spichern* to refuel. For the next three days she cruised the northwest Atlantic, but failed to meet any convoys, as they had been diverted away from the area by the British Admiralty. On May 29 a fault developed with her engines, and she set a course for Brest. As the warships that had participated in the hunt for the *Bismarck* had turned for home by this stage, there were no British units to impede her progress, and she arrived safely in Brest on 1 June. Thus Operation Rheinübung came to an end, a sortie which had brought humiliation to the Royal Navy, then disaster to the Kriegsmarine. Never again would the Germans be prepared to challenge British naval might in such an overt manner. As Grand Admiral Raeder admitted, the loss of the *Bismarck* had a decisive effect on the conduct of the war at sea. While the Royal Navy faced other greater perils during the war, the moral and physical victory she achieved during that week in May demonstrated that seapower, the long-term arbiter of victory in a global conflict, would be the exclusive tool of Britain and her allies.

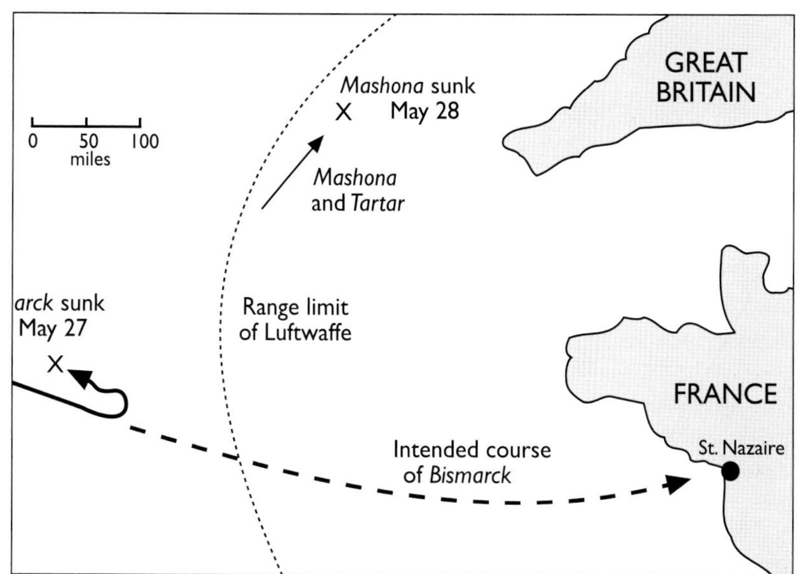

Aftermath

A survivor's story

Kapitänleutnant Baron Burkhard von Müllenheim-Rechberg was the Fourth Gunnery Officer on the *Bismarck*, and its senior surviving officer. He later wrote a fascinating account of his service on board the battleship, and described the events surrounding its sinking. Together with the recollections of other survivors his account allows us to understand what conditions were like during the *Bismarck*'s final moments.

Müllenheim-Rechberg was stationed in the aft gunnery control position, and saw little once the final battle began, as he was busy directing the fire of the battleship's aft guns. When the main fire control director was knocked out, Müllenheim-Rechberg directed the fire of "C" and "D" turrets, ranging on the *King George V*. Minutes later a near miss from a British shell smashed the optics on his rangefinder, forcing the aft turrets to switch to local control, aiming themselves without the benefit of the rangefinders. One by one the guns were silenced; first the forward turrets, then "Caesar" turret, then "Dora". Damage control parties were called to fight fires, counter flooding and to flood magazines. Chief Mechanic Wilhelm Schmidt then recalled the order being given to place scuttling charges, and to prepare to abandon ship. Schmidt tried to work his way onto the upper deck, hindered by flooding, smoke, damage and the listing of the ship to port. He passed medical teams treating casualties before reaching the canteen close to the funnel. Some 300 men were in the compartment, all trying to escape through a single hatchway. One was Seaman Herbert Blum, who recalled emerging onto the deck to see wounded men, some without arms. He was thrown to the deck by an explosion, and both he, Blum and another survivor described a scene of unspeakable carnage, with over a hundred dead sailors scattered around them, with blood everywhere. Other badly wounded men were screaming or vomiting from shock. Seaman Statt saw living, dead and wounded men being washed over the side when the battleship lurched to port, then smashed back against the deck by the waves. Shells were landing on the deck near him, cutting down men as they staggered towards the stern. Great holes were blown in the deck, and men fell into these amid the smoke, plunging down into the maelstrom of fire below. Other survivors describe seeing whole compartments filled with dead, and men driven insane, or to suicide. Müllenheim-Rechberg records the scene:

> The destruction round about was frightful. Everything up to the bridge bulwarks had been erased ... The hatches leading to the main deck (particularly on the port side) were either jammed shut or there was heavy wreckage lying on top of them ... In Compartment XV near the forward mess on the battery deck, two hundred men were imprisoned behind jammed hatches. They were all killed by shellfire. Flames cut off the whole forward part of the ship. One of the starboard 15cm turrets had been hit and its hatch was jammed. No amount of effort from

inside or out could pry it open. The turret became a coffin for its crew ... Hundreds of crewmen lay where they had been hit, in the foretop, on the bridge, in the control stations, at the guns, on the upper deck and on the main and battery decks.

Müllenheim-Rechberg made his way to the quarterdeck, where some 300 men were gathered. Some were singing, but most were busy donning lifejackets, and helping their wounded comrades into the sea. Müllenheim-Rechberg jumped off the starboard side of the quarterdeck, then swam swiftly away from the ship. He looked back to see if he could see any signs of damage as the ship slowly rolled over, but he could see none. Swimmers close to the bow claim to have seen Captain Lindemann standing on the forecastle, waiting for the end. He saluted as the ship rolled over, and went down with his ship. The time was approximately 1039.

The survivors were left floating in the Atlantic. Müllenheim-Rechberg ordered the men near him to stay together and wait to be rescued. He recalled "the fuel oil from our sunken ship that was floating on the surface of the water in a wide, black sheet. Its odor stung our noses. It blackened our faces, and forced its way into our eyes, noses and ears." Eventually he sighted the cruiser *Dorsetshire* approaching. She steered for the thickest concentration of survivors and dropped lines over the side, and a wooden raft. It was extremely difficult for the exhausted, oil-covered men to climb up to safety, and Müllenheim-Rechberg only succeeded on his second attempt, aided by the British seamen who hauled on the rope.

He looked back over the side at the men in the water. "There were hundreds of them, hundreds of yellow lifejackets. Perhaps eight hundred, I estimated. It would take a good while to get them all on board." It was not to be. The perceived threat of a U-boat attack forced Captain Martin of the *Dorsetshire* to get underway before all the survivors could be rescued, condemning the men left in the water. It was a miserable end for those seamen who had endured so much, and were so close to safety.

When the *Bismarck* sank she glided for some distance, before hitting the seabed 4,525m below the surface of the Atlantic. She slid down a slope for another 1,000m before coming to rest in 4,750m of water. There she remained for almost half a century, a haven for sea creatures, her jagged remains softened by marine growth. Her wreck was discovered by a deep-sea exploration team led by Dr. Robert Ballard on June 8, 1989. Ballard's team surveyed the wreckage and the debris field which surrounded her, revealing the full extent of the damage the *Bismarck* suffered during her final battle. Twelve years later the wreckage of the *Hood* was found, some 2,800m below the surface of the Denmark Strait. Again, valuable information was gleaned concerning the cause of the explosion which destroyed the battlecruiser. The explorers treated the two shipwrecks like the war graves they had become, and before they left they laid plaques on the sunken remains, honoring the thousands of men who lost their lives in May 1941. When the teams departed, the once-mighty warships were once again left in peace, amid the cold and darkness of the Atlantic floor.

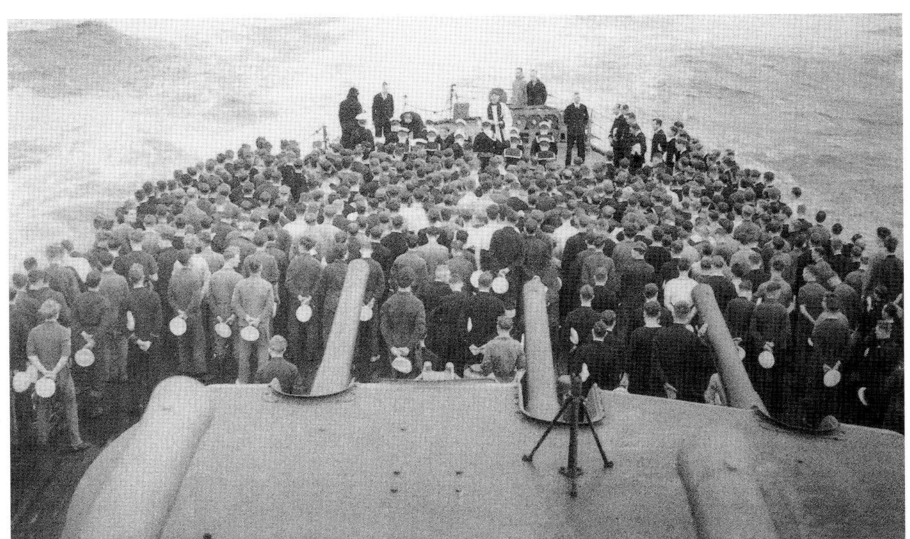

LEFT: Survivors from the *Bismarck* are hauled aboard the *Dorsetshire* while others cling to rafts, awaiting their turn. The *Dorsetshire* was forced to abandon the rescue moments after this photograph was taken. *IWM*

ABOVE LEFT: A funeral service held aboard the cruiser *Sheffield* for crewmen killed during the air attack from *Ark Royal*. *RNM*

Analysis

The recriminations began almost before the last shell was fired. The evening before the final battle, Winston Churchill sent Tovey a signal which suggested that he ensure the *King George V* remain on the scene until the *Bismarck* was sunk, and if need be it would be towed back to port. This ludicrous suggestion demonstrated that although Churchill understood naval strategy, he knew nothing about naval warfare. Risking the flagship this way in U-boat infested water was unthinkable, and Tovey ignored the signal. Later describing it as "the stupidest and most ill-considered signal ever made." It was the first of several clashes between the Prime Minister and the Commander of the Home Fleet. Next, Churchill (through the intermediary of Sir Dudley Pound) demanded that Captain Leach of the *Prince of Wales* and Rear-Admiral Wake-Walker be court martialed for their lack of aggressiveness. Tovey refused, threatening to resign if such a hearing took place. Churchill and Pound also criticized Tovey for losing the *Bismarck* in mid-Atlantic, and Captain Dalrymple-Hamilton of the *Rodney* for failing to give chase with more alacrity. Accusations and counter-accusations continued to be exchanged for months, and it was no credit to Pound that he challenged such interference in naval affairs by a politician. In Germany, Hitler claimed the Kriegsmarine had let him down, and effectively vetoed any further long-range operations.

It is clear that both sides made serious mistakes during the campaign. For the Germans, the first error made by Lütjens was the decision not to refuel the *Bismarck* while she lay in Grimstadfjord. Had she done so, the loss of fuel caused by the hit from the *Prince of Wales* would probably not have forced her to cancel her mission. She would also have had enough fuel to steam at full speed, meaning she would probably have evaded her British pursuers, and reached the limit of Luftwaffe air cover before she was attacked by Swordfish aircraft from their Ark Royal. The Luftwaffe certainly had the potential to strike far out into the Atlantic. Following the sinking of the *Bismarck*, a German long-range bomber sweep in the area the following day failed to find Tovey's battleships, but the German aircraft did locate and sink the destroyer *Mashona* as she headed home. Luftwaffe air cover would have forced Tovey to give up the chase. The second mistake made by the Admiral was the sending of a signal to German Naval Headquarters while she was evading her pursuers. Although the British were unable to determine her location from the resultant radio intercept, they were able to discover the general area in which the *Bismarck* was operating. This told Admiral Tovey two things. First, he was looking in the wrong area of the Atlantic and that the *Bismarck* was further to the southeast; and secondly, that the *Bismarck* was probably heading towards the French ports. This information set the scene for a final phase of the campaign. It also supported evidence gleaned from intelligence sources in the Mediterranean, which pointed to Brest or St. Nazaire being the destination of the German battleship. Even more importantly, the strategic rationale behind Operation Rheinübung was flawed. The *Bismarck* was not supposed to engage enemy warships unless she had no option to do so. This meant that after destroying the *Hood*, the Germans were unable to finish off the *Prince of Wales*. However powerful the *Bismarck* might have been, she had no real chance to wrest control of the Atlantic from the British, temporarily or otherwise. If she had sailed in company with the *Tirpitz* or even the *Scharnhorst* and *Gneisenau*, she might have posed a serious threat to British seapower. Although the loss of the *Hood* was a serious blow to British naval prestige, the loss never really affected the naval balance in the Atlantic. By contrast, the loss of the *Bismarck* two days later was a serious blow to the German Navy, and forced it to abandon any further offensive strategic operations.

As for the British, almost all of the senior commanders left themselves open to criticism. First, Admiral Tovey could have made better dispositions when he ordered his fleet to take up blocking positions between Greenland and the Faeroes. Admiral Holland made the fundamental error of trying to engage the *Bismarck* with his two flawed capital ships by closing the range at an angle which prevented him from using the full weight of his squadron's armament. He also misjudged his approach to the Denmark Strait, and if he had reached his blocking position just 30 minutes earlier, he would have been in a far better tactical position. Similarly, Captain Kerr of the *Hood* engaged at the wrong target, mistaking the *Prinz Eugen* for the *Bismarck*. To the north, Rear-Admiral Wake-Walker failed to support Holland's action by engaging the *Prinz Eugen* with his two heavy cruisers. This might have given the British are slight edge in the engagement. The mistaken attack on the *Sheffield* was a result of poor staff work, and although Somerville could be blamed for the error, the lack of any real damage meant that no further charges were leveled against him or his officers. The criticism aimed at Tovey was largely ill-placed, as he made the best of the intelligence and resources he had at his disposal. His decision to leave the *Bismarck* to be finished off by cruisers was the only possible one given his ad-hoc battleship squadron's chronic shortage of fuel. His handling of the final engagement was skillful, and ensured the destruction of the enemy for the least possible loss.

The hunt for the *Bismarck* was one of the greatest naval operations in history, and its long-term effects were profound. While Admiral Lütjens scored a major victory over the Royal Navy when he sunk the *Hood*, the loss was more of a moral blow than a physical one, as it failed to alter the strategic situation in the Atlantic. The engagement forced the German commander to curtail his mission, and the initiative passed to the British. British merchant shipping was unaffected by the German sortie, and Raeder's stated aim to temporarily challenge the British for control of the Atlantic came to nothing. The loss of the *Bismarck* far outweighed any advantage gained by sinking the *Hood*; an exchange of capital ships which the Germans could ill-afford. Seapower proved the key to success, as the British were able to dominate the Atlantic, bringing overwhelming force to bear against the German raider. It was also the last long-range fling of the Kriegsmarine, who from that point on would rely on U-boats rather than capital ships to attack Britain's sea lanes. With her control of the Atlantic secure, Britain and later the United States would slowly drive these U-boats from the ocean, a final demonstration of the importance of seapower in global strategy. Operation Rheinübung and the pursuit of the *Bismarck* remained a last defiant demonstration of the emotive and physical power of the battleship, a last hurrah for a dinosaur. This last great clash of naval titans passed into history, and naval technology moved on, as naval airpower and submarines became the capital ships of the next generation. Perhaps that is part of the fascination with the events that unfolded during that tense week in May 1941, as a world at war collectively followed the drama to its final and spectacular conclusion.

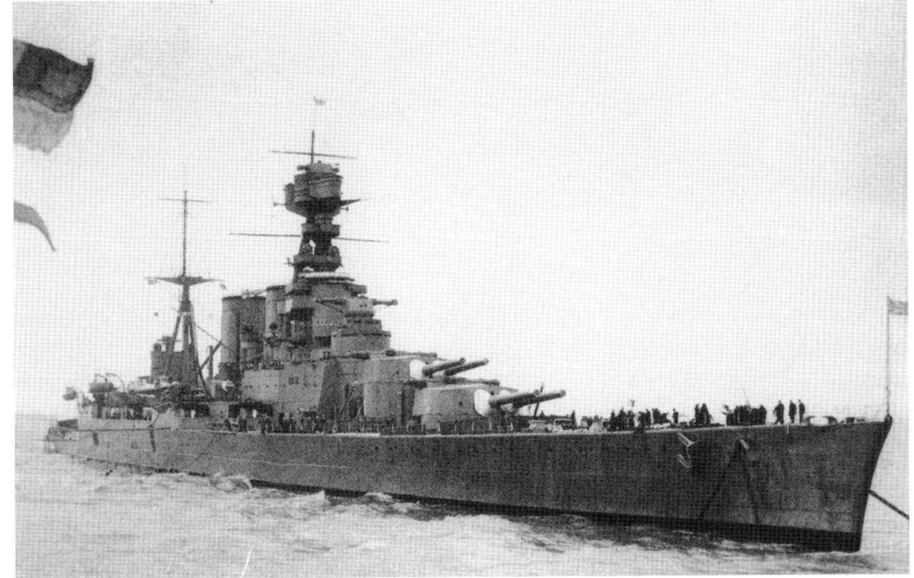

LEFT: The loss of the *Hood* was a major blow to British pride, but it did little to alter the naval balance of power. By contrast the sinking of the *Bismarck* brought an end to German forays into the Atlantic, and ensured the dominance of British seapower in the Atlantic for the remainder of the war. *RNM*

ABOVE LEFT: Admiral Tovey was criticized for his handling of the operation, but he succeeded in cornering and destroying his prey when other less competent commanders might have let the *Bismarck* slip through their net. *RNM*

Reference

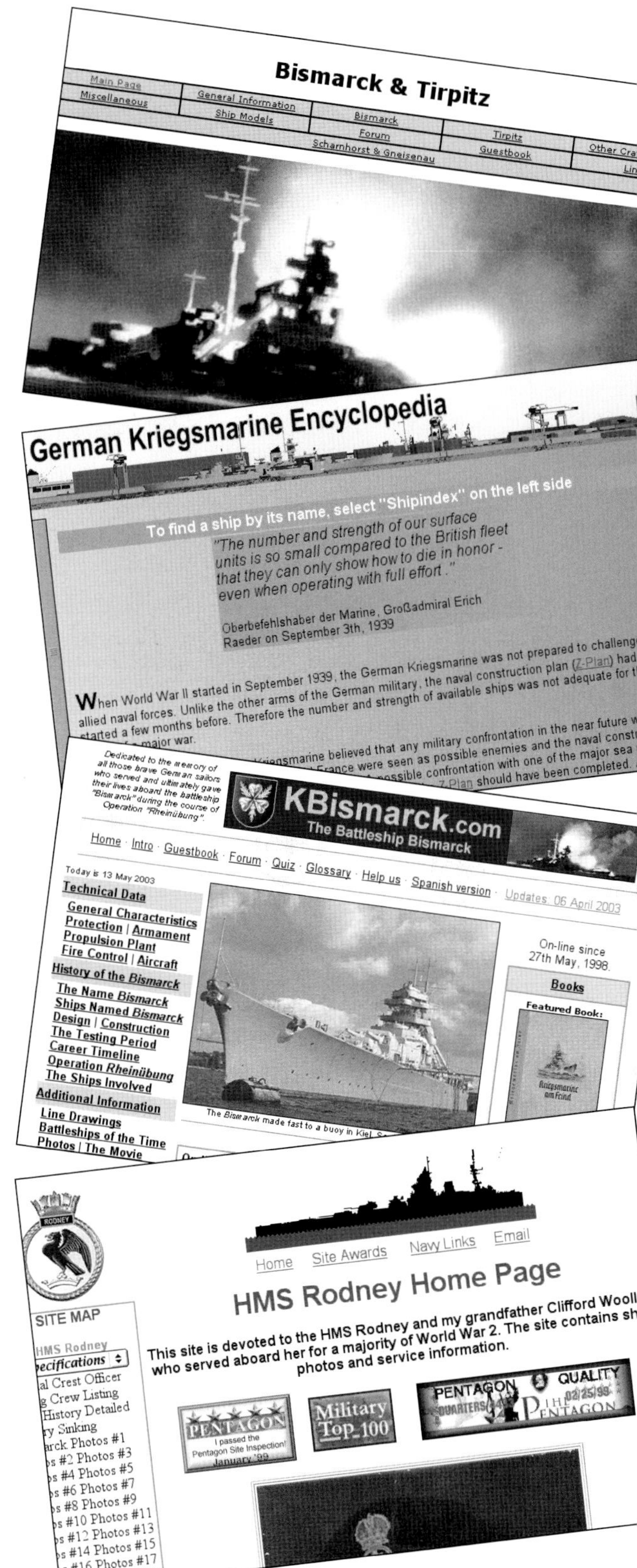

Bibliography

Bekker, Cajus *Hitler's Naval War*, Macdonald and Jane's, London, 1974. Study of German naval strategy, written by a German naval intelligence officer.

Berthold, Will *Sink the Bismarck*, Longmans, London, 1968. One of the first detailed accounts of the operation to be published.

Bradford, Ernie *The Mighty Hood*, Hodder & Stoughton, London, 1959. Highly readable history of the British battlecruiser.

Brennecke, Jochen *Schlachtschiffe Bismarck*, Naval Institute Press, Annapolis, 1960. Translation of the standard German history of the *Bismarck* and her Atlantic sortie.

Busch, Fritz-Otto *The Story of the Prinz Eugen*, Hale, New York, 1960. Useful account of the operational history of the German cruiser.

Chesneau, Roger *Hood: Life and Death of a Battlecruiser*, Cassell, London, 2002. Good general account of the *Hood*'s career, including a chapter on her final battle with the *Bismarck*.

Dönitz, Grand Admiral Karl *Memoirs: Ten Years and Twenty Days*, Weidenfeld and Nicholson, London, 1958. The German admiral's version of the operation, including his rationale for Operation Rheinübung.

Forester, C.S. *Hunting the Bismarck*, Granada Publishing, London, 1963. Dramatic account of the battle, which was later turned into the screenplay for the film *Sink the Bismarck*.

Herwig, Holger H. and Bercuson, David J. *The Destruction of the Bismarck*, Overlook Press, Overlook, 2001. Workmanlike account of the campaign, with detailed coverage of the final battle.

Humble, Richard *Hitler's High Seas Fleet*, Ballantine, New York, 1971. Analysis of German surface ship operations.

Jackson, Robert *The Bismarck*, Spellmount, Staplehurst, 2002. Study of the German battleship along with other German capital ships.

Kennedy, Ludovic *Pursuit: the Chase and Sinking of the Bismarck*, William Collins Sons & Co., London, 1974.

Mearns, David and White, Rob *Hood and Bismarck: the Deep-Sea Discovery of an Epic Battle*, Channel 4 Books, London, 2001.

Müllenheim-Rechberg, Baron Burkhard von *Battleship Bismarck: a Survivor's Story*, Naval Institute Press, Annapolis, 1990. A fascinating and detailed account of the *Bismarck* and her sortie, written by the highest-ranking survivor of her crew. This superb book is probably the best account of the campaign in print.

Rhys-Jones, Graham *The Loss of the Bismarck: an Avoidable Disaster*, Naval Institute Press Annapolis, 2000. Well-written account of the campaign, which explores various theories about the operation and the options available to Admiral Lütjens.

Schmalenbach, Paul *KM Bismarck*, (Warship Profile series) Profile Publications Windsor, 1972. Technical study of the German battleship, containing detailed plans.

Shirer, W.L. *All about the sinking of the Bismarck*, W.H. Allen Publishing, London, 1963. Personal recollections of the *Bismarck* campaign by a British naval officer.

Vian, Admiral of the Fleet Sir Philip *Action this Day*, Frederick Muller Press, London, 1960. The reminiscences include an account of Vian's destroyer attack on the *Bismarck*.

Whitley, M.J. *Cruisers of World War Two: an International Encyclopaedia*, Brockhampton Press, London 1995.

Battleships of World War Two: an International Encyclopaedia, Arms & Armour Press, London 1998.

Winklareth, Robert J. *The Bismarck Chase: New Light on a Famous Engagement*, Chatham Publishing, London, 1998. Highly informed account of the Battle of the Denmark Strait and its aftermath, including new theories concerning the engagement.

Websites

http://www.bismarck-class.dk/index.html Covers the operational history of the warship, her technical specifications and a detailed gallery of *Bismarck* photos and artwork. Recommended.

http://www.german-navy.de/marine.htm General history of the Kriegsmarine, with coverage of the *Bismarck* and her sortie.

http://www.kbismarck.com/ A superbly detailed site, which covers all aspects of the *Bismarck*, including a detailed crew roster.

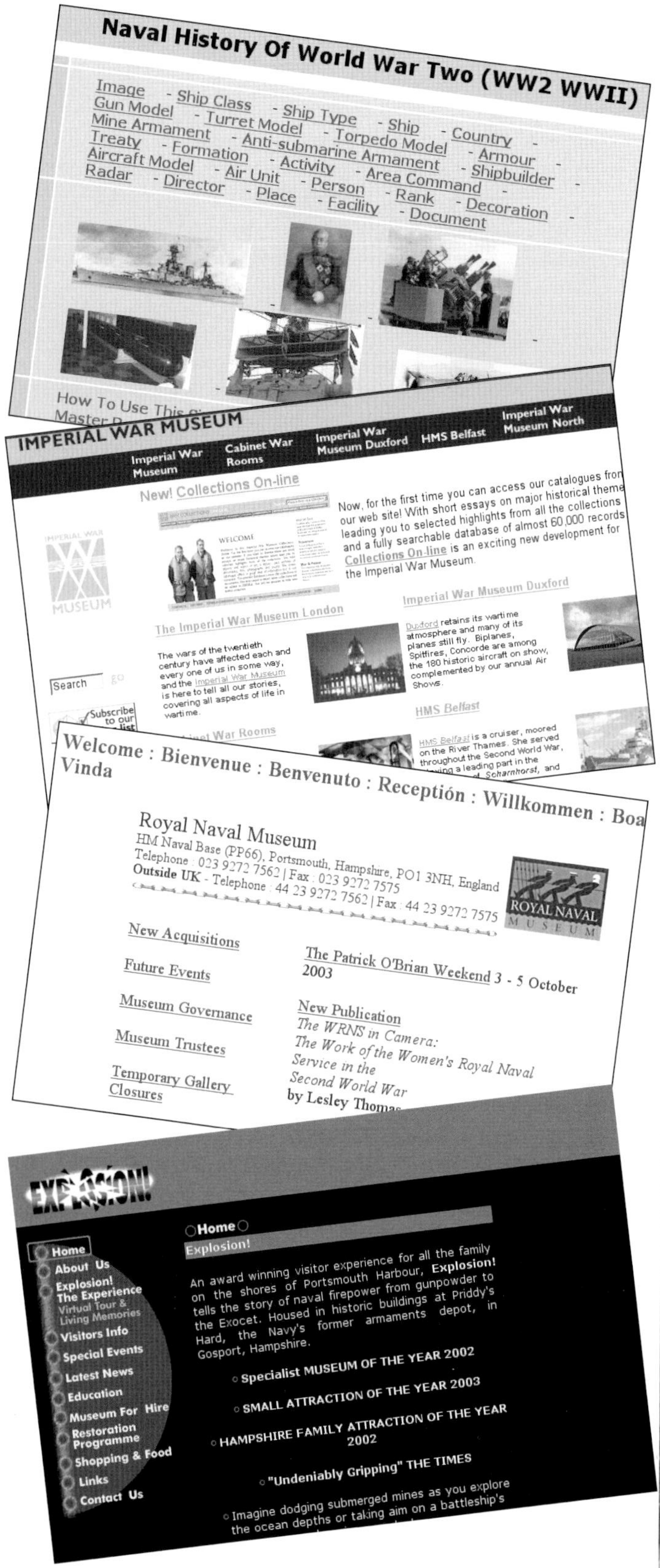

http://www.hmshood.com/ The site of the HMS *Hood* Association: it includes details of her wreck site and a crew database.

http://www.geocities.com/Pentagon/Quarters/4433/index.htm Site covering the activities of HMS *Rodney*, including accounts of her battle with the *Bismarck*.

http://battleshipbismarck.hypermart.net/ Interesting site, but somewhat spoiled by "pop-up" advertising.

http://www.foxcad.com.au/Drawings/Bismarck.htm Contains detailed line drawings and plans of the *Bismarck*.

http://www.schlachtschiff.com/index_00.htm German-language site covering German battleship operations during the Second World War.

http://www.bismarck3d.prv.pl/ A three-dimensional tour of the *Bismarck*.

http://navalhistory.flixco.info/ A naval history of the Second World War, with detailed coverage of ships, weapons and technical data.

Museums

Imperial War Museum, London, UK
http://www.iwm.org.uk/index.htm

Royal Naval Museum, Portsmouth, UK
http://www.royalnavalmuseum.org/

Museum of Naval Firepower, Gosport, UK
http://www.explosion.org.uk/

Fleet Air Arm Museum, Yeovilton, UK
http://www.fleetairarm.com/

National Maritime Museum, Greenwich, London, UK
http://www.nmm.ac.uk/

Deutsches Schiffahrtsmuseum, Germany (German Maritime Museum) http://www.dsm.de

Dresdner Neueste Nachrichten

mit Handels- und Industrie-Zeitung

Bezugspreis: Bei freier Zustellung ins Haus einschl. Trägerlohn monatl. 2.— RM. Postbezug 2.— RM. (einschließl. 34,32 Rpf. Postgebühren) hierzu 36 Rpf. Bestellgeld. Halbmonatl. 1.— RM. Kreuzbandsendung: Inland 75 Rpf., Ausland 1.— RM. wöchentl. Einzelpreis: außerhalb Groß-Dresdens 15 Rpf., in Groß-Dresden 10 Rpf.

Anzeigenpreise: Grundpreis: die 1spaltige mm-Zeile im Anzeigenteil 14 Rpf., Stellengesuche und private Familienanzeigen 11 Rpf., die 79 mm breite mm-Zeile im Textteil 1,10 RM. Nachlaß nach Malstaffel 1 oder Mengenstaffel B. Briefgebühr für Zifferanzeigen 30 Rpf. ausschl. Porto. Zur Zeit ist Anzeigenpreisliste Nr. 10 gültig.

Verlag und Schriftleitung: Dresden A, Ferdinandstraße 4 * Postanschrift: Dresden A 1, Postfach * Fernruf: Ortsverkehr Sammelnummer 24601, Fernverkehr 27981 * Telegramme: Neueste Dresden * Postscheck: Dresden 2060

Nichtverlangte Einsendungen an die Schriftleitung ohne Rückporto werden weder zurückgesandt noch aufbewahrt. — Im Falle höherer Gewalt oder Betriebsstörung haben unsre Bezieher keinen Anspruch auf Nachlieferung oder Erstattung des entsprechenden Entgelts

Nr. 121 — Dienstag, 27. Mai 1941 — 49. Jahrgang

174 800 BRT. in einer Woche versenkt

Japans Flotte für jede Möglichkeit gerüstet — Anwachsende englandfeindliche Kundgebungen in Bombay

Schwer beschädigt!

Sieben britische Einheiten in Gibraltar

× Algeciras, 27. Mai

Im Hafen von Gibraltar trafen, aus dem Mittelmeer kommend, drei britische Kreuzer, zwei Zerstörer und zwei U-Boote, alle in stark beschädigtem Zustand, ein. Es verlautet, daß diese sieben Einheiten am Kampf um Kreta teilnahmen und von der deutschen Luftwaffe Treffer erhielten. Die beiden U-Boote seien nicht mehr tauchfähig.

Nach einer Meldung aus Algeciras ist der britische Zerstörer „Fearleß", aus dem Mittelmeer kommend, Ende vergangener Woche in stark beschädigtem Zustande in den Hafen von Gibraltar eingelaufen.

Vichy über London empört

Koloniale Treuekundgebung

Telegramm unseres Korrespondenten

Bern, 27. Mai

Die französische Regierung hat mit größter Empörung von den neuen Plänen Kenntnis genommen, die England jetzt gegenüber seinem früheren Verbündeten erwägt. Es sei kaum möglich, so wurde in politischen Kreisen Vichys erklärt, ein Gegenbeispiel für die Schamlosigkeit zu finden, mit der die „Sunday Times" jetzt folgende Maßnahmen gegen den langjährigen Waffengefährten und Freund empfehle:

1. die militärische Besetzung Syriens,

2. die Ausdehnung der Blockade auf alle französischen Besitzungen, die die legale Regierung von Vichy anerkennen, und

3. die Bombardierung der französischen Industrie einschließlich jener des unbesetzten Gebietes.

Es gebe für diesen Wahnwitz keine Erklärung mehr. England treibe ein gefährliches Spiel, wenn es sich im Mittelmeer Weygand und Dentz zum Gegner mache. Aus Fez wird hierzu noch gemeldet, daß der französische Oberkommandierende in Nordafrika, General Weygand, nach seinem Eintreffen die europäischen und einheimischen Würdenträger empfangen habe, um ihnen in einer Ansprache die Grundzüge der Politik auseinanderzusetzen, wie sie von Marschall Pétain beschlossen und von der Regierung einstimmig gebilligt worden sei. Es sei Pflicht aller Franzosen, die um die Zukunft ihres Heimatlandes und ihres Imperiums besorgt seien, dieser Politik geschlossen zu folgen. General Weygand richtete einen Appell an die Disziplin und die Einigkeit, damit dem vom Staatschef Frankreichs vorgezeichneten Weg einheitlich Folge geleistet werde.

General Weygand und General Nogues, der Generalresident von Marokko, verließen hierauf Fez, um sich nach dem Tafilalet zu begeben, wo sie mit dem Sultan von Marokko zusammentrafen.

Frankreich kann sich auf diese Kolonien verlassen, wie es die Weygand zuteil gewordenen Kundgebungen bewiesen. Auch Französisch-Somaliland hat einen neuen Beweis für die Ergebenheit an Vichy gesandt, indem es 100 000 Franken für das französische Hilfswerk überwies. Hingegen hat die französische Regierung dem Obersten Collet, der eine tscherkessische Schwadron zum Uebertritt über die syrisch-palästinische Grenze zu verleiten suchte, um in englische Dienste zu treten, die Staatsangehörigkeit entzogen.

Außerdem hat das Militärgericht in Clermont-Ferrand den bisher schwersten Fall von Abtrünnigkeit in Französisch-Westafrika mit schwersten Strafen belegt. Es handelt sich um einen Versuch, den Engländern die Besitzergreifung des französischen Senegal zu erleichtern. Die Angeklagten und zahlreiche Zeugen wurden von Dakar nach Clermont-Ferrand übergeführt. Hauptangeklagter ist ein Leutnant Jean Montever, der eine Anzahl Gruppen organisiert hatte, um einen britischen Landungsversuch in Dakar zu erleichtern. Leutnant Montever hatte auch seine Frau um Informationen über den damals in Dakar liegenden Panzerkreuzer „Strasbourg" ersucht. Im Oktober 1940 floh Montever mit Frau und Kindern sowie seinem besonderen Vertrauensmann Leutnant Bertrand nach Britisch-Gambia. Das Militärgericht verurteilte Montever in Abwesenheit zum Tode, Bertrand zu 20 Jahren Zwangsarbeit; acht Angeklagte waren zugegen, nämlich fünf Militärpersonen, ein Zivilist und eine Frau. Von diesen wurden sieben zu Gefängnisstrafen von zwei bis fünf Jahren verurteilt. Ein Angeklagter wurde freigesprochen. Für alle Verurteilten wurde die Vermögensbeschlagnahme angeordnet, für die militärischen Angeklagten auch die Degradierung.

Handelspartner Griechenland

Ein Aufruf Colakoglus

× Athen, 27. Mai

Der griechische Ministerpräsident, General Colakoglu, erließ einen Aufruf an das griechische Volk, in dem er allen arbeitenden Griechen und insbesondere der griechischen Handels- und Industriewelt befiehlt, sich schnellstens der neuen Wirklichkeit anzupassen und ihre wirtschaftlichen Energien zu verdoppeln. Wörtlich heißt es: „Unsere Handelsbeziehungen zu Deutschland, das früher unser bester Abnehmer war und auch in Zukunft sein wird, sollen demnächst wiederaufgenommen werden. Laßt von Deutschland uns stützen. Laßt uns mit allen Mitteln versuchen, unsere Produktion zu steigern. Wir werden es bestimmt nicht zu bereuen haben."

„Bismarck" in schwerem Kampf

Gegen feindliche Uebermacht — Englische Kreuzerflotte im Mittelmeer aufgerieben

× Berlin, 27. Mai

Das Oberkommando der Wehrmacht gibt bekannt:

Das Schlachtschiff „Bismarck" steht seit Montagabend 21 Uhr wieder in einem schweren Kampf gegen eine feindliche Uebermacht.

Außerdem wird uns zu den großen und schwerwiegenden englischen Kriegsschiffsverlusten der letzten Woche gemeldet, daß bei der erfolgreichen Abwehr der Versuche, die deutsche Aktion gegen Kreta zu stören und zu verhindern

Englands Kreuzerflotte im Mittelmeer aufgerieben

worden ist. England hatte hier mit den Verstärkungen, die in letzter Zeit aus Ostasien gekommen waren, eine Kreuzerflotte von zwölf Einheiten zusammengezogen. Sieben dieser Kreuzer wurden von der deutschen Luftwaffe und vier von italienischen Streitkräften versenkt. Bei Island hat die „Bismarck" Englands größtes Schlachtschiff, den „Goliath der sieben Weltmeere", wie die amerikanische Presse die „Hood" nennt, nach einem Kampf von fünf Minuten vernichtet. In dieser Woche so überaus erfolgreicher Operationen gegen die englische Kriegsflotte sind aber auch im Handelskrieg der britischen Schiffahrt wiederum schwerste Verluste zugefügt worden. Nach den Berichten des OKW. sind in der Woche vom 19. bis 25. Mai durch deutsche Seestreitkräfte 143 300 BRT. und durch die deutsche Luftwaffe 31 500 BRT. versenkt worden. Insgesamt wurden also

174 800 BRT. feindlichen Handelsschiffsraums in einer Woche vernichtet.

Außerdem sind zwei kleinere Handelsschiffe versenkt worden, deren Tonnage nicht bekannt gegeben worden ist. Weitere 15 Schiffe wurden schwer beschädigt. Zu dem Verlust der „Hood" wird noch bekannt, daß sie sich auf der Heimfahrt aus einem nordamerikanischen Hafen befunden habe, wo das Schiff seit Monaten insgeheim zur Ausbesserung von im Mittelmeer erhaltenen Beschädigungen gelegen habe. Vor einigen Tagen sei die „Hood" erst wieder in See gegangen. An der Grenze der nordamerikanischen Gewässer sei dieser Schlachtkreuzer von dem Schlachtschiff „King George V" als Begleitschiff auf der Heimfahrt erwartet worden. Gelegentlich des Kampfes im Nordatlantik sei auch

„King George V." beschädigt

worden. Die deutschen Granaten haben also die Panzer der „Hood" glatt durchschlagen, obgleich die Deckpanzer der „Hood" bis zu 102 Millimeter stark waren. Die Panzer des Kommandoturmes, der Wasserlinie und der anderen verwundbarsten Stellen waren bis zu 305 Millimeter stark. Die Türme waren mit 381 Millimeter dicken Platten umkleidet. Die Versenkung der „Hood" ist damit nicht nur ein Beweis für die ausgezeichnete artilleristische Durchbildung unserer Kriegsmarine, sondern auch für die überragende Güte und ungeheure Durchschlagskraft der deutschen Panzergranaten. Interessant ist in diesem Zusammenhange auch, daß Admiral Hood, der dem jetzt versenkten Schlachtkreuzer den Namen gab, vor fast genau 25 Jahren mit seinem Flaggschiff „Invincible" untergegangen ist. Bekanntlich ist auch die „Invincible", die an der Schlacht vor dem Skagerrak am 31. Mai 1916 beteiligt war, in die Luft geflogen. Der Kommandant des Schlachtschiffes „Hood" war Admiral Holland. [illegible] Mitteilung der britischen Admiralität bekannt, nach der

Admiral Holland und sein Stab als verloren anzusehen

sind. Von der 1340 Mann starken Besatzung des Schiffes konnten nur wenige gerettet werden.

Freyberg sieht schwarz für Kreta

„Die Lage auf der Insel verschlechtert sich" — Admiral Cunningham gesteht die Ohnmacht der britischen Mittelmeerflotte

Telegramm unseres Korrespondenten

Rom, 27. Mai

Der Kommandant der Verteidigung Kretas, General Freyberg, hat an das Hauptquartier General Wavells in Kairo einen Bericht geschickt, in dem es heißt, daß sich die Lage auf der Insel immer mehr verschlechtere. In militärischen Kreisen Roms wird zu den Kämpfen um Kreta hervorgehoben, daß England sich bereits vor Ausbruch des Krieges sehr für eine Befestigung der Insel interessiert und die griechische Regierung zur Ausführung von Verteidigungsanlagen mit den nötigen Geldmitteln versehen hatte. Seit dem 1. November 1940 sei Kreta bereits von den Engländern besetzt worden. Die Engländer begannen zunächst mit den Arbeiten für den Schutz der Flugplätze. In keinem Falle könne man also von einer schwachen Verteidigung Kretas sprechen, vor allem nicht, da auf der Insel ein reguläres Heer stationiert wurde, das durch die von Peloponnes geflüchteten britischen und griechischen Truppen wesentlich verstärkt wurde.

Gerade in diesem Bewußtsein habe die Achse Kreta angegriffen, da es sich um einen der Hauptstützpunkte der englischen Flotte und Luftwaffe im Mittelmeer handle. Man bezeichnet diesen Angriff in Rom als „die zweite Phase der Mittelmeerschlacht". Sie steht am Dienstag im Mittelpunkt des Interesses. „Popolo di Roma" weist in diesem Zusammenhang auf die Aeußerungen von Admiral Cunningham hin, der den Ernst der Lage erkannte und zugeben mußte, daß es der englischen Flotte nicht gelungen sei, den Gegner zu verhindern, Truppen nach Kreta zu schaffen. Diese Erklärungen des Oberbefehlshabers der englischen Seestreitkräfte im Mittelmeer seien, wie das Blatt betont, bezeichnend genug, bestätigen sie doch von amtlicher englischer Seite, daß die englische Flotte jene Kontrolle, deren sie sich so lange rühmte, nicht besitze.

Revolten in Transjordanien

Der Sohn des Emirs führt die Revolte — Erfolgreicher Fortgang der Kämpfe im Irak

× Damaskus, 27. Mai

Die Lage in Transjordanien wird immer gespannter. Emir Abdullah hält sich verborgen oder hat Amman verlassen, seitdem er offen gegen den Irak Stellung genommen hat. Ehemalige arabische Aufständische in Palästina, die ihre Zuflucht im Irak und in Transjordanien genommen hatten, bereiten augenblicklich eine Aufstandsbewegung gegen die britischen Behörden und gegen Emir Abdullah vor. Aus Amman verlautet gerüchtweise, daß diese Revolte vom Erbprinzen Emir Tatal geleitet werde.

Diese Aufstandsbewegung hat denn auch starke Rückwirkungen auf die Kämpfe im Irak, die erfolgreich fortschreiten. So meldet der neue irakische Heeresbericht Nr. 29 u. a.: „Unsere Truppen schlugen mit Erfolg alle feindlichen Angriffe in der Gegend von Ramadi ab. Unter Zurücklassen mehrerer Toter und beträchtlichen Materials zog sich der Feind zurück. Die irregulären nationalen Streitkräfte griffen die feindlichen Stellungen zwischen Ramadi und Ruthba an. Nach zähem Kampf mußte sich der Feind zurückziehen. Wir machten mehrere Gefangene und erbeuteten ein Maschinengewehr. Bei Sinnedelbane belegten unsere Flieger feindliche Flugzeuge am Boden mit Maschinengewehrfeuer. Zwei Hurricane-Apparate wurden zerstört, andere beschädigt. Unsere Flugzeuge eröffneten Maschinengewehrfeuer auf einen Truppentransport südwestlich von Habannia und verursachten schwere Verluste. Das Telegraphenamt in Sinnedelbane wurde durch Bomben zerstört."

Durch diese Meldung widerlegt sich von selbst die Lüge des Londoner Rundfunks, der die Nachricht verbreitete, daß die Engländer in Bagdad eingerückt seien. Zu dieser Siegesmeldung wird in Bagdad festgestellt, daß Engländer tatsächlich in Bagdad eingerückt seien, allerdings nicht als Sieger, sondern, wie so oft bei derartigen „britischen Siegen", in langen Reihen als Gefangene.

Im ganzen Irak herrscht außerdem der größte Jubel über das siegreiche deutsche Seegefecht und die Versenkung der „Hood". Im übrigen begab sich im Auftrage der irakischen Regierung Kriegsminister Schaukat in einer Sondermission nach Ankara.

Feuergefechte in Bombay

× Schanghai, 27. Mai

Die englandfeindlichen Kundgebungen in Bombay haben trotz behördlicher Verbote und der Gewaltanwendung durch die Polizei einen immer stärkeren Zulauf aus der indischen Bevölkerung erhalten. Infolgedessen verschärften sich die Unruhen im Laufe des Montags derart, daß sich die englische Polizei außerstande sah, die Lage zu beherrschen und starke englische Truppenkontingente zu Hilfe gerufen werden mußten. Bei dem Versuch der Besetzung verschiedener Stadtteile stießen die Truppen mit der indischen Bevölkerung zusammen und schossen rücksichtslos in die unbewaffnete Menge. Daher betragen die Verluste der Inder allein am Montag 21 Tote und 151 Verletzte. Ueber 400 Inder wurden verhaftet.

Der Gouverneur von Bombay und der Polizeipräsident fuhren im Panzerauto durch die Straßen der Stadt, um sich über den Verlauf der Kämpfe zu orientieren. Sie mußten feststellen, daß die indische Bevölkerung durch die englischen Grausamkeiten aufs äußerste gereizt ist.

Amerikas zwei Fronten

Der amerikanische Staatssekretär Hull machte am 2. April vor dem Haushaltsausschuß des Repräsentantenhauses in Washington unter anderem folgende Bemerkung: „Entweder werden nach Kriegsende die wirtschaftlichen Kräfte der Welt in der Richtung totalitärer Autarkie organisiert werden, mit ihren unzähligen Methoden und Tricks, die freie Völker empören — oder diese wirtschaftlichen Kräfte werden unter die Führung einer großen Nation kommen wie unsere — und ich kenne keine andere, die dazu in der Lage wäre ...." Diese Bemerkungen sind in zweierlei Hinsicht sehr interessant. Einmal nämlich deshalb, weil amerikanische Kreise anscheinend mit einer zentralen Lenkung der Weltwirtschaft von den USA. aus rechnen, ohne eine Art neuen Völkerbund überhaupt nur noch zu erwähnen. Und zweitens deshalb, weil das britische Weltreich für so erschöpft und ausgeblutet gehalten wird, daß es zu einer führenden Rolle gar nicht mehr fähig ist. Bei den Vereinigten Staaten würde also die absolute Vorherrschaft oder Suprematie in der Weltwirtschaft und Weltpolitik liegen, vorausgesetzt natürlich, daß die angelsächsischen Mächte den Krieg gewinnen. Das Weltbild des Nordamerikaners ist heute eben ein anderes als gestern. Diejenigen politischen Kreise in den USA., die sich überhaupt mit Politik befassen, sehen den amerikanischen Kontinent im Mittelpunkt des Globus mit der Möglichkeit, sowohl im atlantischen Raum, als auch im pazifischen Raum Macht auszuüben. Wie stark heute diese Kreise sind, kann man schwer abschätzen. Daß sie aber unter der Regierung Roosevelts an Einfluß gewinnen, liegt auf der Hand.

Rein geographisch gesehen, hat diese amerikanische Theorie etwas Bestechendes. In Wirklichkeit jedoch fehlen den USA. heute noch die politischen und militärischen Machtmittel, um so weitreichende Pläne durchzuführen. George Washington kannte die Stärke und Schwäche der Union gut, deshalb warnte er sie in seinem Testament ausdrücklich vor Verwicklungen in europäische Angelegenheiten. Wilson setzte sich als erster darüber hinweg und erntete den entsprechenden Mißerfolg. Die USA.-Politik hatte eben keine europäische Erfahrung, um eine derartige transatlantische Gewaltpolitik durchführen zu können. Will Roosevelt durchaus auf den Pfaden Wilsons wandeln, dann muß er sich über die Veränderung der außenpolitischen Lage im klaren sein.

Die Schwäche der USA. liegt eben darin, daß es zwei riesige Fronten zu verteidigen hat. Die beiden Ozeane, die Amerika flankieren, bilden die beste Grenze und Verteidigungslinie, wenn man ihre natürlichen Gesetze beachtet und sich auf die Defensive beschränkt. Sie saugen aber die amerikanische Politik und Strategie in unabsehbare Verwicklungen und Schwierigkeiten, wenn die USA. sich auf unüberlegte Angriffshandlungen über Tausende von Seemeilen festlegen. Es kann keine Rede davon sein, daß die USA. mit ihrem vollen Gewicht England zu Hilfe kommen könnten, solange im pazifischen Raum die politische Hochspannung anhält. Amerika möchte sicher gerne beides zu gleicher Zeit tun, nämlich England helfen und Japan unter Druck setzen. Das ist aber unmöglich, weil die amerikanischen Kräfte dazu nicht ausreichen. Entweder macht man daher nur eins und gibt das andere auf, oder man macht beides halb und verliert beides. Das ist die Zwickmühle Washingtons augenblicklich.

Während im Atlantik sich die Verhältnisse allmählich geklärt haben, liegt über dem Pazifik noch ein dunkler Schleier. Wie weit die anglo-amerikanische Zusammenarbeit hier bereits gediehen ist, ist nicht genau bekannt. Bei der starken Festlegung der amerikanischen Außenpolitik an der Seite Englands, Australiens und der Tschungking-Regierung konnte eine Verschärfung der pazifischen Spannungen erwartet werden. Für die USA. ist die Lage hier gefährlich, denn es steht Japan im Pazifik ohne Zwischenschaltung gegenüber, wie sie im Atlantik noch England darstellt. Im Pazifik muß Amerika selber für den Status quo einstehen und die Hauptlast der Vorbereitungen tragen, da England seine Streitkräfte fast ganz aus Ostasien und dem Pazifik zurückgezogen hat. Nur in bezug auf Flottenbasen und strategische Stützpunkte kann England hier Hilfe leisten. Seit dem Weltkrieg verfügt England über keine Schlachtschiffe mehr im Indopazifischen Ozean, und heute ist natürlich erst recht nicht an eine Korrektur dieses Zustandes zu denken. So sind die Vereinigten Staaten gezwungen, mit dem größten Teil ihrer Kriegsflotte im Pazifik anwesend zu bleiben, was sie daran hindert, wesentliche Streitkräfte in den Atlantik zu senden.

Nach einer Rechnung der „New York Times" ist das gegenwärtige Stärkeverhältnis der Kriegsflotten im Pazifik ungefähr folgendes:

	Schlachtschiffe	Kreuzer	Flugzeugträger	Zerstörer	U-Boote
USA.	12	33	4	90—113	40—72
Empire	0	5—14	1	6—16	12—50?
Japan	10	44	6	126	69

Nach dieser Aufstellung, die den Tatsachen recht nahe kommen dürfte, besteht also keineswegs eine wesentliche zahlenmäßige Ueberlegenheit der angelsächsischen Seemächte über Japan. In Kreuzern, Flugzeugträgern, Zerstörern und wahrscheinlich auch U-Booten ist Japan sogar zahlenmäßig überlegen, nur in Schlachtschiffen nicht. Doch sind die japanischen Schlachtschiffe im Durchschnitt moderner und um etwa 2 Seemeilen schneller als die amerikanischen. Zahlreiche japanische Großbauten stehen überdies vor der Vollendung. Das Jahr 1941 zeigt im ganzen das ungünstigste Verhältnis

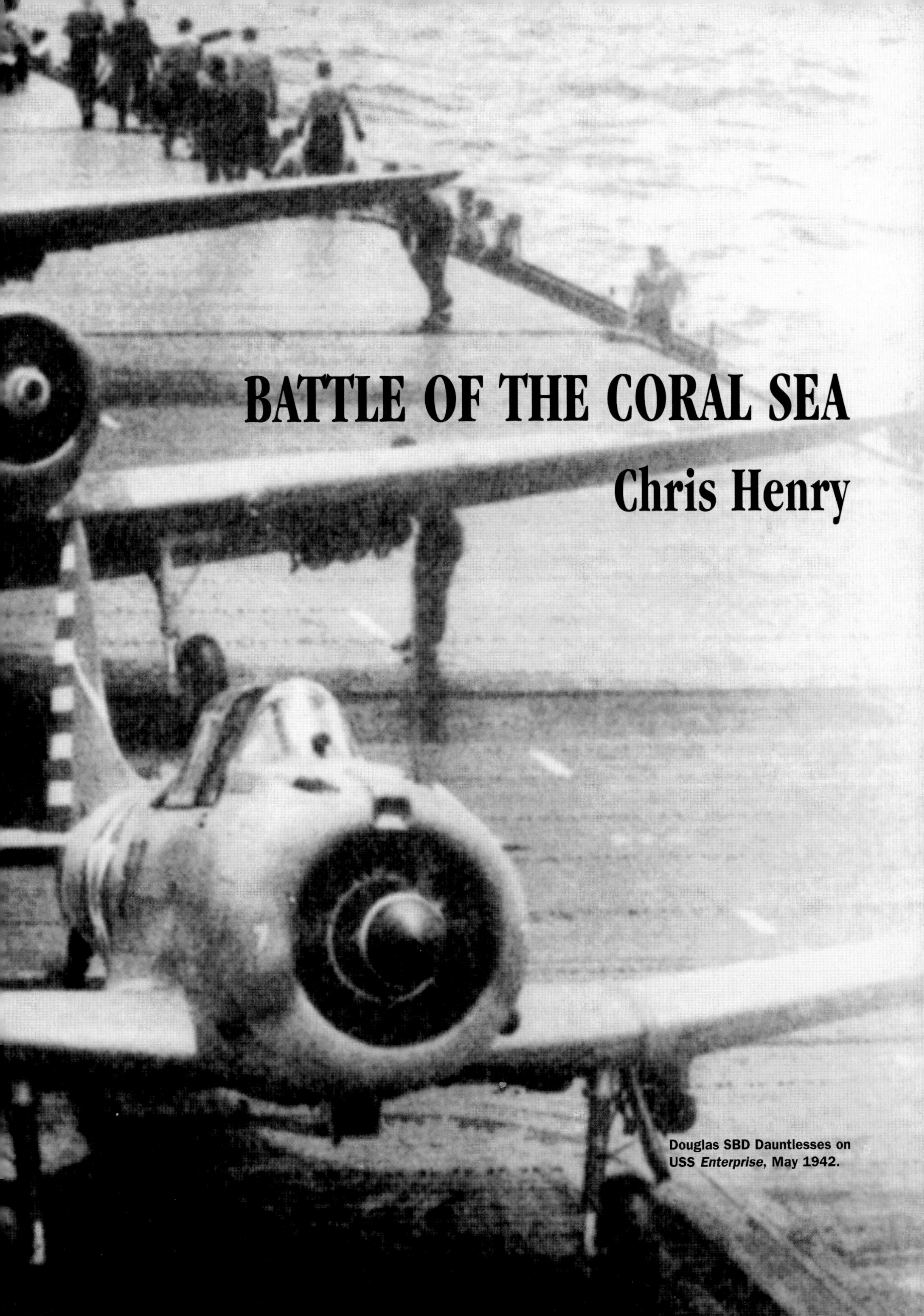

BATTLE OF THE CORAL SEA

Chris Henry

Douglas SBD Dauntlesses on USS *Enterprise*, May 1942.

Introduction

It is hard to believe that an area such as the Coral Sea was ever the scene of a cataclysmic battle. The Solomon Islands and the coasts of Papua New Guinea are more suited to the tranquil lifestyles of the indigenous peoples than as the backdrop to one of the most dramatic naval battles of World War II. For the first time in a battle at sea no large-bore guns roared out and no battleship opposed another. It was the naval aviators and their machines that dealt out death and destruction. The Battle of the Coral Sea is still in some ways overshadowed by the major encounters that punctuate the Pacific War such as Midway, which took place almost immediately afterwards and seems to have been endlessly studied. Yet the Coral Sea is probably the more interesting of the two as it illustrates what happens when two roughly equal sides with similar technology fought a battle for which there was no known precedent. One author describes both sides as groping in the dark and this is certainly the feeling gained from an analysis of the events.

The great naval and amphibious war between America and Japan that raged across the Pacific Ocean during the early period of World War II could justifiably be described as the final act that settled a period of Japanese and US enmity. The roots of this conflict lie before World War II and were the result of the extension of competing spheres of influence. With hindsight, it seems inevitable that the economic juggernaut that was America would smother its opponent in the end, but in 1941 this was not at all clear and the Americans started the war on the back foot.

In the early 1930s The Japanese military had become increasingly involved in politics and by the time of the attack on Pearl Harbor had control over the government of Japan. The Japanese desire to control Asia was both racially and economically motivated. The fundamental driving force was a perceived need for living space and economic stability. Japan was a heavily populated country with few natural resources and these two elements, along with a belief in the racial superiority of the nation, developed into the concept of the Greater Asian Co-Prosperity sphere announced by Prime Minister Matsuoka Yôsuke in August 1940. The Japanese envisioned the Co-Prosperity Sphere as a bloc of Asian nations led by the Japanese and free from the influence of the Western powers. In common with Nazi Germany, Japan was prepared to invade other countries to bolster its own regime, using the resources and populations of invaded countries to sustain itself. In reality, there was no "co-prosperity" and the invaded and dominated nations under Japanese control were forced to do their bidding, supplying workers and resources with no benefit to themselves and suffering extreme privation in the process.

The invasion of China in July 1937, with the subsequent move into French Indo-China in 1940, persuaded the

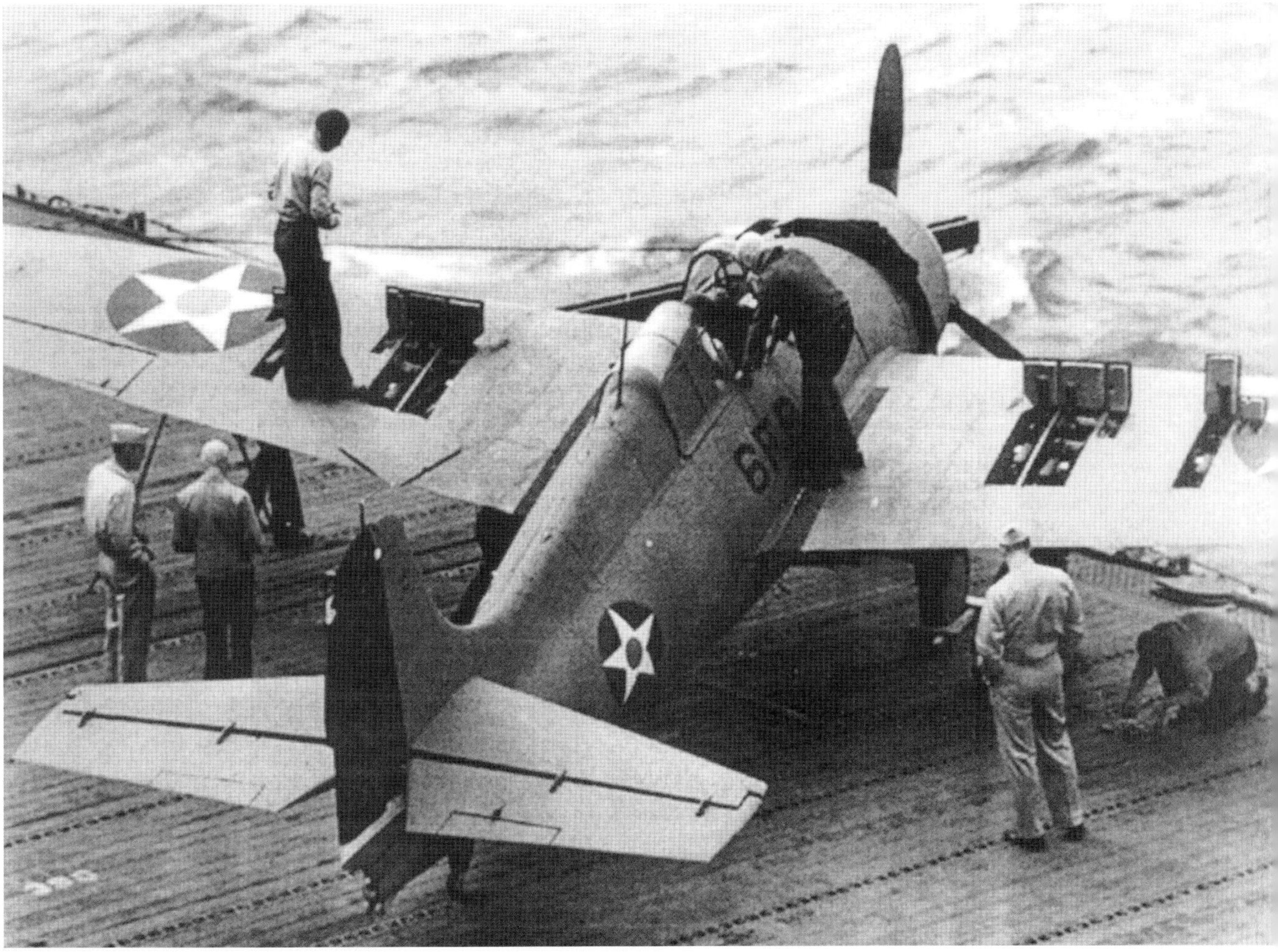

ABOVE: New .50-cal. ammunition for this Grumman F4F Wildcat. The F4F was armed with six machine guns and achieved a high kill rate thanks to its sturdy construction.

LEFT: The Japanese aircraft carrier *Zuikaku* was launched in 1939. She and her sister *Shokaku* were badly mauled during the Battle of the Coral Sea and missed the crucial Battle of Midway because of this.

U.S. that the Japanese were not constrained by their opinions. The Japanese claim was that as an Island nation they had no raw materials, and in some respects it held true. Furthermore, the oil embargo placed on Japan by the U.S. since their intervention in China had exacerbated the supply situation. The army controlled the government and the army saw this as a threat. From this point onwards an increasing emphasis was placed upon an advance across the Pacific. Japan's Navy was young but experienced; it had won two great naval victories during the lifetime of the Imperial Navy. Between 1894 and 1905 the Chinese and the Russians had both been severely defeated at sea by the Imperial Japanese Navy.

The initial surprise Japanese attack at Pearl Harbor in 1941 dealt a savage blow to the U.S. Navy at its most important base. When this was combined with the destruction of British and Dutch naval elements in the region the Japanese genuinely looked as if they could dominate all of the Southeast Asia. It seems clear that they intended to subsume the ex-colonial provinces and then sue for peace. Thus the scene was set for a war that was fought across the length and breadth of the Pacific Ocean. Islands became fortresses and some of the most inhospitable places on earth became battlegrounds. In terms of naval forces the Japanese and Americans were roughly equal at the beginning of the war, though the Japanese had ten aircraft carriers in the Pacific in 1941 compared to the Americans' three. Aircraft were essential for this new kind of warfare and the Japanese had double the number of carrier-based aircraft and at least 400 more land-based aircraft than the allies. Were they to stretch themselves too thinly over the Pacific this advantage would be lost. That is why the carrier battles of the Coral Sea and Midway were critical to Japan's war effort and they had to be victorious in them both. Many works on the Battle of the Coral Sea have admirably dealt with the combat in the air, so this study attempts to redress the balance by covering other aspects of the battle in more detail. As more and more Japanese sources are translated one would hope that their accounts of the air defense of their ships would come to light as this author has yet to find a comprehensive account of the gunnery activities of the Japanese cruisers and destroyers.

RIGHT: Japan was one of the world's great naval powers—in the 1922 Washington Naval Treaty she was allowed to build three capital ships to every five built by the U.S. or Great Britain. By 1942 the Imperial Japanese Navy had more carriers—ten—than either of the big two, all of them equipped with first class equipment and highly trained crew. This is a construction scene from 1939.

Context

Naval warfare at the time

All the great seafaring nations of the world were convinced that the capital ship was the decisive weapon in naval warfare. The battles of Tsushima (1904) and Jutland (1916) were large naval engagements that were decided by the weight of shell provided by battleships. Or at least that was what many naval commentators led the services to believe. Even the Japanese Navy, who were to become the arch exponents of the torpedo bomber, were convinced that a grand naval battle in the traditional style between the Americans and themselves was inevitable. The evidence for this is irrefutable when one considers that they exhausted a great deal of time and resources building the super-battleships *Yamato* and *Musashi*.

The key date from when the two adversaries took divergent paths was 1921. Until that date Britain was an ally of Japan and it was the Washington Naval Treaty of 1922 that attempted to regulate the western and eastern spheres of influence. The Washington Naval Conference was one of the first ever attempts to limit arms expansion and it clearly marks how much weight all the world's great powers put on naval forces. As a result of this treaty, as well as the London naval treaty of 1930, Japan was only allowed a 6:10 ratio in capital ships in relation to the U.S. Navy. Concerned by the strategic limitations imposed on them, particularly by the restriction in the number of capital ships, the Japanese Navy sought other methods to redress the balance, in particular the wholesale-adoption of the aircraft carrier. By 1941, Admiral Isoroku Yamamoto had nine carriers under his control and the Japanese had put their faith in naval airpower. In the first quarter of the 20th century the pioneers of air bombing were a vocal minority. The American pioneer Billy Mitchell had demonstrated as early as 1919 that airpower could seriously damage ships. Despite their success at Pearl Harbor the Japanese still considered that the decisive battle would be between conventional naval forces. The Battle of the Coral Sea would change all that. For the first time two carrier fleets without battleships fought each other without ever seeing each other directly, except through the eyes of their aviators. Naval aircraft and land-based aircraft carried out all the reconnaissance and delivered the killing blows. As such, it is hardly surprising that neither side knew how to deal with the problems of location and identification. That being said, the Japanese had amassed a vast amount of experience in a relatively short time. Following Pearl Harbor in December 1941, Japanese aircraft sank the British battleship the *Prince of Wales* and her supporting battle cruiser the *Repulse*. This attack was another indication to the Japanese that the aerial torpedo could be a battle-winning weapon. By January 1942, Japanese submarines had begun operating in the Indian Ocean, penetrating the inner sanctum of the once-invulnerable British Empire. The USS *Saratoga* also was torpedoed south of Hawaii in another blow to American prestige. In February 1942, the U.S. destroyers *Marblehead* and *Houston* were attacked in the Madoera Straight near Bali and by the end of the month the Battle of the Java Sea had been fought between the Japanese and the combined American, British and Dutch fleet. The

Allies lost two cruisers, three destroyers and the aircraft transport *Langley*. In fact by the end of February 1942, Allied forces had lost control of the seas around Java and the Japanese were pushing forward on all fronts. Probably more significant was the raid by the Japanese First Air Fleet into the Indian Ocean on March 28, 1942. For the British Far Eastern fleet this was too much and they begin a systematic search for the intruders. Running low on fuel they were quickly recalled but sortied from Addu atoll and were attacked by the Japanese First Air Fleet. The First Air Fleet also attacked Columbo, Sri Lanka (Ceylon), and sank a destroyer and an auxiliary cruiser as well as the cruisers *Cornwall* and *Dorsetshire*. On April 9, 1942, the First Air Fleet destroyed merchant shipping and raided into the Bay of Bengal. The British Far Eastern fleet was effectively removed from the area in a tacit acceptance of the power of the Japanese Navy. This catalog of success illustrates how efficient the Japanese Navy and Naval air arm had become.

Strategies and the coming struggle

Only two years after the end of the Russo-Japanese conflict the Japanese were planning to defeat the United States militarily by capturing the Philippine Islands and Guam. These islands had been won for the Americans through the

ABOVE LEFT: By 1942 naval theorists were beginning to realize that the aircraft carrier was the key to naval warfare and that the days of the big-gun battleship were numbered.

LEFT: An F4F prepares for take-off on *Lexington*. A twin 5in. DP mount can be seen in the background.

LEFT: U.S. seapower ensured that the Japanese were incapable of stopping amphibious assaults with seapower, and had to defend their territory on the ground. This is Okinawa, 1945.

RIGHT: USS *Yorktown*, CV-5, at sea, during 1942. Smaller than the Lexington class, *Yorktown* and sister ship *Enterprise* carried more aircraft. *Yorktown* was Rear-Adm. Fletcher's flagship at the Coral Sea.

BELOW RIGHT: Silhouette of a Douglas SBD.3 bomber. Success at the Coral Sea and Midway ensured that over 5,000 SBD Dauntlesses were built during the war.

defeat of Spain in the 1898 war and by capturing them the Japanese intended to provoke the Americans into sending a naval expeditionary force to recapture them. By doing this they would expose themselves to a Japanese attack, which, in the eyes of the Japanese planners, would give them the opportunity to strike when and where they wanted. This was expected to be somewhere near Japan, as this would ensure long American supply lines and Japanese short ones. All of this was thrown into confusion by the Washington Naval Treaty, but the Japanese still intended to keep the basic battle plan prior to World War II, except that they now needed to offset the obvious American superiority in ships.

The answer lay in the use of new weapons of war that would act as force multipliers. The aircraft, the torpedo and the submarine would all be used to destroy the American ships. If the Japanese could whittle down the American fleet by submarine and then aircraft attack, they would then be able to bring the depleted fleet to battle near Japan. The revised plan required new weapons and training techniques to be developed and the Japanese approached the task with relish. By the late 1930s the Japanese naval air arm was an outstanding example of a service that had been created relatively quickly but was extremely efficient.

As the United States acquired dependencies in the Pacific, so the question of how to defend them against an Asian threat was raised. War plan Orange was the plan that laid out how the U.S. would defend against a Japanese attack, and it required that the Philippine Islands be defended until the U.S. Navy arrived to reclaim them. The Philippine Islands were 7,000 miles away from mainland America so it was predictable that any plan would require a large effort on the part of the navy. By the time war arrived, these plans had been altered and refined so that Orange became subsumed in the Rainbow series of war plans. Each Rainbow plan considered ways to protect the U.S. from attack depending upon what forces were available. Rainbow 3 assumed that the United States and the Western Hemisphere north of a latitude of ten degrees south was secure. The Philippines had no real naval base from which to operate and the army few land forces to defend the islands: there were about 17,000 men set against a Japanese invasion force roughly three times the size. Pearl Harbor was the largest naval base in the Pacific but it was 5,000 miles away from the Philippines. Rainbow 3 accepted that these men were to hold the islands until the U.S. Navy could arrive to relieve them. This task was complicated by the fact the Japanese had bases—the Marianas, Marshall and Caroline Islands—from which to sortie along the American supply route. Even as late as 1938 the Orange plan was being refined, but mention of the relief of the islands became more and more vague. Finally, it was decided that the operation was to go through a number of phases that meant the navy would progress across the Pacific rather than head directly for the islands.

The Japanese eventually decided to strike first and attempted to destroy the U.S. fleet at Pearl Harbor in 1941. After a victorious campaign on land and at sea they controlled effectively what they had thought of as the Greater Asia Co-prosperity sphere. Once this area had been occupied the Japanese began to worry about their defensive perimeter. Early raids by the U.S. Navy against the Japanese on the Northern and Southern Marshall Islands as well as Wake Island accentuated this feeling of unease amongst Japanese commanders. Both the USS *Yorktown* and the *Lexington* were used in this way to probe the Japanese and give American morale a boost. But it was in the area of New Guinea where the Japanese were beginning to entrench themselves and at Rabaul on the island of New Britain where they were determined to make a major depot and air base. The conquest of New Guinea was important to the Japanese and surprisingly Australia had become almost as important due to its strategic nature. To the Allies Australia was on the flank of their defense, to the Japanese it represented security for their gains and they intended to have it. Nevertheless the first stage of that progression was the capture of Port Moresby in the early part of 1942. Port Moresby was the principal land base in New Guinea on its south coast and Japanese land forces had been unable to capture it. New Guinea was vital as a pivot for Japanese defensive interests because it formed part of the perimeter they were expecting to hold. Early attacks in March 1942 had affected the Japanese landing on the north coast of the island and the Japanese knew that they would have to hold the port on the south coast to have any chance of defending the area. It was also considered by them that the capture of the base would either act as a springboard for the invasion of Australia or act as an air base that would allow them to control the eastern seaboard of Australia. The plan that was finally adopted was to control any flow of weapons and supplies to Australia and Port Moresby was well situated for this. The Japanese considered endless strategic plans, but the concept of a decisive battle continued to be dominant. Yamamoto, the final arbiter in such matters, was convinced that a decisive battle at Midway was essential to deal the Americans a blow from which they could not recover. Clearly the longer the war went on the easier was for the United States to marshal its colossal economic and industrial power to defeat Japan. The Doolittle raid on April 18 changed everyone's perspective. On that day 16 B-25 bombers flew off the U.S. carrier *Hornet* and traveled 650 miles to drop bombs on Tokyo and other targets. Damage to the city was insignificant, but it was a major blow to Japanese prestige. The inability of military leaders to defend their homeland brought a sense of shame upon the high command.

So the decision to attack Port Moresby and then occupy it was worked up into a complex plan of attack in

RIGHT AND FAR RIGHT: Striking back! On April 1, 1942, 16 B-25s took-off from USS *Hornet* and raided Japan. Commanded by James (latter Lt. Gen.) Doolittle who received a Medal of Honor for the raid, the military effects were negligible. Strategically, however, it was a master stroke that improved U.S. morale and sent an icy wave of apprehension through Japanese ranks.

which several phases were required. Operation MO, as it was known, was composed of several different forces all intended to carry out specific tasks at specific times. Principally there was a transport force to move the Japanese soldiers to the other side of New Guinea. This included the supply vessels and transport vessels. A second invasion force was needed to take over the island of Tulagi in the Solomons, which had a suitable anchorage and would enable the Japanese to set up a naval airbase that could be used for reconnaissance and further attacks on the Coral Sea if needed. A third support force was to set up advanced airbases in the Louisade Archipelago and Santa Isabel. In order to protect and support the invasion force the Japanese provided a substantial group of cruiser and destroyers furthermore there would be a support group of one small aircraft carrier, four cruisers, one destroyer and one tanker for the invasion. A separate carrier force known as the striking force was to counterbalance any American task force at sea and consisted of two large carriers and supporting craft. Reconnaissance was to be carried out by seven submarines and there was a land based aircraft element that was intended to support the whole where possible. It should be noted that while all of this was happening preparations for the big Midway battle were being made so there was no question of the forces of one operation being reused at the other. In fact Midway took place almost immediately after the close of the Coral Sea operation and was probably the most significant sea battle of the Pacific campaign.

The Americans knew some kind of move was in the offing when Japanese force began concentrating at Rabaul. The Americans had carried out several raids into Japanese territory and were aware of Japanese activity in the New Guinea area. Their intention to attack Port Moresby was confirmed by intelligence gathered from intelligence intercepts and the U.S. commander Adm. Nimitz knew something had to be done. Considering that two of America's five carriers were now in the West Pacific having taken part in the Doolittle raid. It was the *Lexington* and the *Yorktown* that were chosen to form the nucleus of the fleet that would oppose any attempt on Port Moresby and Australia. What followed was search for sufficient cruiser and destroyers to support the Task Force. In fact Nimitz went further than just organizing the attack force. He also decided that the two carriers returning from the Pacific raid, namely the *Hornet* and *Enterprise*, should be included in the battle if they arrived at the area of operations in time. Admiral Halsey, who was in charge of the two carriers, was first required to put in at Pearl Harbor and then sail the 3,500 miles to the Coral Sea. They did not arrive anywhere near the islands until May 11, three days after the battle. Nevertheless they still presented a threat to the Japanese, as shall be seen.

The commanders

The first ever carrier against carrier engagement was played under the overall command of two of the great naval strategists of World War II: Admirals Nimitz at Pearl Harbor, and Yamamoto on board the Yamato at Truk. However, the real characters in the drama were Admirals Fletcher and Fitch on the American side, and Admirals Inoue, Goto and Takagi for the Japanese.

The U.S. Navy

At the top of the American tree was Admiral Chester W. Nimitz the Commander-in-Chief of the Pacific Fleet based at Pearl Harbor. Although Nimitz was in overall charge most of the decisions in the field were made by Rr. Adm. Frank J. Fletcher, who was the Commander-in-Chief of the naval and air forces during the battle.

As with many American naval commanders, Frank Jack Fletcher had graduated from the Naval Academy at Annapolis in 1906 and was a veteran of the invasion of Veracruz, Mexico, in 1914. His was to be the task to lead the very first American all-carrier battle. Early in 1941 he was commander of the *Yorktown* task force so he had already had some experience of fighting the Japanese in and around New Guinea. He has been described as a non-dynamic naval officer yet he fought in three major carrier battles in the Pacific and won all of them. It is clear that Nimitz had faith in him and this faith turned out to be justified. Fletcher was cautious when he needed to be but also took risks, which is a prerequisite of any commander at this level of conflict.

Aubrey W. Fitch was another graduate from Annapolis and was considered to be an air specialist, so he took over all air operations when the battle started. In 1930, Fitch went through training to become a naval aviator, and throughout his career he commanded three naval air stations, a seaplane tender and the aircraft carriers *Langley* and *Lexington*, as well as serving as Chief of Staff to

Commander Aircraft, Battle Force, and attending the Naval War College. Earlier in his career he had also commanded destroyers and been involved with aspects of gunnery. He began the war as commander of the *Saratoga* group and carried out raids around New Guinea. Fitch was in command of the *Lexington* group during the Battle of the Coral Sea. Later in the War he became Deputy Chief of Naval Operations for Air.

Adm. Kinkaid served as Fleet Gunnery Officer and Aide to the Commander-in-Chief, U.S. Fleet. He also spent some time as Secretary of the Navy's General Board and as a Naval Advisor at the 1931–32 Geneva Disarmament Conference, giving him valuable insight into the political implications of naval might. Kinkaid took command of USS *Indianapolis* in 1937. Service as Naval Attaché in Italy and Yugoslavia followed in 1938–41. In the months prior to U.S. entry into World War II, he commanded a destroyer squadron before becoming a rear admiral in 1942 when he gained command of a Pacific Fleet cruiser division. During the last half of the year, he commanded a task force built around the aircraft carrier *Enterprise*, participating in the long and difficult fight to seize and hold the southern Solomon Islands.

Herbert Leary, in charge of the Southwest Pacific Group, was a vice admiral at the time of the Battle of the Coral Sea. He had been in command of the *Lexington* task force since February 1942, which was the group that attacked the Japanese air base at Rabaul. He was put under the command of MacArthur on his arrival in Australia to head up the naval forces then in that area, and by May 1942 he was the overall commander of Task Force 44 (Rr. Adm. John C. Crace actually commanded the unit), the destroyers under Macinerny and all the salvage and air groups assigned to the theatre. This included the Task Group TG 17.9, which was basically a seaplane reconnaissance unit.

The American force was divided up into two main Task Forces, which were loose associations of ships pulled together to perform a certain function. The first Task Force was made up of an aircraft carrier group (Rr. Adm. Fitch), a support group (Rr. Adm. T. C. Kincaid and W. W. Smith), a destroyer division (the First under Capt. Early), a carrier escort group and a logistics group (Capt. Phillips). All of these were under the command of Fletcher with Rr. Adm. Fitch.

The second Task Force was under the command of Vice Adm. Herbert F. Leary and included Task Force 44 (Rr. Adm. J. C. Crace RN), a destroyer group (Cmdr. MacInerney), a salvage group and an air reconnaissance task group (Cmdr. de Baun). Also detailed to be involved was a submarine group (Capt. Christie).

TOP: General Douglas Macarthur seen in August 1942.

ABOVE: Rr Adm. Aubrey W. Fitch.

ABOVE LEFT: Admiral C.W. Nimitz.

LEFT: Vice Adm. Frank Jack Fletcher.

The Imperial Japanese Navy

The commander of the Japanese Combined Fleet was Admiral Isoroku Yamamoto, who was the great thinker of the Japanese navy and the architect of the Midway plan. His key defining attribute in many people's eyes was that he had a cosmopolitan and highly sophisticated personality. He had worked and studied in the United States and had a far better idea than most other military commanders of the capabilities of the United States.

The main commander of Japanese forces in the area was Vice Adm. Shigeyoshi Inoue Commander-in-Chief of the 4th Imperial Fleet. Vice Adm. Shigeyoshi Inoue was a brilliant farsighted naval officer whose views on air power were a long way ahead of their time. As a naval strategist he had been head of the Naval Affairs Bureau of the Navy Ministry. As with many senior Japanese naval officers he had studied in Switzerland and France just after World War I. He became a rear admiral in 1936 and Chief of Naval Aviation in 1940. The inability of the Japanese Navy to occupy Port Moresby during Operation MO was largely seen as his responsibility and he was forced to return to Japan after the battle to lead a life of relative obscurity as commander of the naval college. During this battle Inoue was based at Rabaul and his headquarters were on board the cruiser *Kashima*.

Rr. Adm. Takeo Takagi graduated from the Naval Academy in 1912 and was something of an all-rounder, having served both as a staff officer on surface vessels and as an expert in torpedo warfare. He commanded the

strike force during the Battle of the Coral Sea and became the commander of the Sixth Submarine Fleet in 1943. He was killed on Saipan in 1944.

Rr. Adm. Aritomo Goto was the commander of the 6th Cruiser Squadron during the battle; he had commanded this unit from the beginning of the war. He fought at all the major actions in Rabaul and the Solomons but did not long survive the Coral Sea, being killed at Cape Esperance in 1942.

Rr. Adm. Chuichi Hara was commander of the 5th Carrier Division, which included the carriers *Shokaku* and *Zuikaku*. He missed the Battle of Midway because of the involvement of his force in the Coral Sea. In 1944 he became commander of the Fourth Fleet and survived till the end of the war. Hara's position during the battle reveals one of the peculiarities of Japanese command style, the adherence to strict rules of seniority. Hara would have been a wise choice for command of the entire Mobile Force, but Takagi got the post on the basis of seniority. Hara was to have exclusive command of the air operations in an irregular arrangement probably reflecting Takagi's lack of experience as an air commander.

In a book such as this it is common to deal with the high ranking commanders and their influence on events. But at the lower levels there are many commendable individuals, especially those who led the various air groups, without whom things could have gone very badly wrong. Commanding an air unit takes a special kind of control and awareness. On the American side officers such as Cmdr. W. B. Ault on the *Lexington* had to control the movements of all their air assets, he was killed during the battle. On the Japanese side the *Shokaku*'s Lt. Cmdr. Takahashi was a highly experienced and capable individual who orchestrated the attacks on the *Lexington* and the *Yorktown*.

ABOVE LEFT: A 1945 view of Vice Adm. Thomas C. Kincaid aboard his flagship, USS *Wasatch*.

LEFT: A 1945 view of Vice Adm. Frederick C. Sherman aboard USS *Wasp*.

ABOVE RIGHT AND RIGHT: Fleet Adm. Isoroku Yamamoto, C-in-C of the Imperial Japanese Navy's Combined Fleet until his death. He was shot down by P-38 Lightnings over Bougainville on April 18, 1943, following the interception of a radio signal giving details of his location. His death was a great blow to Japanese morale.

OPPOSITE, ABOVE LEFT: Lt. (jg) Robert M. Elder, who won the Navy Cross.

OPPOSITE, ABOVE RIGHT: Another Navy Cross winner—Lt. Cdr. Dewitt S. Shumway.

OPPOSITE, BELOW: Adm. Elliot Buckmaster at the launching of the new USS *Yorktown*, January 21, 1943.

LEFT: Fleet Adm. Chester W. Nimitz (Right), Adm. Sir Bruce Fraser RN, and Adm. Raymond A. Spruance (Left) at a lunch on December 17, 1944.

BELOW: Captured Japanese newsreel possibly showing Adm. Goto watching his aircraft take-off. Note the "scoreboard" at left.

The opposing forces

Surface ships

Aircraft carriers

The two great Japanese carriers, *Zuikaku* and *Shokaku*, that made up the 5th Aircraft Carrier Division were the main striking forces of the Japanese Navy during the battle.

They were medium sized carriers with a displacement of 25,675 tons and a maximum speed of 34 knots. Both Japanese aircraft carriers were started in 1937 and *Shokaku* was completed on August 8, 1941, at Yokosuka Navy Yard. The *Zuikaku* was completed on August 25, 1941. Their dimensions were as follows:

	Shokaku	*Zuikaku*
Displacement	29,800 tons	25,675 tons
Length	820ft	844ft
Beam	85ft	85ft
Armament (both)	16 x 127mm (5in.) 40-cal. DP M1660, 42 x 25mm AA guns	

The aircraft compliment of the carriers was as follows: 16 Zero fighters, including four spare machines, 18 Type 99 bombers, including six spares, and 18 Type 97 bombers, including six spares. Slightly later the complement was increased to 18 fighters and 27 of each type of bomber.

The *Shoho* was much lighter escort vessel, she was built at Yokosuka yard and, as with many carriers of the period, was a conversion of an earlier ship, the *Takasaki*.

	Weight	Length	Beam	Armament
Shoho	11,262 tons	660ft	59ft	8 x 127mm (5in.) 40-cal. DP M1660, 8 x 25mm AA guns

On the American side the two major carriers were the USS *Lexington* and the *Yorktown*. The *Lexington* was finished on October 3, 1925, by the Fore River ship building company. She had a displacement of 33,000 tons was crewed by a complement of 2,122 sailors. She was originally intended as a battlecruiser, but following World War I was converted to an aircraft carrier. It was possible to carry 90 aircraft aboard but this seldom happened in practice and routinely carried just 71 in four squadrons: 36 Douglas Dauntless SBD.2-3 dive-bombers in two squadrons, 12 Douglas TBD Devastator torpedo bombers and 23 Grumman F4F.3 Wildcats.

	Lexington	*Yorktown*
Displacement	33,000 tons	19,900 tons
Length	830ft	761ft
Beam	105.5ft	83.25ft
Armament (both)	8 x 8in. 55-cal., 12 x 5in. AA 4 x 6-pdr saluting 8 x 50-cal. MGs	8 x 5in. 38-cal., 16 x 1.1in. AA 16 x .50-cal. MGs

Above: Japanese Yubari-class light cruiser.

Above Right: Japanese carrier *Shokaku*—one of the casualties of the battle.

OPPOSING FORCES
Naval forces and air force available at the Battle of the Coral Sea

JAPANESE
5th Carrier Division (Hara)
Zuikaku
Shokaku
5th Cruiser Division
Myoko
Haguro
Destroyers
Ariake
Yugure
Shiratsuyu
Ushio
Akebono
Tanker
Toho Maru

Landing Forces
Tulagi Group (Shima)
Minelayer
Okinishima
Seaplane tender
Kawa Maru
22nd Destroyer Division
Kikuzuki
Yuzuki
Transports
Asuman Maru
Tama Maru
Two minesweepers plus auxiliary vessels.

MO group (Kajioka)
Cruisers
Yubari
Destroyers
Oite
Asanagi
Uzuki
Mutsuki
Yunagi
Yahoi

18th Cruiser Division (Marushige)
Cruisers
Tenryu
Tatsuta
Seaplane transport
Kamikawa Maru
Gunboats
Keijo Maru
Seikai Maru
Nikkai Maru
Minelayer
Tsugaru

Covering Force (Goto)
Cruisers
Aoba
Kako
Kinugasa
Furutaka
Aircraft carrier
Shoho
Destroyer
Sazanami
Fuel Tanker
Hiro Maru
Submarines
Two RO class
Five I class

Aircraft resources
***Shokaku* Air Group**
18 A6M.2 Zero fighters
27 Aichi D3A Val dive-bombers
27 Nakajima 97 B5N Kate torpedo carriers
***Zuikaku* Air Group**
18 A6M.2 Zero fighters
27 Aichi D3A Val dive-bombers
27 Nakajima 97 B5N Kate torpedo carriers
***Shoho* Air Group**
16 A6M.2 Zero fighters
19 Nakajima 97 B5N Kate torpedo carriers
25th Air Group
44 A6M.2 Zero fighters
41 Mitsubishi Nell bombers
13 Kawanishi HK6 reconnaissance flying boats
Lae
16 A6M.2 Zero fighters
Buna
7 Mitsubishi Nell bombers
Shortland
3 Kawanishi HK6 reconnaissance flying boats
4 light seaplanes
Tulagi
6 A6M.2 Zero fighters
Truk
44 A6M.2 Zero fighters
41 Mitsubishi Nell bombers
Deboyne
12 light reconnaissance seaplanes

UNITED STATES FORCES
Task Force 17
Task Group 17.2 (Attack Group)
Heavy cruisers
Minneapolis
New Orleans
Astoria
Chester
Portland
Destroyer screen
Phelps
Dewey
Farragut
Aylwin
Monaghan

Task Force 44 (TF 17.3)
Heavy cruisers
Australia
Chicago
Light cruisers
Hobart
Destroyer screen
Perkins
Walke
Farragut

Task Group 17.5 (Carrier Group)
Aircraft carriers
Yorktown (CV-5)
Lexington (CV-2)
Destroyer screen
Morris
Anderson
Hammann
Russell

Task Group 17.6 (Fueling Group)
Oilers
Neosho
Tippecanoe
Destroyers
Sims
Worden

Task Group 17.9 (Search Group)
Seaplane tanker
Tangier
Submarine patrol group
Seven patrolling submarines
Aircraft resources
VP71 – 6 Catalina PBY flying boats
VP73 – 6 Catalina PBY flying boats

Yorktown air group
VF42 – 21 Grumman F4F Wildcat fighters
VB5 – 19 Douglas Dauntless SBD.2/3 dive-bombers (bombing role)
VS5 – 19 Douglas Dauntless SBD.2/3 dive-bombers (scouting role)
VT5 – 13 Douglas TBD.1 Devastators torpedo carriers
Lexington air group
VF2 – 23 Grumman F4F Wildcat fighters
VB2 – 18 Douglas Dauntless SBD. 2/3 dive-bombers (bombing role)
VS2 – 18 Douglas Dauntless SBD.2/3 dive-bombers (scouting role)
VT2 – 12 Douglas TBD.1 Devastators torpedo carriers

ABOVE: A 1937 view of CV-5 *Yorktown*.

LEFT: CV-2 *Lexington*—another prewar photograph, this one dated 1933.

Cruisers

There were both American and Australian heavy cruisers present at the Battle of the Coral Sea. The concept of the cruiser in the U.S. Navy was as a larger version of the destroyer, though there were differences notably in the size of main armament and armor protection. In American service these vessels ranged from 8,000–18,000 tons and had between six and ten 8in. guns as well as secondary AA armament. Light cruisers were armed with 6-in. rather than 8-in. primary armament with a secondary armament often equal to the heavies. One of the principal differences between the Japanese and American cruisers at this stage in the war was that the Japanese retained torpedoes on their heavy cruisers as standard. The U.S. heavy cruisers were mainly of the Minneapolis, Portland and Northampton classes their details were as follows:

	Displacement	Length	Beam	Armor	Armament
Minneapolis class	9,950 tons	588ft	61.75ft	5in. side, 3in. turret	9 x 8in., 8 x 5 in. AA, 2 x 3-pdr, 10 x MGs
Portland class	9,800 tons	584ft	66ft	3–4in. side, 3in. turret	9 x 8in., 8 x 5in. AA, 2 x 3-pdr, 10 x MGs
Northampton class	9,050 tons	570ft	66	3in. side, 1.5in. turret	9 x 8in., 8 x 5 in. AA, 2 x 3-pdr, 8 x MGs

The Australian cruisers present at the battle were the *Australia* and the *Hobart*:

	Displacement	Length	Beam	Armor	Armament
Australia	10,000 tons	630ft	68.5	4in. deck, 2in. turret	8 x 8in., 8 x 4in. AA, 4 x 3-pdr, 4 x 2-pdr pom poms, 4 x MGs, 8 x Lewis guns.
Hobart	6,980 tons	555ft	56.25ft	3in. side, 1in. turret	8 x 6in., 8 x 4in. AA, 4 X 4-pdr, 10 x MGs.

RIGHT: The flightdeck of this U.S. carrier is a hive of activity as a Douglas SBD comes in to land.

BELOW: USS *Marblehead*, CL-2. This ship was attacked by Japanese aircraft in 1942 and severly damaged.

OPPOSITE, TOP: IJN carrier *Zuikaku* seen in 1944 with a Grumman TBF Avenger overhead. The TBF entered service in spring 1942 and first saw action at Midway. The *Zuikaku* and her sister *Shokaku* were the first Japanese carriers planned after the naval limitation treaties of the postwar period lapsed. *Zuikaku* was sunk at Luzon on October 25, 1944.

OPPOSITE, CENTER: IJN destroyer *Ushio* in Yokosuka Habor, September 13, 1945.

OPPOSITE, BELOW: A Japanese minesweeper.

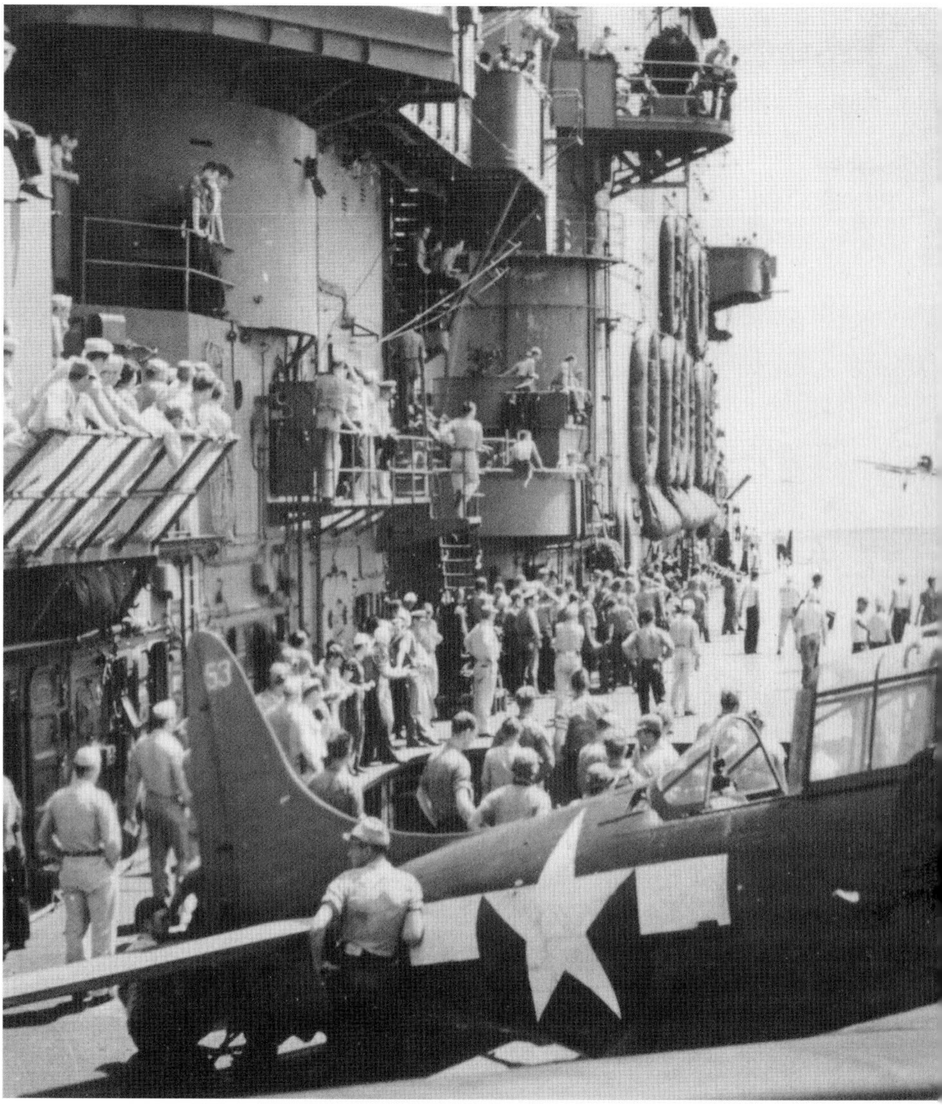

3

ABOVE: The cruiser USS *Chester* seen in 1930.

RIGHT: The cruiser USS *Minneapolis* seen in 1934.

OPPOSITE, ABOVE: The Japanese cruiser *Myoko*.

OPPOSITE, BELOW: The Japanese cruiser *Haguro* seen in 1936.

Japanese cruisers such as the *Aoba* were really 1920s designs. At 7,100 tons she could manage a speed of 33 knots maximum. Her armament was 6 x 8in. guns in three twin turrets, 4 x 4.7in. anti-aircraft guns, 10 x machine guns and 12 x 21in. torpedo tubes. The armored decks and belt were 2in. thick. In contrast the *Myoko*, Admiral Takagi's flagship, was much more heavily armored and gunned. Her main armament was 10 x 8in. 50-cal. guns in five twin turrets. She also had six 4.7in. AA guns and 8 x 47mm AA guns, plus 8 x machine guns and 8 x torpedo tubes. She had a much more substantial belt of 3in. and a 2–3in. armored deck. The other Japanese cruisers fell into Myoko, Kako and Yubari Classes:

	Displacement	Length	Beam	Armor	Armament
Myoko class	10,000 tons	630ft	62.5ft	3in. side, 3in. turret	10 x 8in., 6 x 4.7in. AA, 8 x 47mm AA, 8 x MGs
Kako class	7,100 tons	595ft	50.75ft	2in. side, 1.5in. turret	6 x 8in., 4 x 4.7in. AA, 10 x MGs
Yubari class	2,890 tons	435ft	39.5ft	2in. side	6 x 5.5in., 1 x 3in. AA, 2 x MGs

Destroyers

The workhorse of both navies during this battle was the destroyer, without which no large capital ship could be defended. A typical example of this was the *Anderson* of Task Force 17. She was one of the Sims-class that had been part of the pre-war destroyer program. At 1,570 tons she was armed with 5 x 5in. guns, four torpedo tubes and depth charge racks. These ships were inclined to be top heavy but their use in aircraft defense was to be critical. American destroyers of the Farragut, Sims, Porter and Mahan classes were all present at the battle and their comparative characteristics were as follows:

Class	Sims	Farragut	Porter	Mahan
Displacement (tons)	1,570	1,395	1,850	1,500
Length	341ft	341.25ft	381ft	341.25ft
Beam	35ft	34ft	37ft	34.75ft
Armament	Sims—5 x 5in. 4 x MGs, 12 x 2in. TTs			
	Farragut—5 x 5in., 4 x MGs, 8 x 21in. TTs			
	Porter—8 x 5 in. 38-cal., 8 x 1-pdr, 2 x MGs, 8 x 21in. TTs			
	Mahan—5 x 5in. 4 x MGs, 12 x 2in. TTs			

The destroyers could reach speeds of between 36 and 37 knots, whereas the maximum speed of a carrier such as the *Shoho* was only 28 knots.

The Japanese destroyers of the Hatuharu class and the Hubuki class had the following characteristics:

	Displacement	Length	Beam	Armament
Hatuharu class	1,368 tons	337.75ft	32.5ft	5 x 5in., 2 machine guns, 6 x 21in. TT
Hubuki class	1,700 tons	371.5ft	33.75ft	6 x 5in., 4 AA machine guns, 9 x 21in. TTs

Both classes were capable of a maximum speed of 34 knots.

LEFT: Two-man Japanese submarine that grounded near Bellows Field on December 7, 1941, and was later brought to Pearl Harbor. Another was rammed and sunk in Pearl.

FAR LEFT: The destroyer USS *Farragut* seen prewar in 1934.

All of these specifications are drawn from sources written in 1941 and as such do not take into account the upgrades that many vessels underwent between the end of 1941 and 1942. The *Lexington* in particular was up-gunned with many smaller caliber anti-aircraft weapons, as were many Japanese ships.

Submarines

Some mention of submarines must be made here even though they played no direct role in the battle. There were submarine groups attached to the naval forces of both sides. The Japanese had seven allocated to Operation MO of which five were I class and two were RO class. They were known as the patrol group and raiding group respectively. Submarines were excellent reconnaissance vessels and they could be used in all sorts of different roles. As lookouts they could cover a known area of the sea undetected whilst reporting back enemy sightings. The Americans had a submarine group of seven vessels patrolling the southeastern approaches to Australia.

Anti-aircraft guns

Probably the most interesting aspect of the Battle of the Coral Sea was the fact that it was air power and air power alone that decided the issue. The large main gun armament of each ship was of secondary importance to the air defense weapons. This has often been overlooked during this battle so it is my intention to analyze the differences in the anti-aircraft defenses of the two fleets.

It was clear that, from the point of view of aircraft defense, the fleet that could put up the most accurate, effective anti-aircraft barrage would be the one that would be best defended. This needed a combination of good morale and training for the gunners, accurate fire direction equipment and the right type of weapon. Traditionally the anti-aircraft defense of a ship was divided between the long-range high-altitude guns, such as the 5in. 38-cal. so favored by the Americans, and the low-level short-range guns such as the 20mm Oerlikon.

The American 5in. 38-cal. gun was the commonest weapon for primary air defense. There were three main mountings for it: the pedestal mount, the base ring and the dual-purpose (DP) twin. This weapon was designed to counter bombers attacking on the level at distance. These aircraft needed a long run to their target and if they were engaged at long range their attack runs would be upset.

LEFT: The Japanese 1st Destroyer Squadron on maneuvers in 1939.

RIGHT: A U.S. Navy 5in. 38-cal. gun.

The days of the proximity fuse were in the future and long time delay fuses were used with this sort of weapon. From the gunnery report of the *Lexington* it is clear that time-fused shells were preset:

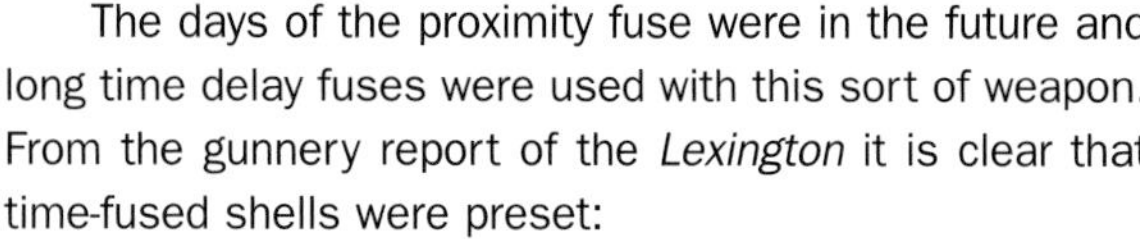

> Subsequently, certain of the 5in. group control officers attempted to designate fuse settings to be used [the 5in. ammunition was all pre-set to either 5.2 seconds, 3 seconds, or 2.2 seconds]. It is considered that they erred in so doing. The surviving 5in. were used against torpedo planes. They were not mobile enough against the shallow glides and dispersed bearing of the dive-bombers.
> (*Naval Intelligence Combat Reports*)

In the 1930s the dive-bomber was perceived as the main aerial threat and that is how it turned out to be. A high-angle, automatic weapon was thought to be the counter. Both the Americans and the British used the Bofors gun, which was a Swedish design made under license. During the Battle of the Coral Sea none of the Allied ships were armed with it. Although both the Japanese and Americans favored a 5in. heavy anti-aircraft gun they used very different sorts of light anti-aircraft weapon. Initially the US favored the Browning .50-cal. machine gun and the homegrown 1.1in. heavy machine gun for their anti-aircraft defense at close range, but they soon realized that these guns, particularly the latter, were unreliable and complicated to use. Therefore, by 1940 it had been decided to install the Bofors and the Swiss-designed Oerlikon 20mm anti-aircraft guns. Any photographs of American vessels in the Pacific after 1942 shows them bristling with these weapons. In fact Oerlikons were beginning to be installed at the start of 1941. The Oerlikon needed no power supply and could be bolted to the deck almost anywhere on a ship. It had a spring recuperator, could easily be repaired and had a high rate of fire. However, the smaller 20mm projectile did not have the destructive capacity of the 40mm round. From July 1942 onwards, American ships were armed with the larger 40mm weapon.

The gunnery report on the *Lexington* quotes the following armament: 5in. guns, 1.1in. machine guns, 20mm Oerlikons and .5in. Browning stacks. The crews operating these guns seem to have been in control and alert throughout the battle, in fact the gunnery officer O'Donnell stated of his men:

> The fire discipline and distribution of the automatic weapons was splendid. No enemy plane was seen to

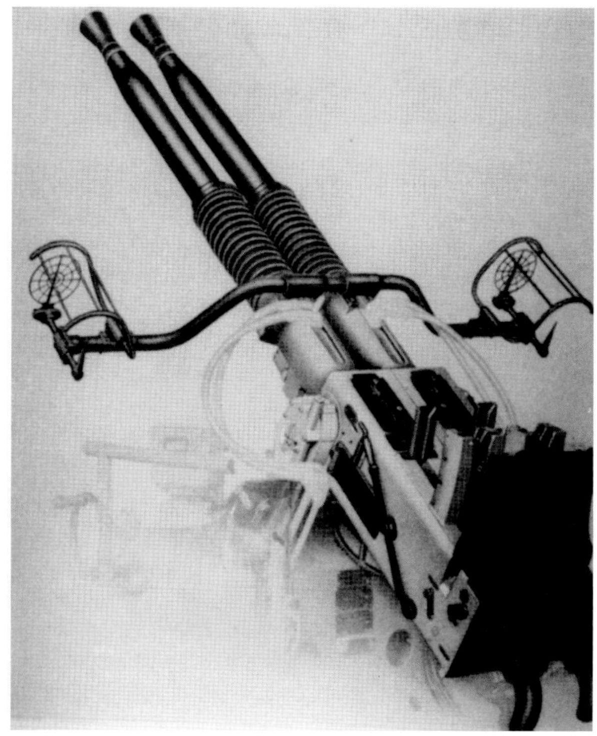

LEFT: A pair of 40mm AA guns in a single mounting. This weapon became the principal close-range AA defense weapon on U.S. ships after 1942.

OPPOSITE, ABOVE LEFT: 5in. AA guns on USS *Enterprise* firing at a target drone during a simulated torpedo attack, March 1942.

OPPOSITE, ABOVE RIGHT: Marines standing by the 20mm guns on USS *Yorktown*.

OPPOSITE, BELOW: Guncrew of a 1.1in. AA gun on USS *Enterprise* preparing to fire, April 1942.

BELOW: Testing a 20mm. AA gun on USS *Jouett*, 1942.

attack without being fired upon. The accuracy of the fire was fairly good, as nearly as could be judged.

The air defense of the Japanese fleet relied on a wide range of weaponry. Probably the most popular weapon was the Type 89 40-cal. 12.7cm gun, though other 4.7in. and 3.9in. weapons were used. Part of the reason for this was that the Japanese, like most other countries, were using older designs as well as those that were specifically designed to be fired at a high angle for anti-aircraft defense. The Type 89 was one of the few weapons that was specifically designed for the purpose and its main target was the dive-bomber. Although larger caliber guns could engage the slower moving and horizontally attacking torpedo bombers, dive-bombers posed the greatest threat to the fleet. The Type 89 could fire 14 rounds per minute at 90 degrees elevation. Two other larger caliber weapons were developed during 1937 and 1938, and these were the Type 98 10cm (65-cal.) and the 8cm (60-cal) high angle weapons.

The gun itself was only one part of a system that had to make sure that a shell arrived at the right time near a fast-moving and erratic target. This form of prediction required a complicated fire control system that could calculate the speed and direction of an aircraft compared that to that of the ship and then order the right guns to fire at the target. It is not the intention of this book to go into the complexities of fire control, it is sufficient to say that what were needed for the guns to fire accurately were an elevation angle, a training angle and a fuse time for the guns. By the time of the Battle of the Coral Sea the Type 94 HA angle fire direction equipment was being used on Japanese vessels. It consisted of a rangefinder and director on the superstructure of the ship and a calculating computer deep in the bowels of the vessel, as was the case with Allied vessels. This area was known in Allied parlance as the transmission station and was one of the most vital parts of the ship, which explains its location in a protected metal box. There was an earlier version known as the Type 91, this was not as satisfactory but was also in use during the battle.

Japanese light anti-aircraft weapons were based on Hotchkiss designs and, as ever, the Japanese had studied the design and development of foreign weapon systems in minute detail. They relied on the heavy 25mm gun as an equivalent to the American Oerlikon and a 8mm gun for close-range defense. In 1935 the Japanese decided to

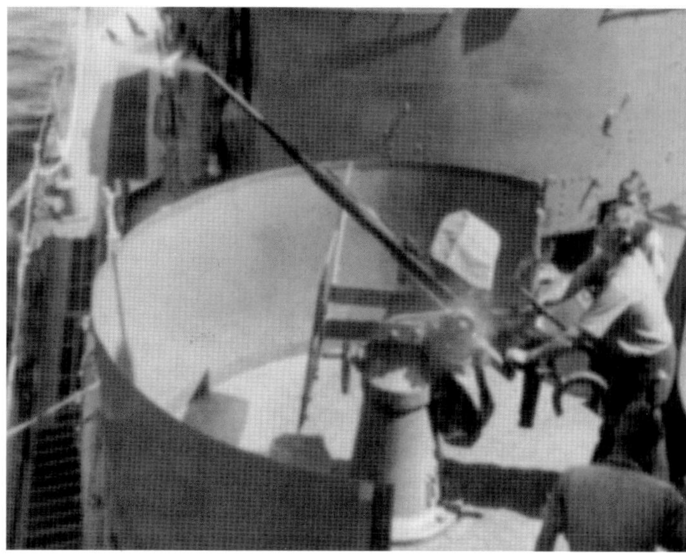

replace their British made 2-pdrs because of their slow rate of fire, unreliable nature and difficulties of construction. A design based upon the French Hotchkiss machine gun was selected as the replacement. Japanese modifications included the replacement of some parts by castings and the use of German Rheinmetall-type flash suppressors. The 25mm Type 96 was widely used throughout the Japanese Navy, with about 33,000 guns being produced. It had an effective rate of fire of 110-120 rpm and there were single, double and triple mountings. There are few real accounts of its defensive use during the Battle of the Coral Sea but the Japanese considered this gun to be an excellent weapon. The magazines for the Type 96 held only 15 rounds, so frequent stoppages for changes of magazine were required. The Japanese were the only major navy of World War II not to develop close-range anti-aircraft machine guns larger than 25mm (1in.).

A 13.7mm machine gun was widely used on Japanese ships throughout World War II. Its design was again based upon a French Hotchkiss machine gun and it was similar in design to the 25mm gun, though its magazine held 30 rounds.

Aircraft

Fighters

The main U.S. fighter used at the Battle of the Coral Sea was the Grumman F4F Wildcat, which had been in service since 1940 having replaced the previous series of biplanes. As a fighter it was robust and could be used to devastating effect in the right hands. Its Wright R1830-76 engine enabled it to fly at a maximum speed of 330mph, though its climb rate was poor compared to the Japanese Zero. It had four .50-cal. machine guns and could carry a 200lb bomb load. Although the Wildcat was in many ways inferior to the Japanese Zero its inherent survivability, coupled with the innovative defensive tactics used by U.S. pilots, ensured that it held its own in aerial combat. One such tactic was known as the Thatch Weave, as Lt. James Thatch developed it. The formation required a gap of about 550–750yds abreast between friendly aircraft. If an enemy aircraft latched on to either aircraft, both pilots turned towards each other. This resulted in the wingmans's guns coming to bear on the aircraft pursuing the primary aircraft. Repeating this maneuver forced the pursuing enemy aircraft to either break off the pursuit or face multiple head-on attacks from the wingman.

Against the Wildcat stood the Japanese A6M Zero fighter. This exceptional aircraft had been built to a design concept that sacrificed everything for speed and maneuverability. The designers, Mitsubishi, had created an aircraft that caused the Americans severe problems in combat. The Zero had a similar maximum speed as the F4F but its climb rate was greater and it was much lighter. The Model 21 was armed with two 20mm cannon and two 7.7mm machine guns. It could also carry a 250lb bomb. The one great drawback to the Zero was its lack of both armor protection and a self-sealing fuel tank. This combination led to it being extremely combustible when hit.

Comparative performance:

	Power	Max. speed	Climb speed	Range	Armament
Grumman F4F Wildcat	1,200HP	329mph	2,000ft per minute	844 miles	4 x .50-cal. MGs and a 200lb bomb load
Mitsubishi A6M2 Zero	940HP	331mph	2,571ft per minute	1,470 miles	2 x 20mm cannon, 2 x 7.7mm MGs and a 250lb bomb load

Dive-bombers

The Americans had a very reliable accurate dive-bomber in the Douglas SBD Dauntless. Stability, a vital attribute for dive-bombers, was a prominent feature of the Dauntless's flying characteristics and ensured that it stayed in the American arsenal for longer than many other aircraft. It carried a bomb load of one 900lb bomb and two 90lb bombs, and was armed with two forward firing machine guns and two flexible machine guns. This was a substantial range of armament for a bomber and the Dauntless was used as a fighter on several occasions. The main drawback of the Dauntless was that it was very slow in horizontal flight. There was also a problem when the aircraft dived from high to low altitude. According to Barret Tillman:

> The SBD.1-4 was armed with a three power telescopic sight, a holdover from the open cockpit aircraft of the 1930s. The pilot looked through the tube, lining up the crosshairs on the target while keeping a ball much like that of a turn and bank indicator centered in its groove. The centered ball told him the aircraft was level in the dive, otherwise the bomb would go off on a tangent when released.However, the sight was prone to condensation and could fog up at this critical moment.

In organizational terms, the 1942 dive-bomber squadrons usually consisted of 18 aircraft flying in three divisions of two three-plane sections. Each section flew in an inverted V formation. Weather often affected the way in which the unit could work but visual contact could be made at 30–40 miles from the target in clear weather at 18,000ft. When the dive-bomber went in for an attack he went to what was called pushover, which is the point at which the plane started its dive. Pushover altitude was at about 15,000 feet and the aircraft were normally spaced

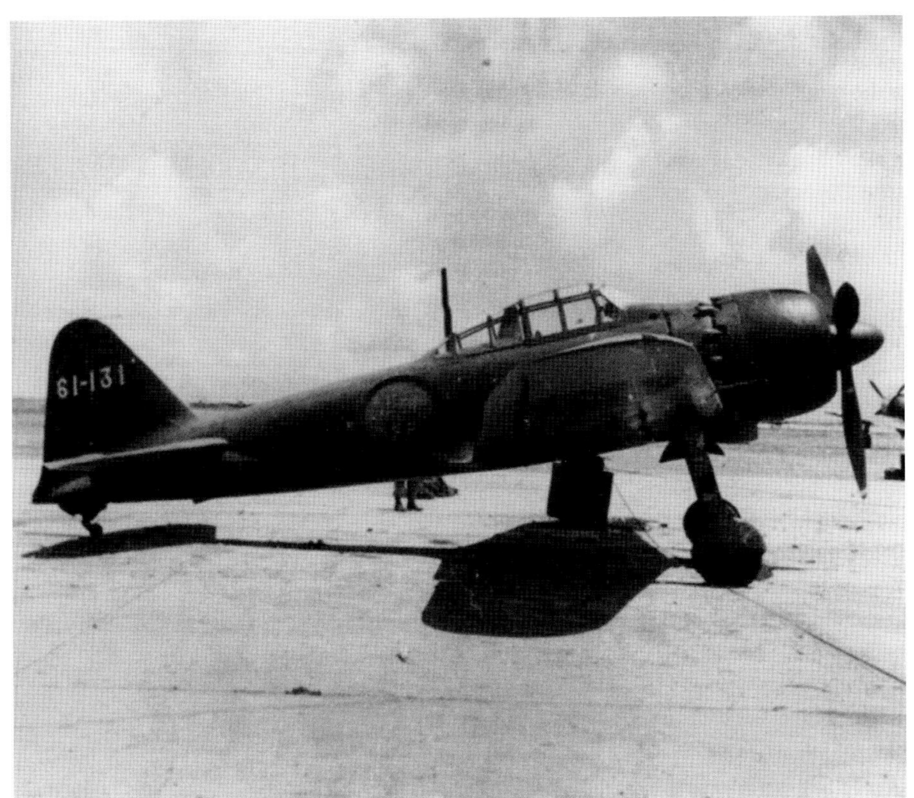

LEFT: The Mitsubishi A6M Zero-Sen, codenamed "Zeke" by the Allies, was the best-known of Japan's fighters. Over 10,000 were built and it was used as a carrier- or land-based fighter, fighter-bomber, dive-bomber, and, latterly, as a suicide bomber.

OPPOSITE, TOP: U.S. Navy .50-cal. machine gun mounting.

OPPOSITE, CENTER: October 1942 shot of a Zero in U.S. colors being evaluated above San Diego.

OPPOSITE, BELOW: Aichi D3A1 Navy Type 99 carrier bomber. The mainstay of the Japanese naval airforce in 1942.

1,500 feet apart; one diving after the other. On its descent the dive speed was about 276mph. This was controlled by the dive brakes easily recognizable on a Dauntless as the flaps with holes in them. When the Dauntless was being chased by a Japanese fighter using the dive brakes was one way of making the attacker overshoot. The bomb was usually released at about 1,500–2,000ft above the target.

The Dauntless acted as a scout as well as a bomber and a carrier group carried four squadrons of the scout and bomber variants.

The Japanese had not been slow in appreciating the value of the dive-bomber on land or at sea and when they produced their first monoplane dive-bomber, the Aichi 99 Val, it proved to be a formidable weapon, at least for early part of the war. It had a fixed undercarriage and a crew of three men. It is believed that the Japanese had based some of the features of the Aichi Val on those of the Ju 87 Stuka and on the basis of their experiments produced an all-metal aircraft. The Val had a maximum speed of 267mph and a range of 930 miles. It was said to be extremely accurate and very stable as a dive-bomber. It remained an important weapon in the Japanese armory throughout the war.

Comparative performance:

	Power	Max.speed	Climb speed	Range	Armament
Douglas Dauntless SBD.3	1,000HP	246mph	9,000ft in 6 minutes	1,100 miles	2 x .50-cal. MGs, 2 x .30-cal. MGs, 1 x 900lb and 2 x 90lb bombs
Aichi 99 Val	1,300HP	267mph	9,000ft in 5 minutes	930 miles	2 x .30-cal. MGs, 1 x flexible .30-cal. MG, 1 x 500lb and 2 x 120lb, or 4 x 120lb bombs.

Torpedo bombers

At this stage in the war the main U.S. torpedo plane was the Douglas TBD Devastator, which came to the fore in 1935. By the time of the Pacific War it was an antiquated aircraft. it was slow in horizontal flight and easy to shoot down, as the early battles showed. The aircraft required three crew to operate it and very few of these aircraft scored a hit during the Battle of the Coral Sea.

The main Japanese torpedo plane was the Nakajima 97 Kate. This was the first fully Japanese designed torpedo plane and it had a crew of three. It was designed so that it could carry out horizontal bombing and low level torpedo attacks. Most of the torpedo bombers that entered the war for the combatant nations were obsolete before they actually carried out any attacks, the British Swordfish and the Devastator in particular, but the Kate was state of the art in 1939. It could carry a torpedo weighing 1,600lb and had a maximum speed of 235mph and a cruising speed of 163mph, which compared favorably to the 128mph that the Devastator could muster.

Comparative performance:

	Power	Max.speed	Climb speed	Range	Armament
Nakajima 97 Kate	1,000HP	235mph	9,000ft in 7 minutes	634 miles	1 x .30-cal. moveable machine gun, 1 Type 96 torpedo or a bomb load up to 1000lb
Douglas TBD Devastator	900HP	205mph	700ft per minute		1 x .30-cal. machine gun fixed, 1 x .30-cal. machine gun flexible, 1 Mark 13 torpedo

Torpedoes and bombs

Two weapons stand out as being particularly effective against ships during the Battle of the Coral Sea: the aerial bomb and the torpedo. The latter, along with the mine, was responsible for the greatest number of ship losses of World War II and was understandably feared by surface commanders. When it was delivered by air its extended range dramatically increased its potency.

In the United States pre-war torpedo designs were almost exclusively dominated by the company E. W. Bliss and Co. (known as Bliss-Leavitt) whose weapons were still in use at the beginning of the war. The Mk 9 was the last torpedo manufactured by them whilst the Mk 10 was the

Above: Douglas TBD Devastator launching a Mk 13 torpedo in a prewar trial.

Left and Above Left: Douglas SBD Dauntlesses on the deck of USS *Enterprise*, May 1942. Note the early-war identification stars.

last designed by them. Bliss and the Navy were at loggerheads in the early part of the century over the intention of the company to sell their ideas abroad and from 1907 the U.S. Navy began to develop its own production and testing facility known as the NTS or Naval Torpedo Station. Mks 11 and 12 were pure NTS products, but altogether only a few hundred were built. It was the Mk 13 torpedo that was to be used by the Americans as the main armament for their aircraft. It was 14.24ft in length and had a diameter of 22.5in. Its maximum speed was 33.5 knots, slow compared to other submarine-launched weapons. The Mk 13 structure was designed to survive being launched at a speed of 100 knots and from a height of 50ft. Accessories were required to maintain satisfactory aerodynamics and prevent damage on entry into the water.

American torpedoes of WWII

	Mark 11	Mark 13	Mark 14	Mark 15
Weight	3,512lb	2,216lb	3,280lb	3,840lb
Length	22.6ft	14.24ft	20.5ft	24ft
Speed	27knts	33.5knts	46knts	33.5knts
Range	15,000yds	6,300yds	4,500yds	10,000yds
Warhead	500lb	578lb	644lb	825lb

In Japan the aerial torpedo had reached a high state of technical development. The Japanese had opted for a pure oxygen system of propulsion, which made their torpedoes perform far more spectacularly than those of the Americans. There were several models in use at the time of the Battle of the Coral Sea, Types 91 to 96. These torpedoes were very similar in range and weight and the Type 91 Mod 2 had a length of 17.7ft, weighed 1,841lb and could travel at 41 knots. It was first deployed in April 1941, and carried by the Kate torpedo bombers that attacked Pearl Harbor. This torpedo was far faster than that employed by the Americans and therefore much harder to maneuver away from. In addition to this the Japanese had developed other mechanisms to protect the torpedo when dropped into the water from height. American commentators said that they could see wooden boxes protecting the head and tail of the torpedoes when they were being attacked.

In contrast to the complexity of the torpedo a bomb is a simple device. Normally it is a steel shell filled with high explosive, sometimes with a base fuse and sometimes with a nose fuse. Even with a small explosive charge an aerial-delivered bomb can be a devastating weapon. Many were designed to pierce armor and, with a delayed action fuse, they could penetrate into the bowels of a ship before exploding. Bombs were often converted naval munitions and when attacking ships the preferred weight during this battle was about 1,000lb on both sides. The Aichi Val dive-bomber could carry one 500lb bomb under its fuselage plus (D3A1) two 120lb bombs, or (D3A2) four 120lb bombs under its wings. The Douglas SBD Dauntless could carry one 1,000lb or 500lb bomb under the fuselage or two 250lb or 100lb. bombs under its wings.

Japanese torpedoes of WWII

	Type 93 Mod 1	Type 93 Mod 3	Type 95 Mod1	Type 96
Weight	5,952lb	6,173lb	3,671lb	3,671lb
Length	30ft	30ft	23ft	23ft
Speed	36knts	36knts	45knts	48knts
Range	40,000yds	30,000yds	12,000yds	4500yds
Warhead	1,080lb	1,720lb	1,091lb	1,091lb

Morale and fighting experience

It should be remembered that the crews of the two U.S. carriers were at a state of very high morale during this battle. There is a good reason for this; the *Lexington* had taken part in reprisal raids against the Japanese in the central Pacific. These were isolated successes set against the backdrop of the series of defeats suffered by the British, Americans and Dutch in early 1942. The "Lady Lex," as she was known, was a relatively new ship and her captain Frederick C Sherman was very popular with the crew. The one drawback of the crew was their inexperience and this would show during the battle. The *Yorktown* under Capt. Buckmaster had also been part of the reprisal raids under Fletcher and had attacked islands in the Marshall chain, her crew too were said to be riding high on their new-found success.

The Japanese aviators had much more experience than their U.S. counterparts. As a good example of their activities the history of a fighter squadron assigned to the *Shokaku* shows how they performed. Originally assigned to Kyushu in October 1941, part of the unit was involved in the attack on Pearl Harbor. As part of the 5th Carrier Division they took part in attacks on Rabaul and Lae on January 8, 1942. In March 1942 they were in the Indian Ocean and they raided Trincomalee before their involvement in the Battle of the Coral Sea. Similarly, the fighter groups of the *Zuikaku* were continuously involved in action from the Pearl Harbor until the beginnings of the Coral Sea. The experience gained by these operations undoubtedly gave the Japanese an advantage.

ABOVE: Japanese torpedo-bombers were better than those of the U.S. Navy at the start of the war, the Kate being a much better aircraft than the Devastator.

LEFT: Torpedo bombers on the deck of USS *Enterprise*.

BELOW: Only some 129 Douglas TBD Devastators were built and losses were heavy due to poor defensive armament, but it could carry a 21in. torpedo or 1,000lb bomb and inflicted heavy damage on Japanese forces at the start of the Pacific war. This one is about to land on USS *Enterprise* in May 1942.

Logistics

It is an often-ignored fact that the supply and maintenance of vessels at sea is as important to the success of an action as the offensive capabilities of a fleet. Large vessels such as an aircraft carrier or battlecruiser are not endowed with huge fuel tanks and need to be re-supplied irregularly. Ammunition, food and other essentials can only be stored on board up to a point. Therefore any task force had to have a supply train in tow. Before 1943 the U.S. Navy had a shortage of supply vessels and the later war organization was not fully in place. As an example of the amount of fuel used a carrier task force of three carriers, two heavy cruisers, light cruisers and destroyers would use 50 tons of fuel oil in one hour traveling at 12 knots. This meant that a tanker of say 9,600 tons capacity would need to refuel the ships every eight days. The *Lexington* used 4.9 tons an hour and had a fuel tank of 3,600 tons capacity. The *Shokaku* used 6.2 tons an hour and had a slightly larger tank at 4,100 tons. At the other end of the scale a Fletcher-class destroyer used 1.1 tons an hour with a tank capacity of 492 tons. If one takes into account the need to fuel aircraft a second supply problem becomes obvious: aircraft fuel also needed to be stored onboard. The *Shokaku*'s original compliment of 72 aircraft needed 187,000 gallons of aviation fuel, of which 2,600 gallons of fuel were allocated to each aircraft allowing roughly nine flights. The *Yorktown* carried 178,000 gallons allowing an average of 6 or 7 sorties per aircraft. It has also been estimated that the ammunition required for an Essex-class aircraft carrier was about 325 tons, including two torpedoes per bomber and 18 bombs per dive-bomber.

The complexities of supply and distribution were enormous. Food, ammunition, engine spares, and all the

Right: DD-456 USS *Rodman* is refueled at sea. This image gives a good view of her 5in. guns.

other needs of the navy had to be carried with them. In an area such as the Coral Sea the local ports were frequently not big enough to deal with supplying large amounts of stores. Therefore both sides had to use a small number of ports and facilities for their operations. Rabaul was the base of operations for the Japanese and this in some ways counterbalanced the fact that their landing force under Rr. Adm. Koso Abe had a whole fleet of small supply ships attached to it. With an average speed of 12–15 knots these ships were sitting ducks for American naval aviators. Rabaul needed to be supplied from Japan and the distance was roughly 2,900 miles. At an average speed it took a merchant ship 48 days to arrive at the Solomon Islands from the nearest of the home islands. The threat of enemy submarines and bad weather fronts in the Pacific meant that commanders could not rely on a shipment from Japan arriving in one piece. The Japanese controlled most of the good ports in the Pacific area in 1942 and so the allies relied on being supplied from Australia or—more realistically—from Midway and then the United States itself. Therefore large fleet trains were required to sail with the fleet and supply it. In the case of the battle of the Coral Sea the Logistics force consisted of the tankers *Neosho* and *Tippecanoe* protected by two destroyers. There was also a seaplane replenisher called the AV8 *Tangier* based at Nouméa on the island of New Caledonia.

As a final point about how the destruction of the supply train could affect the ability of naval vessels to wage war, we can look at what happened to the problems after the tanker *Neosho* was sunk. The damage sustained by the *Yorktown* during the battle meant that she leaked fuel and the need to retire from the battle area to carry out repairs and replenishment would be essential. There were only so many places that the Task Force could go: south and west to Australia or to Tongatabu, which is what Fletcher eventually did. Although the naval command had dispatched two oilers to Fletcher's group under Halsey there was serious risk that these vessels could well be sunk by Japanese aircraft or vessels on their way to rendezvous.

THIS PAGE AND OPPOSITE: Refueling at sea was of major importance to both sides during the Pacific war, albeit a risky business at times as these pictures of USS *Neosho* (AO-23) show. The photograph opposite shows *Neosho* refueling the *Yorktown* at sea on May 1, 1942, just before the battle. *Neosho* was one of the casualties of the battle, scuttled on May 11 after being crippled by bombs dropped from "Val" bombers from *Zuikaku* on May 7.

The battle arena

The Pacific Ocean is a vast area of water. We know much more about the geography and climate than was known in 1942 and so to commanders of both sides it was with some trepidation that they planned for the battle. Dominating the area are two large landmasses—New Guinea and Australia. The former is an island to the northeast of Australia that was, and still is, in many areas impenetrable. The Owen Stanley mountain ranges separate the two halves of the island, northern and southern, and it is completely covered in rain forest and jungle—hardly the kind of place to carry out a military campaign. The Japanese occupied Rabaul on New Britain and it was their inability to cross the Owen Stanley Mountains that forced them to sail to Port Moresby. The Coral Sea is an area southeast of Papua New Guinea and to the south of the Solomon Islands. On its eastern side New Caledonia encloses it. It is approximately 1,000 miles from Townsville on the eastern coast of Australia to the island of Santa Isabel in the Solomons and approximately 1,000 miles to New Caledonia to Samarai on the tip of New Guinea. These four points roughly enclose the Coral Sea in 1,000,000 square miles of ocean. It is effectively very close to the Australian mainland, hence its strategic significance. During the 19th century many ships were wrecked in the area due to constantly shifting sand cays, and the reefs and islands have often been named after the ships that foundered there.

All of the islands in the Solomons group are particularly tropical, crowned with dense jungle and some mountains. The Japanese decided to make their seaplane base at Tulagi, which lies to the north of Guadalcanal. Its sister island, Florida, is east of Tulagi but is very close to it. To the southwest of the Solomon Islands lie the Louisade Archipelago and the strategically important area known as the Jomard Passage. This was the area through which the Japanese had to pass to get to Port Moresby, their invasion objective. The weather is similar to the tropical maritime Tasman air mass, but it is warmer, coming from further north in the Coral Sea and tropical western Pacific Ocean. This air mass affects the Central and North Queensland coast most of the year, and can bring heavy rainfall if associated with tropical cyclones or tropical depressions. High humidity and frequent rains mean that It is a normally good source of moisture for eastern Australia generally and the eastern seaboard especially. The same types of weather pattern can create huge cloud formations and snap tropical storms. For a naval air force this changing climate could be a useful asset or a huge disadvantage.

The distances across these areas are vast although they look small on the map. Within the Coral Sea itself and close to the coast of Australia there are numerous small Islands. They are still uninhabited today, apart from a large population of sea birds, and the occasional meteorologist on Willis Island. Unmanned weather stations, beacons, and a lighthouse are located on several other islands and reefs. Occasional tropical cyclones sweep over the islands from November to April, leaving the sand and coral-based mass with little or no vegetation. To the extreme east of the area lay the Island of New Caledonia the capital of which was Nouméa. The Americans used it as a base because it had reasonably good port facilities and could be used to dominate the Coral Sea by air. Originally the French occupied it. Several of the American warships involved in this campaign were sent from Nouméa.

It is quite clear that the weather had a very significant effect on the Battle of the Coral Sea. Fletcher's ships encountered winds blowing up to 30 miles an hour from the southeast and a huge bank of cloud cover almost 300 miles wide obscured both sides from each other, hindering reconnaissance and Combat Air Patrols alike. By May 5 the cloud cover was still very low and eventually Fletcher's ships emerged from the clouds to brilliant sunshine. The same weather front that had covered Fletcher effectively did the same for the Japanese.

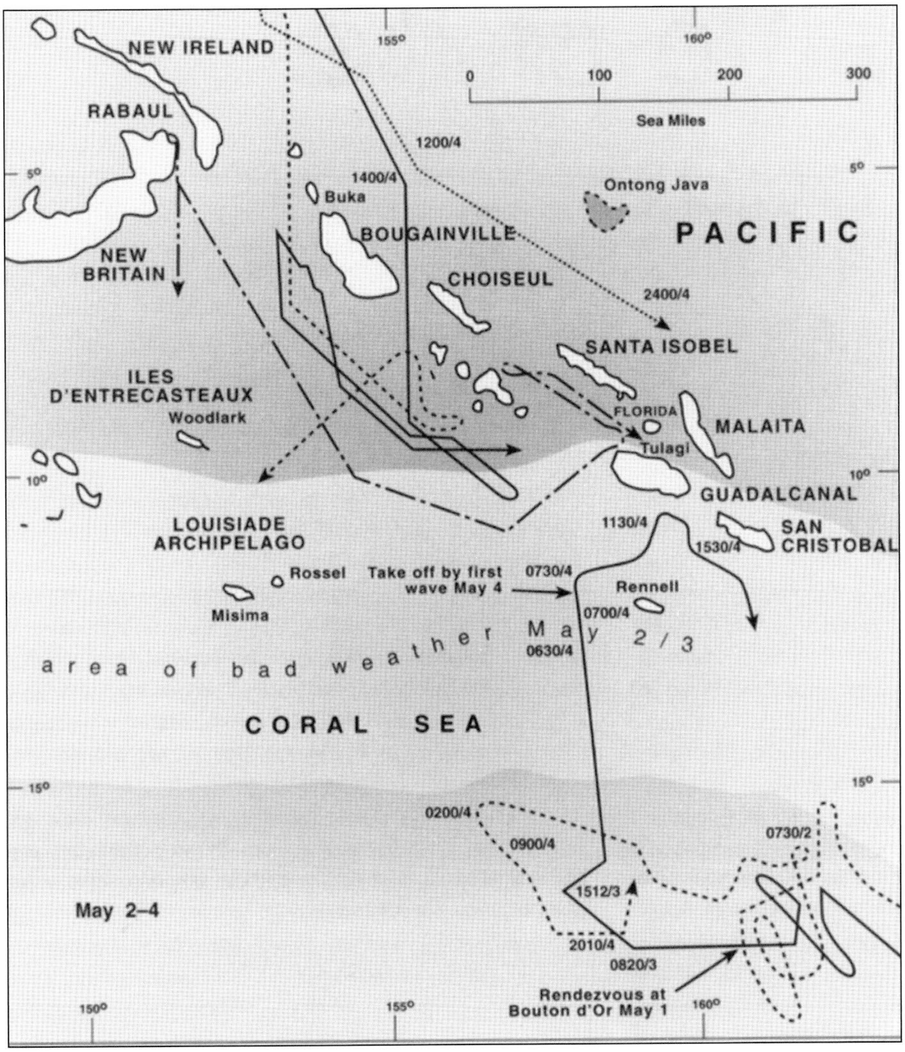

LEFT: The battle arena—the movement of forces between May 2 and 4, 1942. From the south (bottom of map) the solid line shows the path of Task Force 17; the dotted line shows the path of Task Force 11. From the north (top) the dotted lines represent the course followed by theJapanese Striking Force (above Saint Isobel) and Marumo's Support Group (to Louisade Archipeligo). The solid line shows the path of Goto's Support Group. From New Britain Admiral Shima's Naval Group moves to Tulagi and the Japanese force bound for Port Moresby heads south.

BELOW: Land-based Zero seen at Rabaul. Captured in January 1942, Rabaul gave the Japanese control of the New Guinea/Solomons area and was a major objective of the Allies. It would become pivotal in the Japanese base system. Attacked by air from October 1943, Rabaul would surrender only on September 6, 1945.

The Battle of the Coral Sea

Reconnaissance

The beginning of any battle starts with a reconnaissance of both sides to detect and identify the opposing forces. This is not easy on an ocean the size of the Pacific where weather fronts can dramatically affect visibility and thousands of small islands provide vantage points for hiding vessels. The Battle of the Coral Sea was punctuated by reports that were wildly exaggerated and believed when they should have been treated with some caution. Reconnaissance was exceedingly important and in some ways it worth looking at how it was done on both sides. The Japanese had an advantage in they had the Kawanishi 97K Mavis seaplane. The range of this aircraft was 4,193 miles ensuring that it could explore very large areas of ocean. The Americans did not have this sort of aircraft and relied heavily on other types that were more suited to their main combat role. The only other sorts of aircraft available to them were the bombers under McArthur's command in Australia or the 12 PBY Catalina flying boats that were based on the island of Nouméa

Comparative aircraft ranges

Aircraft	Range
Kawanishi 97 H6K Mavis	4,193 miles
Mitsubishi AM6 Zero	1,470 miles
Nakajima 97 Kate	634 miles
Aichi 99 Val	930 miles
Grumman F4F Wildcat	844 miles
Douglas SBD Dauntless	3,100 miles
Douglas TBD Devastator	652 miles

The taking of Tulagi and Fletcher's response

The Japanese occupied the island of Tulagi in the eastern Solomons with relative ease on May 3. The first the Americans knew of it was the report of a reconnaissance plane from Australia given to General MacArthur's Headquarters at 1900hrs on May 3. It was clear from this and other reports that the Japanese had been active since the morning and had, at the very least, landed troops. This gave them a distinct advantage with regard to reconnaissance in the area, since their long-range Mavis seaplanes would soon begin operating from there. American plans had not foreseen this activity and the response was something of a knee-jerk reaction.

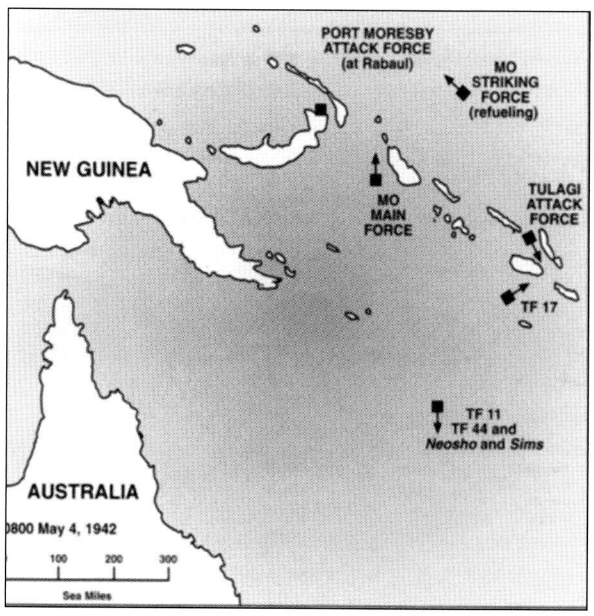

Opposite: Position of forces at 0800hrs on May 4.

Left and Below: Photographs and map of the attack on Tulagi—two in a sequence continued overleaf. The large land mass is Florida Island.

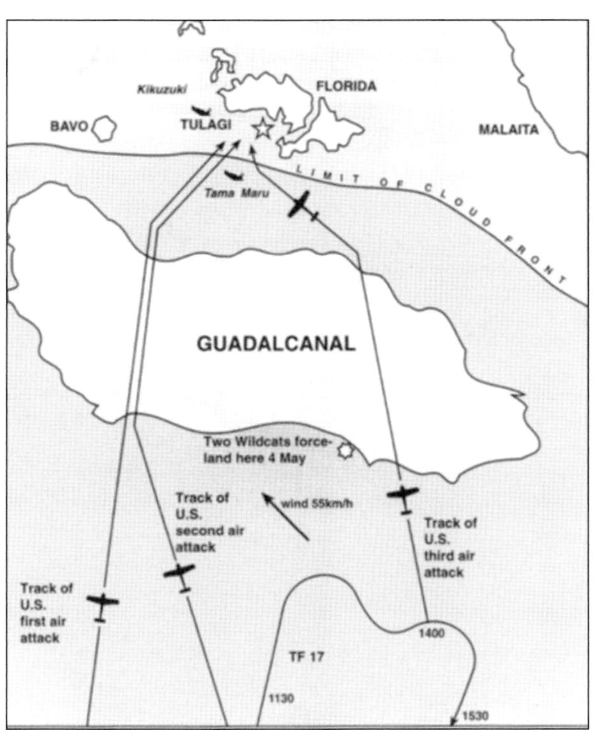

An air attack was clearly the obvious solution to this situation and, although it would betray the Allied presence in the area, it was felt that it was needed. However, there were complications. Firstly an area of bad weather had approached the Americans, it was about 300 miles wide and started from the north of the task force covering the area between it and Tulagi. While it was advantageous to mask an American approach it also hindered air operations. Since early morning both carrier air groups had been progressing to the west. It appears that communication between Fletcher and Fitch was somewhat sporadic. Refueling had begun to take place at about 1300hrs on May 3 and this had a bearing on what happened next because Fletcher was forced to use the *Yorktown* only as the basis for his attack on Tulagi. So the *Yorktown* sailed north to begin operations traveling at speeds of between 24–27 knots. At about 0600hrs on May 4 she was about 100 miles southwest of the coast of Guadalcanal. Half an hour later she headed in to the wind and launched 11 or 12 (depending on the source) Devastators of Squadron VT5 and 28 Dauntless dive-bombers of Squadrons VB5 and VS5, the former with Mk 13 torpedoes and the latter with 1,000lb bombs or in the scouting role. In addition, six Wildcat fighters were sent to escort the bombers while the remaining fighters formed a Combat Air Patrol above the carrier. Squadron VS5 under Lt. Cmdr. Burch was the first over the island at 0815hrs. Seeing the relatively undefended ships in the harbor they dived in immediately to attack and the unfortunate destroyer *Kikuzuki* bore the brunt of it, along with two small minesweepers in the area. The *Kikuzuki* was mortally damaged by a 500lb bomb that penetrated to her engine room and the crew abandoned ship. It is normally claimed that two minesweepers were sunk and the minesweeper *Okinoshima* was certainly damaged. When the second group, VT5, arrived at the scene they launched all of their torpedoes, one of which destroyed the minesweeper *Tama Maru*. Two patrol ships were also sunk. Fifteen minutes later at 0830hrs, VB5 under Lt. Short arrived to add to the carnage but found only a couple of minor vessels to attack. The Americans all returned to the ship at around 0930hrs and immediately rearmed for a second attack. According to Morison, the second strike consisted of 27 dive-bombers and 11 torpedo planes. This second attack may have been a waste of time but it is clear that Fletcher did not believe the exaggerated claims of his pilots and therefore resolved to ensure that the target was destroyed. Having been caught off guard once, the Japanese were more prepared for the second attack and engaged the approaching U.S. planes with heavy machine-gun and anti-aircraft fire. The U.S. planes pushed through and destroyed two Kawanishi Mavis seaplanes. Again the Devastators had difficulty hitting the target in a pattern that was to be carried through to Midway and beyond, the Navy's first monoplane torpedo-armed aircraft was proving to be something of a lame duck.

A lot of effort was expended for not much return when the second wave returned to the *Yorktown* they informed Fletcher that three more seaplanes were anchored off Makambo Island in Tulagi harbor. Consequently four Wildcats were dispatched to destroy them, which they did

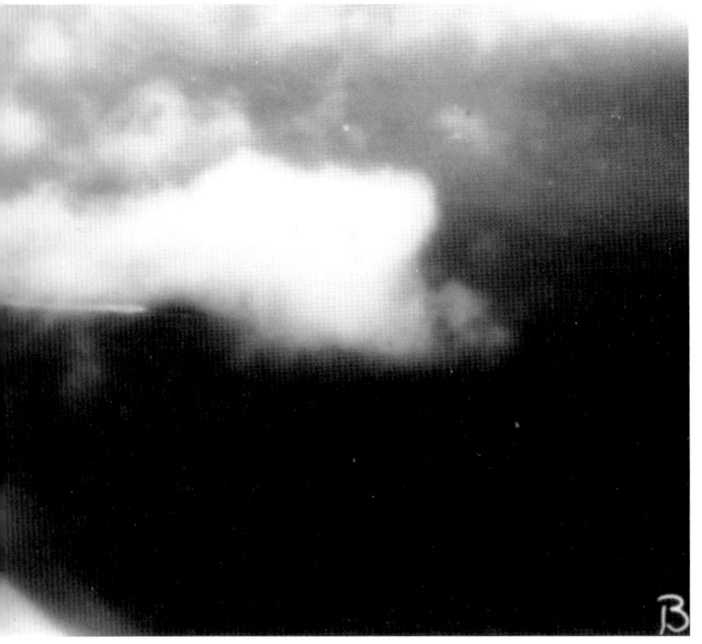

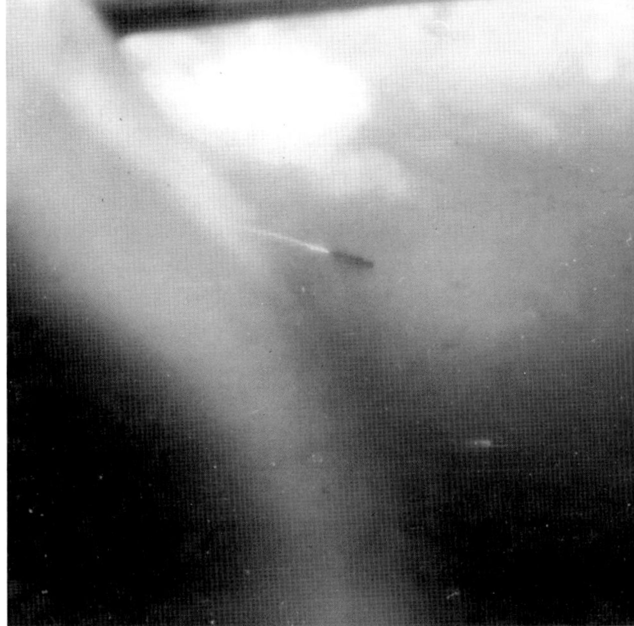

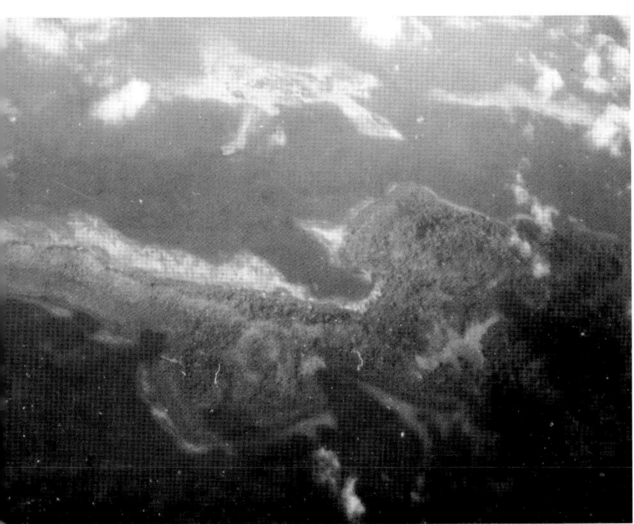

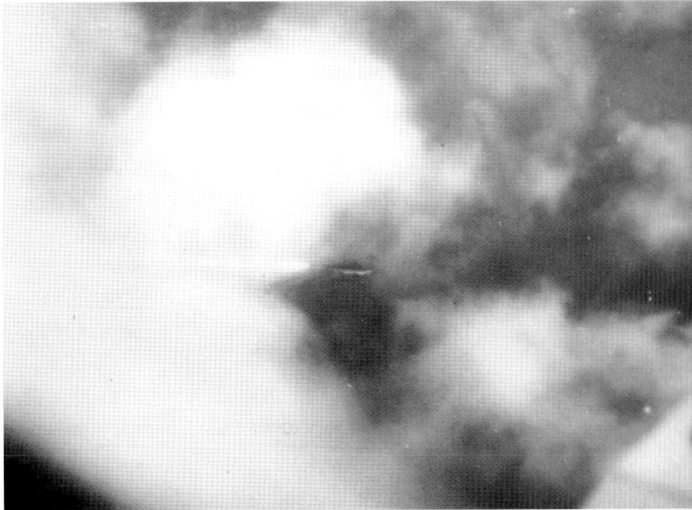

attacking the destroyer *Yuzuki* at the same time. Fletcher was still not satisfied with the third raid and decided to mount a fourth one at 1400hrs. Twenty-one Dauntless dive-bombers left the ship at 1400hrs and proceeded to make the fourth and final attack of the day. Four landing craft were sunk and not much else was achieved before the aircraft returned to the *Yorktown* at 1630hrs. Despite the victorious claims of his pilots Fletcher knew that there was precious little to cheer about. Few significant vessels had been sunk for the expenditure of a lot of effort and ammunition, though the destruction of the seaplanes had weakened the Japanese ability to carry out long-range reconnaissance. According to Japanese records they lost one destroyer, two patrol boats and a transport. In addition one transport was badly damaged, a further destroyer was damaged and a further minesweeper was damaged along with at least four seaplanes. So the first phase of the battle was over but the main combat beckoned and the Japanese now knew the Allies were in the vicinity. From the Japanese point of view, Operation MO had been detected at a vulnerable stage and they now knew there was going to be a carrier battle – the first in history.

May 5 continued with preparations for the forthcoming operation; it was a day of waiting and watching. For the Japanese their various naval groups were dispersed. The group under the control of Admiral Takagi, which included the large carriers *Zuikaku* and *Shokaku*, was refueling at North Bougainville. Goto's cruisers were further north. They were to eventually travel south through the gap between Bougainville and Choiseul Island. Takagi was informed of the American raid on Tulagi at about 1200hrs and this forced him to sail southeast, close to Malaita Island.

OPPOSITE AND ABOVE: Sequence of photographs taken during the attack on Tulagi.

BELOW: Movement of forces on May 7.

Task Force 44

It is unusual in any battle to split one's forces in the face of an approaching enemy. Yet this is exactly what Fletcher did in the early stages of the Battle of the Coral Sea. Task

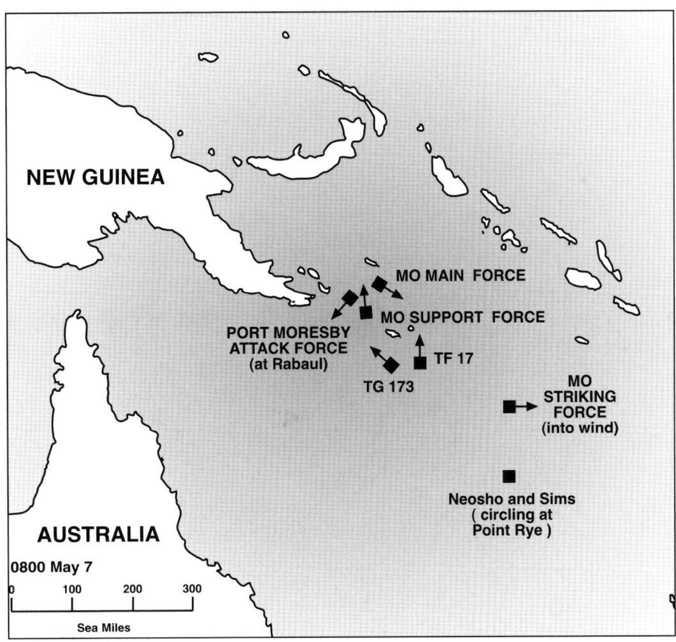

Force 44 consisted of three cruisers, USS *Chicago*, RAN *Hobart* and RAN *Australia*, and three destroyers, USS *Walke*, USS *Farragut* and USS *Perkins*. They were due to rendezvous with Fletcher's force on May 4 at 0800hrs. The Australian/American force was under the command of the British Admiral J. G. Crace. In 1939 John Crace, then Rr. Adm. R.N., was seconded by the Admiralty to take command of the Royal Australian Navy as Rr. Adm. commanding Australia Squadron.

At the outbreak of World War II, the government of Australia placed their Navy under the direction of the British Admiralty, thus giving Rr. Adm. Crace a severe organizational headache since control of the theatre resided with an organization thousands of miles away that were not fully informed of regional developments. He was on the point of asking for a transfer back to the Royal Navy when the Japanese attack on Pearl Harbor forced him to reconsider. Political considerations meant that Crace would lead the Australian and American contingent. Once the Tulagi occupation force was detected it was clear that a new rendezvous would have to be made and the *Yorktown* duly proceeded towards Tulagi whilst Crace's force, along with that of the *Lexington*, were left behind. After the sorties against Tulagi, the *Yorktown* rejoined the *Lexington* on the morning of May 5. They began sailing northwest by west on the evening of the 5th and by early morning on May 7 they were about 100 miles south of Rossel Island in the Louisade Archipelago. It was at this point that Crace was ordered to take his ships and continue northwest to the Jomard Passage. This was intended to stop the Port Moresby invasion force from coming around the southeastern tip of New Guinea to Port Moresby by way of the passage. According to Samuel Morison, Fletcher declared that this move was intended to block the passage even if the carriers were defeated in battle by the Japanese. However, this seems unlikely as if the Japanese were successful they would surely have been able to bring enough force to bear to force the passage. By this time the Australians were accompanied by a third American destroyer, USS *Perkins*. This left Fletcher with two problems: firstly, he was reducing the anti-aircraft capability that he needed to defend his carriers against Japanese attacks and, secondly, he was exposing Task Force 44 to attacks by Japanese land-based aircraft. It has been argued that this bold move Fletcher was a tactical mistake. This is in some ways missing the point. The Japanese had a complex and multi-layered plan and had split their forces into different groups to achieve different objectives. There was no point in Fletcher defeating the carrier force if the landing force was to arrive at Port Moresby with little resistance. Therefore he did what was likely to stop them arriving at their objective by using his own blocking force. The Japanese spotted Task Force 44 at about 0810hrs and their response was not long in coming.

Crace realized that his force was liable to come under Japanese attack and formed a lozenge formation in order to protect his ships. They were traveling at 25 knots when the first attacks began between 1400hrs and 1430hrs. Commodore Dacre Smyth of the *Australia* describes them

> Having been sent to the Jomard Entrance, our cruiser force was without air cover. Being under constant

threat from Japanese shore-based and carrier aircraft, our position was parlous. Quoting from my midshipman's journal: "Radar reports from Chicago were frequent during the forenoon, and several unidentified 'planes were sighted. At 1424hrs 11 'planes appeared, and fire was opened on them. They turned away. A few minutes later, a U.S. Navy Dauntless dive-bomber appeared. It had lost its carrier, and asked for directions. As it disappeared ahead, having been told to go to Port Moresby, a formation of some 12 two-engined aircraft appeared on our port bow, bunched together and flying very low."

Although the first Japanese attack on Crace's force was pressed home with typical Japanese vigor it was surprisingly badly delivered. Torpedoes were dropped at ranges of between 1,000 and 1,500yds, after which the aircraft flew on and fired on the ships with machine guns and cannon. Three aerial torpedoes were launched at *Australia* and it seems that five of the attackers were shot down. It appears that Crace's handling of the ships, their weaving tactics and the fearful anti-aircraft barrage put the attackers off. It is worth at this point just analyzing what sort of air defense the Australian ships and their American counterparts could call upon. In 1941 the defensive armament of the cruiser *Chicago* was 8 x 5in. anti-aircraft guns, 2 x 3-pdrs and 8 machine guns. The *Australia* had 8 x 4in. anti-aircraft guns, 4 x 3-pdr anti-aircraft guns, 4 x 2-pdr pom poms, 4 x machine guns and 8 Lewis guns. The *Hobart* was similarly armed, though with fewer small caliber guns. A typical American destroyer armament such as that on the *Phelps* was 8 x 5in. 38-cal. guns, 8 x 1-pdrs and 2 machine guns. By 1942 they would all have carried more guns. Certainly the Americans were adding small caliber guns to their ships on an ad hoc basis and the trend during the war was to increase firepower as much as possible. The firing cycle of a typical 38-cal. gun was around 3–4 seconds so the rate of fire could be 15rpm. Assuming all the guns were firing this gives a possible rate of fire of 129 rounds from the heavier caliber guns, with considerably more from the smaller caliber guns. The closer the Japanese got to their targets the more guns were able to hit them and the more difficult the task became. This may explain why some of their attacks were carried out at high altitude.

The Japanese Admiral Yamada was based at Rabaul and it was he who ordered the attack from the 25th Air Group. He had been wrongly informed that there was at least one battleship with Crace's fleet and, conscious of the threat that a ship of that size would cause to the landing at Port Moresby, he sent his fleet of bombers and torpedo planes to attack. The failure to destroy any of Crace's vessels effectively allowed the Allies to block the Jomard Passage and therefore the Japanese invasion fleet. There were in fact four separate attacks on the Task Force: the first consisted of 11 single-engined bombers then there were two successive attacks of Mitsubishi 96 Nell bombers, one of 12 planes and the other of 19, and finally, and more worrying, a group of B-26 Martin Marauders from the 19th Bombardment Group based in Townsville, Australia. The last attack prompted Crace to contact McArthur's command in protest.

The immediate consequence of the action by Task Force 44 was that Admiral Inoue gave orders to the landing group to reverse course at 0900hrs on May 7. They were to wait north of the Jomard Passage until the battle had been resolved.

The attempt to take Port Moresby required a great deal of air cover; therefore the Japanese 25th Air Group under Yamada was carrying out attacks on Port Moresby on this day. This again restricted the Japanese ability to detect the Americans, since their main scouting force was being used on this offensive mission.

LEFT: The Royal Australian Navy cruiser *Hobart*, the lighter of the two Australian cruisers involved in the battle.

BELOW: Carrier operations May 5–6.

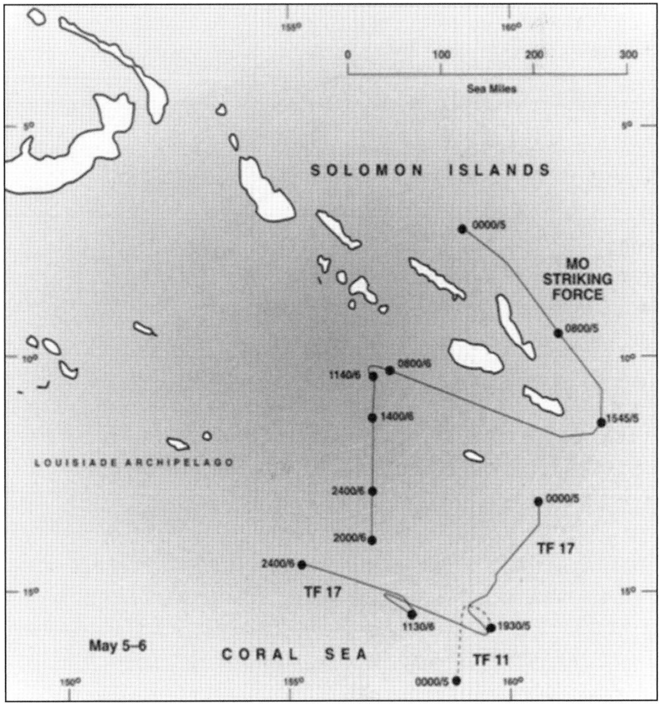

May 6 began for the Americans with the order from Adm. Fletcher to form a single group at 0730hrs that was to become known as Task Force 17. This meant that the commander of Task Force 11, Adm. Fitch, came under the direct command of Fletcher. However, as Fitch was far more experienced in the offensive use of air power he became the overall air commander at this point. The long Japanese wait for news of the Americans' location was finally broken on the morning of May 6 when a Mavis reconnaissance plane spotted the American task force and transmitted its position. It is thought that Takagi did not receive this information until the 7th, which may explain his delayed reaction to events that were about to occur.

Events of May 7

The preliminary skirmishes of the Battle of the Coral Sea were over and between May 5 and 6 a frantic search had taken place for the main battle fleets of either side. The Americans had a huge advantage in this due to their ability to decode Japanese transmissions. By 1940, the U.S. Army's Signal Intelligence Service had cracked Japan's top diplomatic code enabling U.S. forces to decipher massive amounts of high-level Japanese intelligence. Assigned the code name "Magic," this data source allowed the President and a small number of military officers access to high-quality information concerning Japanese military activities and diplomatic policies. As with any intelligence gained from the enemy the Magic information was not always used wisely and it was difficult to judge the amount of information to use without running the risk of betraying the source. Perhaps the most serious shortfall was due to the fact this information was not analyzed in any depth or used in conjunction with material collected by independent sources and means. However, Fletcher had been informed that there were carriers in the vicinity and that Japanese forces were converging on Port Moresby. Naval Intelligence too played a large part in keeping the Americans informed of Japanese intentions. The Office of Naval Intelligence was able to read part of the Japanese Navy's JN-25 code, the one dealing with operational matters. In conjunction with the ability to read the Japanese codes the Americans could detect radio transmissions between ships and shore-based stations, the level of traffic was a good indication of imminent action.

All this meant that the Americans had an intelligence advantage that, without doubt, assisted them during the Battle of the Coral Sea. The second U.S. advantage was that their ships, or at least some of them, had radar. Early radar trials had taken place in the Caribbean in January 1939, with sets mounted on the battleships USS *New York* and USS *Texas* and aircraft could now be spotted at

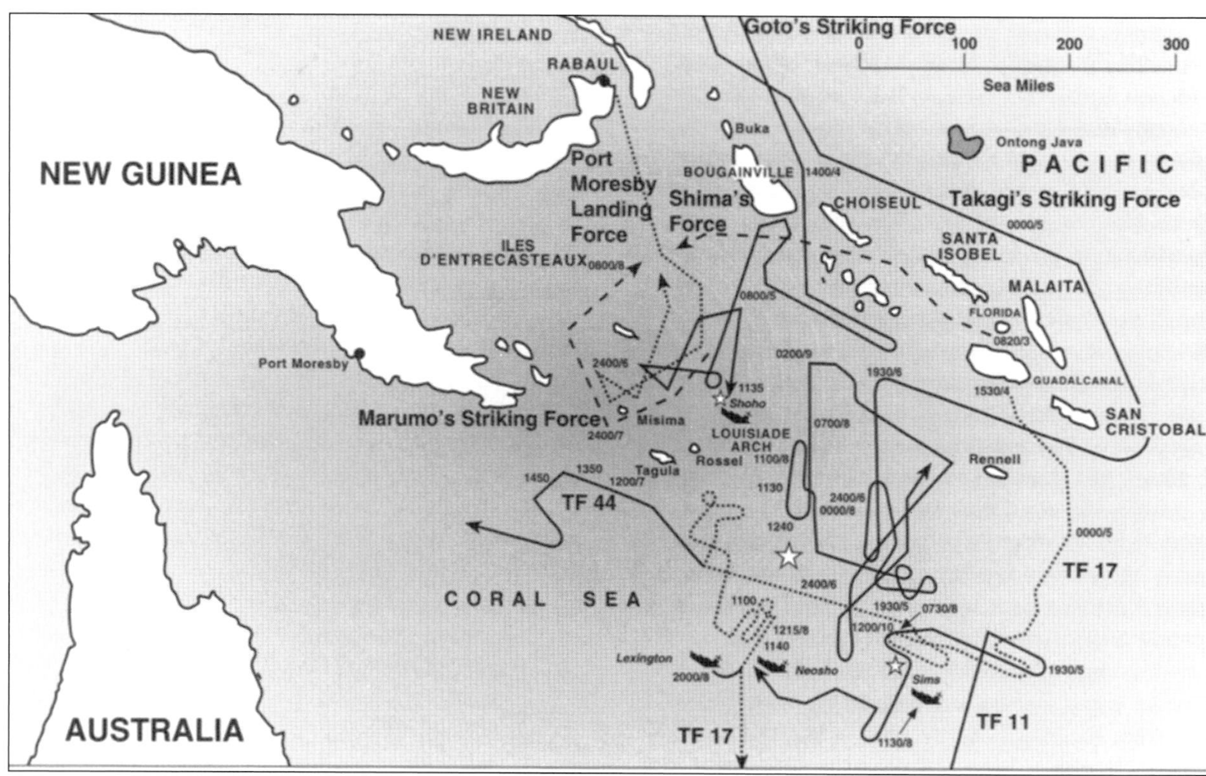

a range of 48 miles and vessels at 10 miles. It was also possible to detect surface vessel attacks at night, projectiles could be tracked in flight and radar was even used for navigation by ranging peaks on nearby islands. The Navy ordered RCA (Radio Corporation of America) to build 20 sets to their requirements. These sets were put into operational use as CXAM on capital ships, such as battleships and carriers.

Although these early radar sets were fairly primitive, their effectiveness was clearly illustrated on May 5 when a Wildcat fighter was directed onto its target by the radar of the *Yorktown*. This enabled the Wildcat to shoot down a Kawanishi H6K seaplane and delay the detection of the carrier group.

The attack on the Shoho

The *Shoho*, a Japanese escort carrier was covering the naval forces heading for the Jomard Passage during May 6, she was then ordered to wait 90 miles northeast of Deboyne Island. The *Shoho* was a light carrier that was capable of carrying 28 aircraft. She was the converted *Tsurugisaki* and was built at Yokosuka Yard. She had a displacement of 11,262 tons and was armed with 8 x 5in. 40-cal. guns and 8 x 25mm automatic anti-aircraft guns. The *Shoho* was typical of the series of converted ships that became escort carriers in the Imperial Japanese Navy.

On the morning of May 7 just before dawn she launched four reconnaissance aircraft. These machines were intended to provide screening cover for the landing force. It just so happened that Fletcher's force now headed north into area of bad weather. This enabled him to hide from the Japanese. though the clouds were just high enough to allow him to launch some aircraft. The previously mentioned reconnaissance planes were shadowing the Americans whose Combat Air Patrol had been reinforced to try to drive them off. At 0735hrs scout sections of flight VB5 spotted the cruisers *Furutaka* and *Kinugasa*. Real contact came about at 0815hrs when two carriers and four heavy cruisers were reported about 200 miles northwest of the Task Force's position. What is interesting in this battle is the propensity of both commanders to believe that they had found the enemy. This is fully understandable but Fletcher had exercised extreme thoroughness when attacking Tulagi and yet somehow he was prepared to accept the first report of the scout confirming the Japanese Fleet's presence. This may have been because they were expecting the Japanese to be in the vicinity of the report. Both carrier crews and aircrew frantically prepared themselves for what would be the

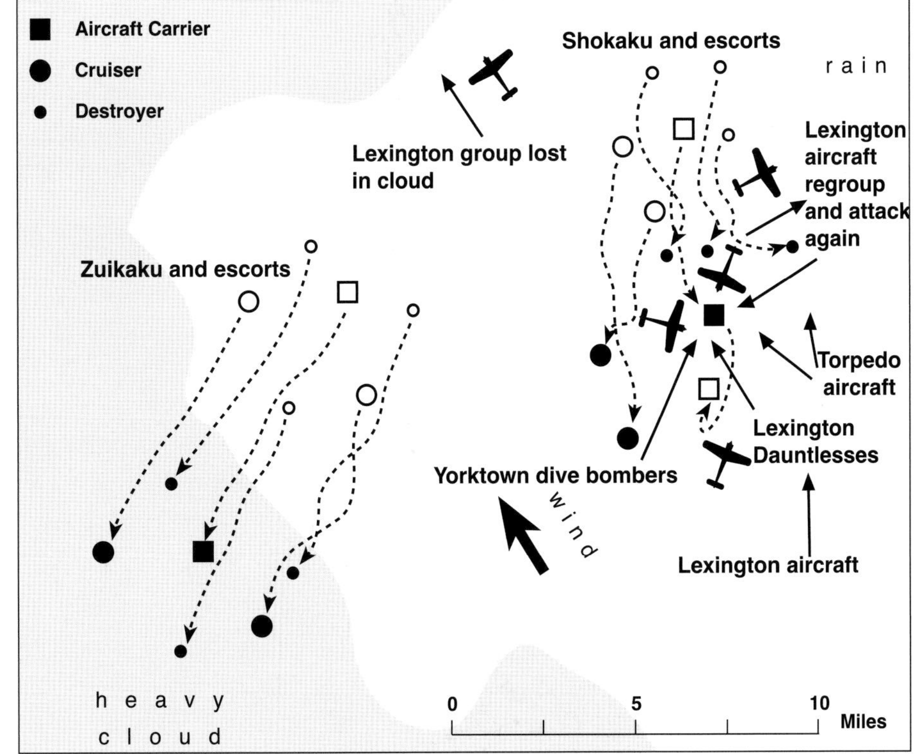

LEFT: Movement of the Japanese fleet before and after the attack on May 8.

FAR LEFT: Operations of both forces May 5–8.

first carrier against carrier attack in the Pacific War. There was at this juncture a lack of fighter cover so that of the four flights on the *Lexington* only ten were fighters, Grumman F4F Wildcats, 25 were bombers and 12 were torpedo planes. This air group carried out what was known as deferred departure, when all the aircraft formed up together before leaving for the target. They left at 0947hrs commanded by William B Ault. The *Yorktown* group consisted of eight Grumman F4F Wildcats, 25 SBD Dauntless bombers and 10 TBD Devastators, and they began to leave the ship at 0944hrs. This second group was less cohesive as the torpedo bombers had a 20-minute head start. In all 93 aircraft were winging their way to the *Shoho*. Fletcher, however, must have felt exactly like Hara when the scouting planes returned at around 1030hrs. The pilot who had reported in denied any knowledge of having seen a carrier and it was quickly discovered that his message had been wrongly coded! It was to be the army aircraft of McArthur's command that had sighted a carrier and several other ships near the original position. In addition the commander of flight VB2 of the *Lexington* also discovered the *Shoho* and escorts near the island of Tagula, so the force was redirected to that position. The Americans were also expecting a backlash once their attack had gone home so the Combat Air Patrol was stiffened by adding all the Dauntlesses on anti-torpedo aircraft patrol to the protective screen above the fleet. This was not unusual since the Dauntlesses were used for scouting, bombing and even as fighters when the need arose.

The *Shoho* was commanded by Capt. Izawa Ishinosuke who was at that moment preparing for an attack himself, even though his aircraft were being recovered. The launch of the attack planes ordered by Inoue was complicated by the fact that the *Shoho* was a converted depot ship and so had design limitations. Lt. Cmdr. Ault and the three command Dauntlesses of the *Lexington* group carried out the first attack on her at around 1107hrs near Misima Island. There were four Japanese cruisers covering the *Shoho*: the *Kakao*, *Furutaka*, *Aoba* and *Kinugasa*, as well as the destroyer *Sazanami*. Together they were able to muster a decent anti-aircraft barrage, there was also a small Japanese Combat Air Patrol, but this had been dispersed by the need to chase other aircraft notably VS2. The first attacks all missed the target partly due to a sharp turn to port made by Capt. Izawa. The next group to attack was Dixon's VS2, who had been pursued by fighters and whose dives were interrupted by them. The *Shoho* continued to turn to port and, although scouts claimed she was hit there was no confirmation. At this point three further fighters were launched from the *Shoho*.

The next wave came in under the command of Lt. Cmdr. Hamilton:

> Lt. Cmdr. Weldon Hamilton, the dive-bomber skipper, was at the front of his formation, which had climbed up to 15,000 feet and was slightly ahead and above Dixon's scout bombers, who were at 12,000. Underneath these two groups were Brett's torpedo

planes. The fighters split up, four pairs in the high-level group flying slightly above and behind Hamilton, and the other four idling along with the torpedo squadron. "We began from 16,500 feet and pushed over in our dive at 12,000. The Jap was exactly downwind as I nosed down, simplifying my problem tremendously. My bomb, which was the first 1,000-pdr to hit struck in the middle of the flight deck's width, just abaft amidships. As I looked back the entire after-portion of the flight deck was ablaze and pouring forth heavy smoke."

A second bomb hit the *Shoho* further forward just after Hamilton's attack causing explosions and confusion in the fires and wreckage. One can see the amount courage needed for this kind of attack when one considers the interview with the experience of Ens. Leppla.

> When I looked into the cockpit I found that other shots had gone through the Plexiglas cockpit covers, missed the pilot and gunner by inches, and then completely smashed some of the instrument board. One bullet tore off the heel of the pilot's shoe, and another, after coming through the plane and buzzing around the cockpit like a bee went through the leg of his flying suit and was found stuck in the knee of his trousers. *(Queen of the Flatops)*

The next attack was from the torpedo bombers approaching from the southwest and they decided to split

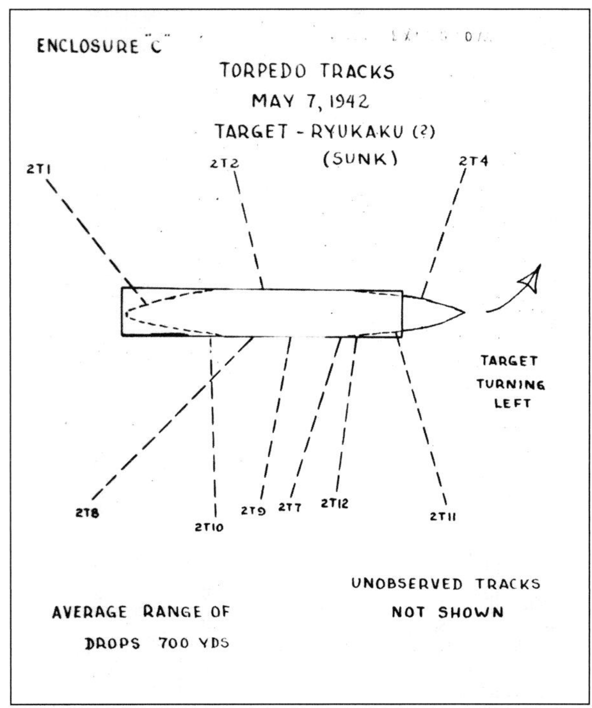

ABOVE: Although named as *Ryukaku*, this shows the hits on *Shoho* that led to its demise.

BELOW AND BELOW LEFT: A sequence of photographs (continued overleaf) showing the *Shoho* taking hits during the battle, May 7. The photographs are by an aircraft off USS *Lexington*. Note the TBD-1 visible to the right of the large splash in the photograph on page 54.

their forces and go at the ship simultaneously. This meant that torpedoes could be launched from either side of the ship preventing it from maneuvering away. Because of their low-level attack they were vulnerable to anti-aircraft fire and the cruisers were putting up a wall of lead. The release height for the American torpedoes was only 100ft—it was a decidedly risky proposition. Squadron VT2 were the first in to attack from the stern and the torpedo of Lt. Thornhill hit the *Shoho* on her port side. VT2 probably hit the *Shoho* five times, over 5,500lb of explosive that destroyed her engine room and tore holes in her side. She began to lose speed and, whilst fires were raging on her decks her below decks area was awash with water.

The *Yorktown* group was 15 minutes behind the *Lexington* group and they proceeded to give the coup de grace to the ship. Within five minutes she was a steaming, burning wreck. Even after this she had to endure a further torpedo attack from VT5 of the *Yorktown*, who may well have been better directed against the cruisers all of whom seem to have escaped from the encounter unscathed. The order to abandon the *Shoho* was given at 1131hrs and the ship sank at 1135hrs. Only about 100 men of the crew survived picked up by the destroyer *Sazanami*. The rest of the battle dissolved into a series fighter combats and the attacking planes finally assembled at 1140hrs for the journey back to their respective carriers. At 1210hrs Cmdr. R. E. Dixon of squadron VS2 of the *Lexington* sent the signal "Scratch one flat top! Signed Bob" to the Task Force. But, and it was big but, the relief that the carrier commanders felt at that moment was to be short lived. The Americans had actually identified the *Shoho* as a carrier of the Ryujo class and one can still see captions on official U.S. photographs quoting her as the *Ryukaku*.

There were others who did not make it back to the ship Edward Allen and Ens. Quigley were hit by anti-aircraft fire whilst in a dive and were forced to land on Rossel Island, only being rescued some 18 days later.

> "I was stunned a little but the water coming in revived me. We got the rubber boat out and took the chart board. We rowed for 45 minutes but got nowhere cos the current was too strong." They saw an outrigger and three of the wildest natives you can imagine.

The end of this attack was followed by the long return flight to the U.S. carriers, who promptly received them at 1335hrs. Three aircraft had been lost during this attack. In his usual thorough way Fletcher was already thinking of a second attack. The aircraft were prepared and ready to go an hour later but the order was never given. It seems that a combination of factors stayed his hand at that time.

FAR LEFT AND LEFT: Two more views of the crippled *Shoho*. TBD Devastators can be seen in the photograph on page 56.

The loss of the Neosho *and the* Sims

Fletcher had detached the destroyer *Sims* and the oiler *Neosho* on May 6 to go to their next refueling station, they arrived there at about 0810hrs the following morning. It was at this time that they saw two approaching aircraft. Takagi's force had been making a search southwards since the early hours of the morning. Takagi did not know the whereabouts of the American carriers so he was moving westward covering the MO invasion group. At 0600hrs Hara's carriers launched 12 Type 97 aircraft to search for the U.S. fleet. The planes were looking for the Americans in a southerly direction to a range of about 250 miles away from their carriers. After one and a half-hour's search the *Zuikaku* received a message from the easternmost aircraft that he had seen an aircraft carrier and a cruiser. In fact it was the *Neosho* and the *Sims*. Aircraft were already being prepared for a possible action and efforts were redoubled to make sure they could catch the Americans. A further aircraft was sent to keep contact with the ships while the rest were readied for the attack. The first wave of Kate bombers took off at 0800hrs. In all the attack consisted of 78 planes: 36 dive-bombers, 24 torpedo planes and 18 fighters under the control of Lt. Cmdr. Kakuichi Takahashi. The search aircraft from the carriers had not been the only ones looking for the American fleet. At 0815hrs Task force 17 was found south of Rossel Island. Once this message was received further confirmation came at 0830hrs. Both sightings were very close to each other and it was thought that the Japanese striking force was sending its aircraft to Rossel Island when in fact they were heading south.

The attacking Japanese forces arrived at 0935hrs over the spot where the American ships had been seen. After a short search only a solitary destroyer and tanker were found rather than a grand U.S. fleet. The search appeared to be fruitless and, rather than return empty-handed, Kakuichi decided to attack the solitary ships. At 0945hrs the first wave of aircraft screamed towards their targets, but with little success. The *Sims* began weaving in order to avoid bombs; the *Neosho* followed about a mile behind. Kakuichi did not arrive over the scene until a little later with 36 dive-bombers. The *Sims* was forced to turn and support the *Neosho* with her anti-aircraft guns, thus exposing her rear to attack. The skill of the Aichi Val pilots was decisive and they hit the *Sims* with three armor-piercing bombs that exploded in her engine room. This left her motionless and with no means of escape. The following description was given by the survivors after the action:

> Four planes broke off from one wave of *Neosho* attackers and directed their attack at the *Sims*, diving on her in succession from astern. All of these planes were single-motored, had fixed landing gear, and had

a silhouette similar to that of Japanese dive-bombers. The first released a bomb which landed in the water about amidships to port; the second released a bomb which landed on Number Two Torpedo Mount and exploded in the forward engine room; the third released a bomb which apparently hit the after upper deck house and went down through diagonally forward, exploding in the after engine room; the fourth plane is believed to have made a direct hit on Number Four Gun, but this cannot be definitely established. Numbers Three and Four Mounts and the after 20mm guns were put out of commission by the bomb hits, but the forward mounts in local control and one 20mm gun continued firing at the planes until all of them were out of gun range. The total number of rounds fired by the *Sims* cannot be ascertained, but one survivor states that over 200 rounds were fired from Number Two Mount alone. During this last attack, the paint on the barrel of Number One Mount blistered and caught fire; the crew, however, continued to fire with the complete length of the barrel in flames. Several planes were brought down by gunfire during this attack. *Neosho* survivors told *Sims* survivors that the planes that attacked the *Sims* were never seen to emerge from the blast of their bomb explosions. It is believed that the bombs dropped were about 500lb size.

CSM R. J. Dicken had to swim out to the boat from the ship and his comments were noted in the same report quoted above

He noted that there was no oil on the water at this time. On taking charge of the boat Dicken proceeded around the bow to the lee side of the ship aft. As the motor whaleboat approached, the ship seemed to break amidships and start to sink slowly. The stern went under first and appeared to draw the bow aft, pulling it down stern first. All hands began abandoning ship in life jackets, swimming for the rafts. Just as the water level reached the top of the stack and began running down into it, a terrific explosion occurred. What remained of the ship was lifted 10 to 15ft out of the water, and the surface of the water around the ship was covered with oil. This great explosion was followed by another smaller one, which survivors definitely identified as a depth charge explosion. The remaining forward section then settled slowly, sinking in about five minutes. One man who couldn't swim was seen hanging onto the anchor until the stem disappeared into the water. Survivors estimate that the ship sank in about 15 to 20 minutes after receiving the first direct hit. Under conditions of stress such as existed at the time, minutes would seem like hours and it is quite possible that the ship sank much more rapidly than these men estimate.
(*Naval Intelligence Combat Reports*)

The *Neosho* did not long survive the destruction of the *Sims* as she received seven bomb strikes and one aircraft that crashed into her stern and set the ship alight. There were many efforts of heroism during the attacks on the *Neosho*. Chief Watertender Oscar Verner Peterson was a case in point, he literally burnt himself to death to try and save the ship. Without assistance because of injuries to the other members of his repair party and severely wounded himself, Peterson closed the bulkhead stop valves and in so doing received additional burns that resulted in his death. He was awarded the Medal of Honor posthumously for his efforts.

The *Neosho* did not sink straight away and, even though she had lost her rudder, she drifted for four days until the destroyer *Henley* from the salvage group found her.

Immediately prior to the attack on the *Sims* and *Neosho*, the Japanese admirals realized that they had made a serious error. They had dispatched a large attacking force onto a pair of vessels that were not worth the effort. Although destroying the two ships was militarily useful, it was clear that valuable time had been lost. Now that the main American force was located the aircraft had to return, rearm and get organized for the major assault. A large force such as the Japanese had dispatched was almost impossible to recall. The cost in ammunition, fuel and other resources was also very high. Although it was surprising that Admiral Hara did not get more confirmation before launching such a large attack, this was not the only mistake of the day. Around 1500hrs a reconnaissance report was received that indicated that the U.S. Task Force had altered course and headed south. At this point the Americans were believed to be 330–360 miles to the west of the Japanese Fleet. Takagi knew that if he was to launch an afternoon raid he might well steal a march on the Americans, but it would mean returning in the dark, a factor that would be significant later in the battle and that was to be significant for later developments. At 1630hrs in the afternoon of May 7, 12 Aichi Type 99 dive-bombers and 15 Kate Type 97 torpedo planes left the carriers on yet another sortie. They were expected to make a three and a half-hour flight to the target. Considering the weather front that the Americans were engulfed in it would be a matter of enormous skill or complete luck if they found the American ships at all. According to several authors, it was at the limit of their search pattern that they realized that they were not going to find the Americans. What they did not realize was that they were much closer than they thought, they had been detected on the *Lexington*'s radar at about 48 miles out. Obviously the Americans had a Combat Air Patrol on station, but they were low on fuel and so there was a frantic scramble to get more fighters aloft when the Japanese were spotted by the radar. The first unit attacked was Lt. Cmdr. Shimazaki's group of nine Type 97 Kate torpedo planes from the *Zuikaku* and in the ensuing melee attacks five Japanese aircraft were shot down for the loss of one American plane. These fighter aircraft were recalled to refuel and a second wave of seven further Wildcats from VF42 under Lt. Flately were dispatched. This group encountered Kate torpedo-bombers from the *Shokaku* commanded by Lt. Ichihara Tatsuo. In this battle the Japanese lost a further two planes and one severely damaged (which eventually ditched) whilst the Americans lost another Wildcat piloted by ensign Lt. Knox.

Below and Below Right: Two drawings showing the tactical dispositions of Japanese forces during the battle—*Shoho* and escorts (below) and *Zuikaku* and *Shokaku*.

A further Aichi Val was shot down but the light was failing fast and soon it was almost impossible to see. After taking a severe mauling from the Americans, the Japanese decided to jettison their weapons and returned to their own carriers. They had taken a risk in sending the bombers and torpedo planes without fighter cover and had paid the price. Between 1830hrs and 1845hrs, the American fighters returned to their ships while the Japanese fled back to theirs. Night had closed in and the Americans were clearly having trouble recalling their planes. At about 1850 four additional aircraft appeared apparently trying to land on the *Yorktown*, one of them signaling with an Aldiss lamp. These aircraft turned out to be four extremely disorientated Japanese aircraft, which were immediately set upon by a Wildcat that was near to the *Yorktown*. The Japanese were forced away but the situation had caused some alarm and the pilots of two Wildcats, Ens. W. W. Barnes and Dick Wright, were both fired upon in the act of landing.

Events of May 8

After all the events of the 7th, May 8 would be a day of reckoning, or at least that was how it seemed to many of the officers on both sides that day. Both had made less than spectacular attacks on bogus targets and both

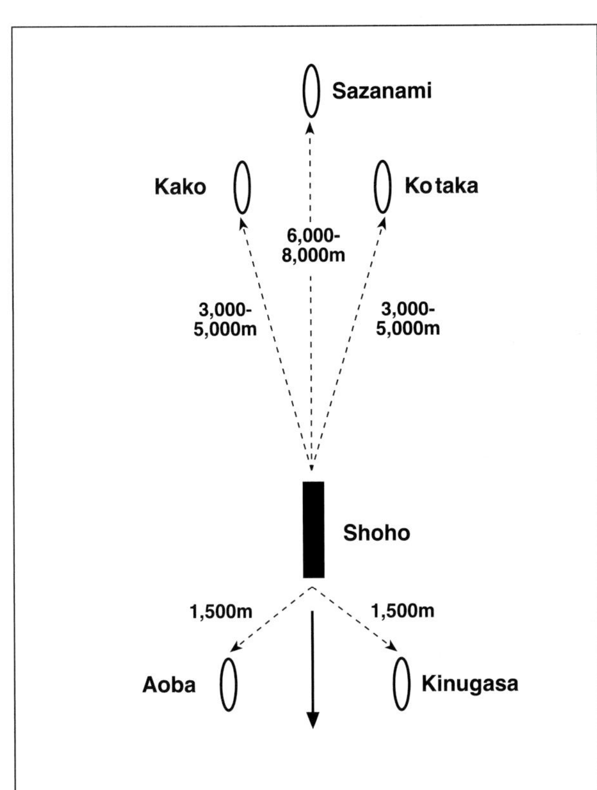

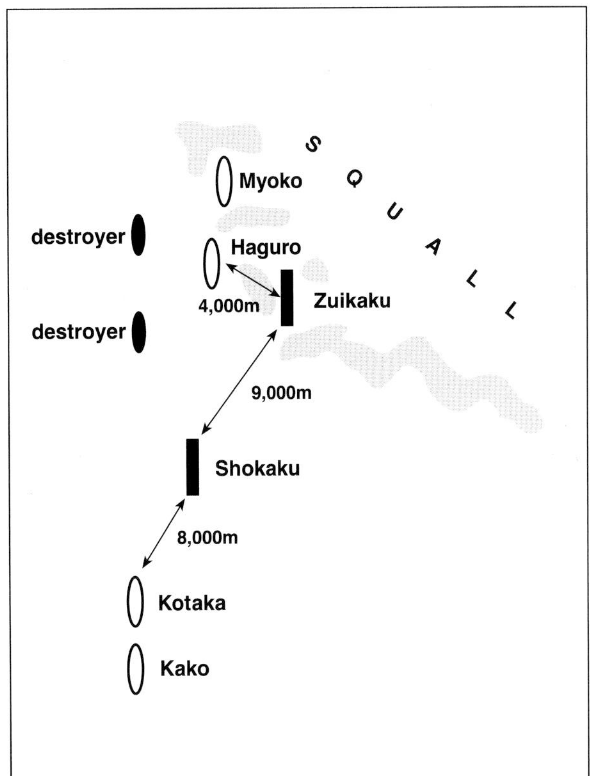

realized that it was still possible to strike the killing blow if the opportunity was given to them. The weather was clear and there was a sense that major action was imminent. The Japanese were 100 miles east-southeast of Rossell Island going north. Fletcher and Task Force 17 were 200 miles southwest of this position heading south. In terms of weather the tables had been turned; the Americans were in clear daylight whereas the Japanese were happily concealed in cloud cover. They also changed their formation; each carrier was escorted by two heavy cruisers and two or three destroyers but the two groups sailed about 10 miles apart. This was done so that if one were detected the other might not be as well and this is exactly what happened. Very early in the day Hara had decided to carry out a search and at 0615hrs sent seven planes off to search in a southerly direction to a radius of 200 miles. Conveniently for the Japanese, Hara had the assistance of the land-based aircraft of the 5th Air Attack force from Rabaul and Tulagi. Three Kawanishi's from Tulagi were to cover the northern Coral Sea and four other land-based planes were to look at the Louisades. This airborne reconnaissance was absolutely essential and whoever spotted the other's fleet first would have the advantage of first strike. Both forces were making course changes: the Americans headed west at 0116hrs, whilst the Japanese headed southwest at 0700hrs before Hara launched an attack group of planes at 0822hrs to search the area in which he expected the Americans to be. Fletcher's force now consisted of five heavy cruisers, seven destroyers and his two carriers. According to Morison both sides had almost equivalent numbers of aircraft: 121 Japanese and 122 American. This is not the whole story and Lundstrom states that there were only 95 aircraft available to the Japanese at the time of the battle, consisting of 37 fighters, 33 dive-bombers and 25 torpedo carrying planes. The Americans were also keen to send up aircraft to track down the Japanese fleet and at 0625hrs the *Lexington* launched 18 aircraft with that express purpose. Incredibly, both sides spotted each other almost simultaneously. At 0833hrs a Japanese spotter plane relayed a message that it had spotted the American carriers. This message was intercepted by the Americans and translated so that they too knew they were being sought out, whilst Lt. J. G. Smith saw the Japanese preparing for takeoff at roughly the same time and gave the composition of the Japanese force. Lt. Cmdr. R. E. Dixon of VS2 flew out to try to maintain this contact but failed to find Smith. He eventually found the Japanese at 0930hrs and realized that the location of the ships was wrong. He maintained contact for another hour and a quarter. Exactly 23 minutes after the first sighting the Americans gave the order to launch their attacks. The planes of the *Yorktown* left at 0915hrs and arrived at the target at 1100hrs. As usual the Dauntlesses, flying faster than the lumbering Devastators, were first to arrive flying at about 17,000 feet. At this point the *Shokaku* was visible to the attackers but the *Zuikaku* was not as she had been hidden under the clouds. The *Yorktown*'s bombers were the first to attack the *Shokaku* when VT5 attacked at 1100hrs. The attack of the torpedo bombers initiated by Lt. Cmdr. Taylor was a failure as the pilots launched their torpedoes too far away from the carrier. As a result no explosions were seen and this left the Americans with just the dive-bombers to carry out the attack. They succeeded where the torpedo bombers had failed and two hits were made on the *Shokaku*; one on the starboard side of the flight deck and the other on the stern. This latter bomb destroyed the engine repair workshop on the lower flight deck. As all of this was happening the fighters were engaged in a struggle either to support the attacks or to counteract the Japanese air patrols.

More torpedo-carrying aircraft then arrived from the *Lexington*, four Dauntlesses from VS2 and six Wildcats from VF2. This second attack was organized by Cmdr. W Ault, the Air Group commander who was missing believed dead after the battle. The cloud cover that hid the *Zuikaku* also gave some vital cover to the U.S. attack. As the torpedo bombers approached the *Shokaku*, followed by the Dauntlesses, six of the escorting fighters peeled off to engage in a duel with an equal number of Japanese fighters. This left the *Shokaku* stripped of defensive cover and completely exposed to torpedo attack.

The *Lexington* flight, which flew off ten minutes later, ran into confusion. The three Widcat fighter escorts supporting 18 Dauntlesses of VB2 got lost in cloud and returned to the Lexington without doing anything. For some reason they had been given the wrong destination information and therefore were unable to find the Japanese, after circling for a while they were forced to jettison their weapons and return to the carrier. The torpedo flight VT2 was also directed onto the initial position of the Japanese fleet as first sighted and therefore could not find them. They then flew in a box search and eventually found the Japanese at 1140hrs. Again the Devastators released their weapons from an approach from 6,000ft allowing the Japanese commanders time to maneuver away from the torpedoes. The dive-bombers fared little better, landing just one further bomb on the *Shokaku*. This hit her on the starboard bow starting a fire and preventing her from launching aircraft. 108 Japanese sailors were killed and 40 wounded in this attack. Because she could not launch aircraft some of her planes were transferred to the *Zuikaku*.

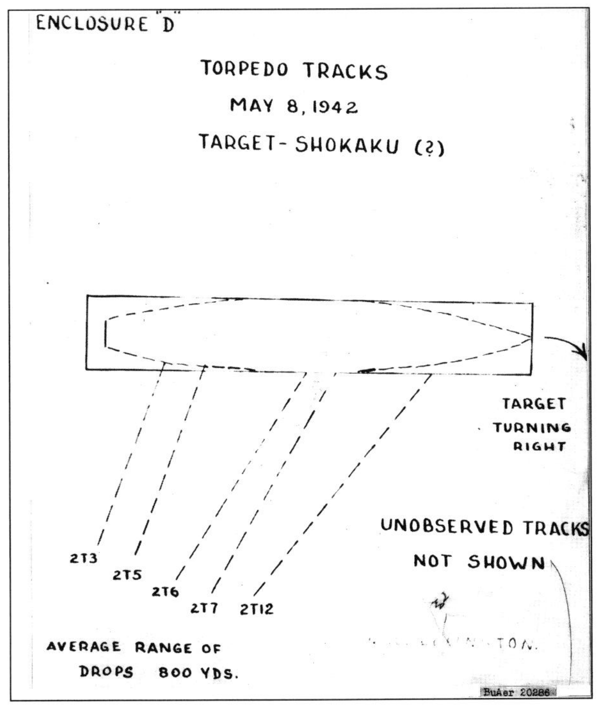

As soon as the Japanese ships saw the torpedo bombers they went into a zigzag movement to spoil the aim of the torpedo bombers and, once again, no successful hits were recorded. The dive-bombers, however, were much more successful in a task that was daunting to say the least in the face of hostile aircraft and anti-aircraft batteries. The citation of Lt. Powers of the *Lexington*, who was killed in a dive-bombing attack on this day, gives an impression of the situation in the skies over the *Shokaku* on May 8.

> He led his section of dive-bombers down to the target from an altitude of 18,000ft, through a wall of bursting anti-aircraft shells and into the face of enemy fighter planes. Again, completely disregarding the safety altitude and without fear or concern for his safety, Lt. Powers courageously pressed home his attack, almost to the very deck of an enemy carrier and did not release his bomb until he was sure of a direct hit. He was last seen attempting recovery from his dive at the extremely low altitude of 200ft, and amid a terrific barrage of shell and bomb fragments,

ABOVE LEFT: The torpedo tracks that led to hits on *Shokaku*, May 8.

LEFT AND OVERLEAF: The start of a sequence of photographs taken by aircraft from *Yorktown* of *Shokaku* under attack, maneuvering in a vain attempt to evade the bombs. See also pages 62–67.

smoke, flame and debris from the stricken vessel. (*Medal of Honor citation*)

The Japanese authors Hata and Izawa claim that the *Shokaku* Combat Air Patrol shot down 21 torpedo bombers and dive-bombers during this attack. Petty Officer Takeo Miyazawa is said to have shot down one torpedo bomber and crashed into another to prevent the destruction of the carrier itself. They also claim that the ten-plane fighter compliment of the *Zuikaku* did similar execution destroying a total of 11 bombers/torpedo planes and 13 fighters. These figures seem a trifle fanciful when one considers the total number of losses recorded by the Americans.

The Japanese had actually launched their attack before the Americans, with their attack force consisting of 70 aircraft. The Americans expected an attack at and had estimated that the Japanese planes would arrive at about 1100hrs. In fact they turned up about five minutes before predicted when the radar of the *Lexington* saw a group of aircraft 70 miles to the northeast. Unfortunately, one patrol had just been recovered and there were only eight aircraft on Combat Air Patrol. They were also low on fuel and so had to be kept near the carriers and could not be vectored out to the Japanese attackers. The carriers immediately changed course to 125 degrees and sped up. A further nine Wildcats were launched of which five were sent to intercept the Japanese. It was a case of too little too late and they arrived at their attack point at the wrong height to make a successful intercept, while the Japanese fighter escort also made it difficult for them to molest the attacking bombers. Things were desperate and the shining example of this is the fact that 23 Dauntlesses were in the air being used as fighters. Coming in from the northeast the Japanese torpedo bombers came in on both bows of the *Lexington* in a textbook attack. They launched their torpedoes at a distance of about 1,300yds and at between 50 and 200ft. The effectiveness of the American 5in. anti-aircraft fire was

ABOVE AND ABOVE RIGHT: Two more views of the sequence of photographs of *Shokaku*.

RIGHT: Movement of USS *Lexington* and *Yorktown* on May 8.

demonstrated when one of the aircraft disintegrated into a ball of flame throwing the airmens' bodies into the sea. However, whichever way the *Lexington* moved it was difficult to avoid torpedoes, which is exactly what the Japanese had hoped for. Lt. Cmdr. Paul D Stroop had been up since 0330hrs that morning:

> We began seeing enemy aircraft overhead and they came down in a very well coordinated attack, with torpedo planes and dive-bombers. I can remember standing on the bridge and watching the enemy dive-bombers come down. These were fixed landing gear dive-bombers, [Aichi99 Val] and you were convinced the pilot in the plane had the bridge of your ship right in his sight. Fortunately, they were not strafing, because if they had been, I'm sure that they would have made the topside untenable.

Of the torpedo attack he stated "if you were

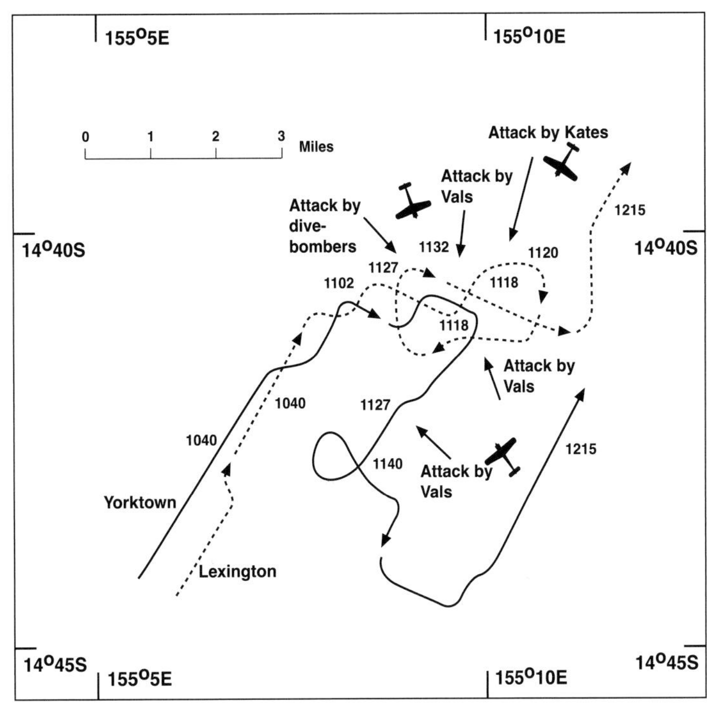

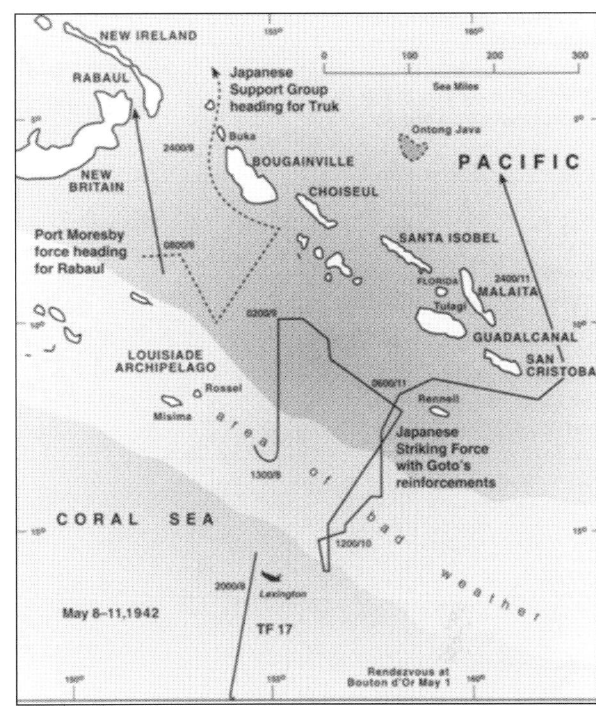

ABOVE: Movements of the fleets May 8–11.

LEFT: Another view in the sequence of photographs of the *Shokaku*.

in the general vicinity of a hit, you could be hurt; the shock to the deck you were standing on was enough to break people's legs if a torpedo hit in the general vicinity."

Accordingly, one torpedo hit the port side of the ship at 1120hrs and a second hit the port side opposite the bridge. The attack was extremely well coordinated with both bombers and torpedoes hitting at similar times.

While all of this was occurring the *Yorktown* was also receiving unwelcome attention. At almost the same time as the *Lexington* was hit three torpedoes were launched on her port quarter. She was more maneuverable than the *Lexington* and was thus able to avoid the torpedoes, which in fact only came from one side. However, she was attacked about five minutes later by dive-bombers and one of their projectiles hit her near the bridge penetrating down to the fourth deck and causing serious casualties, though this did not stop her from carrying out operations.

A complete description of the damage to the *Yorktown* makes sobering reading:

> The bomb which struck the *Yorktown*'s flight deck penetrated a vertical distance of 50ft from the point

FAR RIGHT: *Lexington* seen from *Yorktown* on May 8—one of a sequence of photographs taken of CV-2—see following pages.

RIGHT: The torpedo attack on TF17, 1118–1121hrs, May 8.

BELOW RIGHT: The dive bombing of TF17, 1121–1124hrs, May 8.

In these drawings, the ships are identified by pennant numbers as follows:

AIRCRAFT CARRIERS
CV-2 *Lexington*
CV-5 *Yorktown*

HEAVY CRUISERS
CA-27 USS *Chester* (Northampton class)
CA-32 USS *New Orleans* (New Orleans class)
CA-33 USS *Portland* (Portland class)
CA-34 USS *Astoria* (New Orleans class)
CA-36 USS *Minneapolis* (New Orleans class)

DESTROYERS
DD-349 USS *Dewey* (Farragut class)
DD-355 USS *Aylwin* (Farragut class)
DD-360 USS *Phelps* (Porter class)
DD-411 USS *Anderson* (Sims class)
DD-412 USS *Hammann* (Sims class)
DD-414 USS *Russell* (Sims class)
DD-417 USS *Morris* (Sims class)

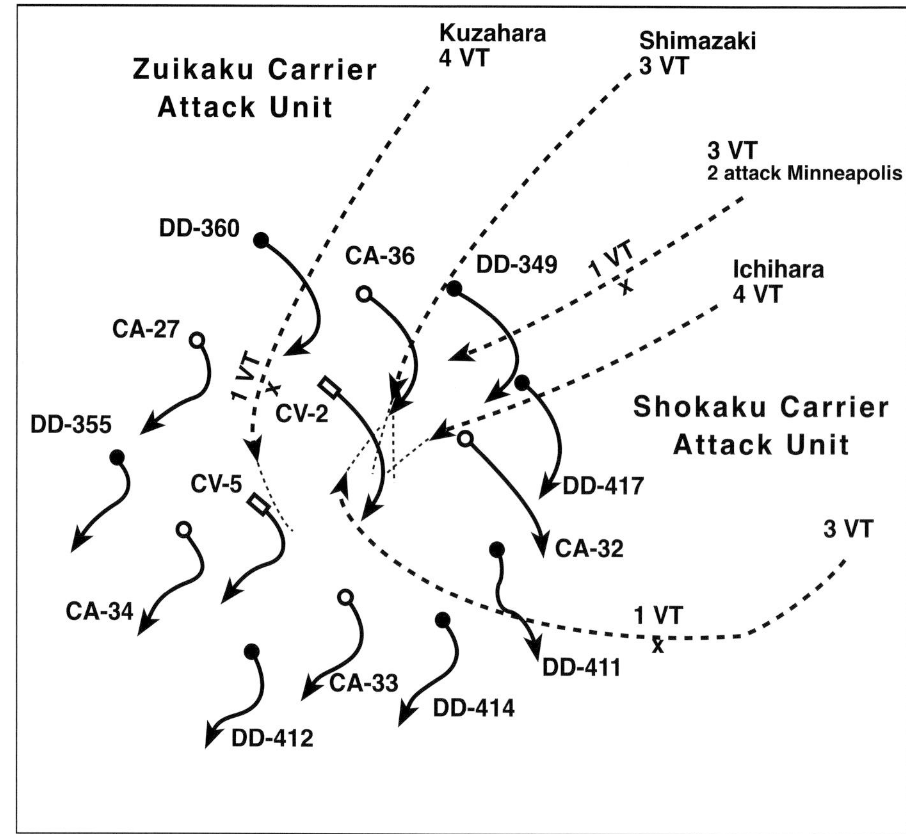

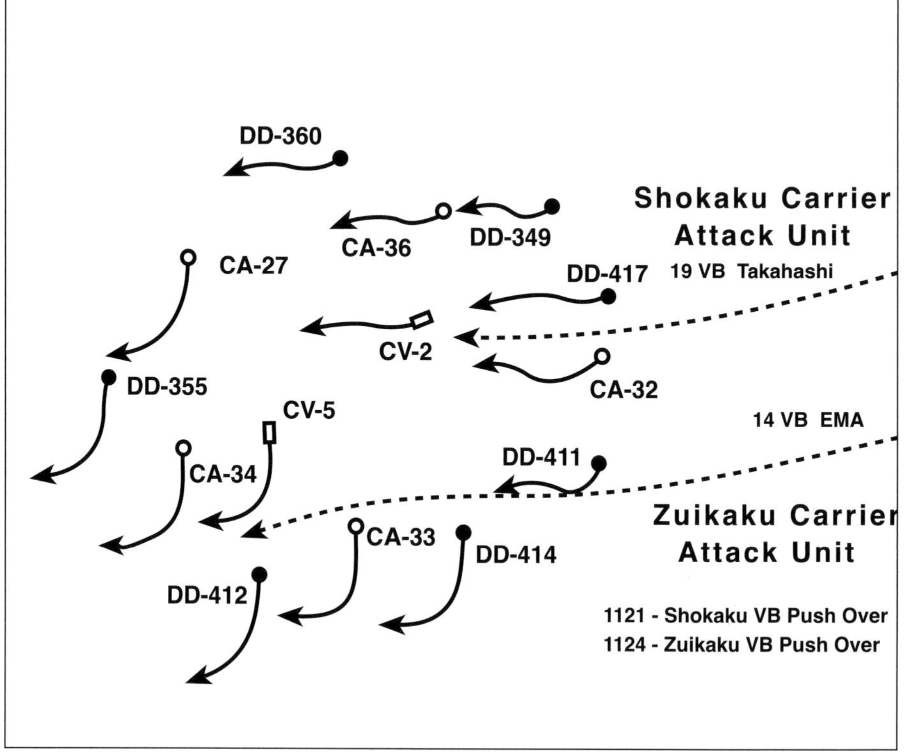

of impact to the point of detonation, piercing a total thickness of 1.68in. of steel deck plating. The hole in the flight deck was clean. The holes in the hangar and second decks were jagged and somewhat larger. The ship's shell was not punctured. The flight and galley decks were not harmed, but the hangar deck was bulged across its entire breadth from frame No. 100 to frame No. 115. A hole 4ft in diameter was blown up through the second deck 8ft inboard of the bomb impact hole, and the entire deck in the marine living compartment was bulged upward. Also, the transverse bulkheads of this compartment were badly bulged forward and aft. However, they did not rupture, and all doors remained secure, though severely warped. When the bomb hit the second deck it pierced the general lighting and battle light and power circuits for the damaged area, causing short circuits. Several people in the fire parties were shocked, one seriously. A hole 6ft in diameter was blown out of the third deck, with the deck turned and peeled back over an area of 35 square feet. The entire deck in compartment C-301-1L was bulged upward, and the ship's-service store and office, soda fountain, engineer's office, and laundry issue room were wrecked.

The fourth deck was not ruptured but was dished downward over an area of 40 square feet. The inboard bulkhead of the forward engine room access truck, and the after bulkhead of the laundry storeroom were shattered. Two watertight doors were severely damaged and a large hatch cover was thrown about 15ft up into the No. 2 elevator pit. The transverse bulkheads and doors joining four compartments were blown out.
(*Naval Intelligence Combat Reports*)

All of this is nothing compared to the difficulty that the *Lexington* was in. Unbelievably the attacks had lasted just 25 minutes. The problem was that the destruction unleashed on either side had made the rest of the day a struggle for survival, especially on board the *Lexington*. Sailors are trained to deal with fire. It is the one great threat to a ship carrying huge amounts of explosives and fuel and the response aboard the *Lexington* was magnificent. She had received hits from at least two torpedoes and four bombs. One of these bombs was apparently a 1,000lb device that had hit the after end of the port forward gun gallery. Its impact killed the crew of the No. 6 gun as well as a number of men on nearby guns. Several men also were killed inboard in the main passageway on the main deck; this was because the bomb was thought to have set of a stack of 5in. gun rounds in the vicinity. Fire broke out on the gun gallery, in the admiral's cabin and the surrounding area. The second large bomb to hit was a 500lb weapon that hit the gig boat pocket on the port side killing many men. A third and considerably smaller bomb hit and exploded inside the stack. Initially it was believed that more than two torpedoes had hit the ship, then it was realized that two large caliber bombs had hit near the port side aft. Flying fragments from one or more near hits aft on the starboard side also killed and injured several machine gunners in the sky aft and the after signal station.

The *Lexington* had received some punishment but it was thought that she could be saved, although immediately after the battle she had a 6–7 degree list to port. It was reported that three of her boiler rooms were full of water and that there were three large fires raging. In fact by 1230hrs the fires were out and everybody on board thought that the worst was over, when a huge explosion rocked the ship at 1247hrs. It turned out that the pipes that carried petrol around the ship had been shaken and that sparks generated by a generator rotor had set the whole thing off. Explosions then began to rock the ship in stages. The communications links around the ship were damaged and this prevented one group of firefighters from finding out what the other was doing

Adm. Fletcher reassumed tactical command from Fitch at 1510hrs but, following the explosions on board the great carrier, time was slipping away. It was planned to take her serviceable planes aboard the *Yorktown* and send her back to Pearl Harbor for repairs quickly as possible. One of the problems was that the firefighters inside the ship needed breathing apparatus and many of the men not so equipped could not assist in the difficult areas without being overcome by fumes. Cmdr. Seligman described the events on board at the time:

> Lt. Cmdr. Edward J. O'Donnell, the gunnery officer, had procured two additional hoses from aft. These were led into the scuttles of the 5in. ammunition hoist to starboard, and the last available hose was led into the dumb waiter of the food distribution room in an attempt to flood the C.P.O. [Chief Petty Officer] country. Good pressure was maintained on these hoses for a short time and it was hoped that sufficient water could be gotten below to flood the area on fire forward of the quarter deck and check the spread of the blaze. Under existing conditions it was impossible to combat it otherwise. "I ordered life rafts made ready and preparations made to abandon ship," Captain Sherman related. "Fire

fighting efforts were still being made until the engineering plant was abandoned, when all water pressure was gone."
(*Naval Intelligence Combat Reports*)

It was at this point that Sherman requested assistance of the destroyers through Adm. Fitch. The Admiral directed destroyers to come alongside, as it was time to get the personnel at risk off the ship. The destroyers provided fire hoses and water to combat the fires while the crew climbed down ropes off the ship. The destroyer *Morris* risked a great deal by coming as close as she did. But it was all to no avail: the torpedo warheads were threatened by the fire and, at a temperature of 60 degrees centigrade, the threat was too much. At 1630hrs the ship stopped. At 1830hrs the torpedo warheads finally exploded. The ship was abandoned with Sherman and his entourage the last to leave. It was the destroyer *Phelps* that finally finished off the *Lexington* by firing four torpedoes at her. She sank at around 2000hrs in the evening taking her remaining aircraft and deceased crew with her.

But what of the other ships belonging to the carrier groups? The destroyers and cruiser whose job it was to defend the great carriers. Luckily for them, the Japanese were not interested in destroying these ships as the carriers were the greater prizes. In terms of their response we can look at the views of the commander of the *Portland*, Capt. Perlman who stated that:

All fire, except in the instance of one torpedo plane that was shot down approaching the *Yorktown*, was "generally without damaging effect, inasmuch as lead-offs were too small and planes were out of effective range. However, the volume of fire was apparently disconcerting to the pilots, who released torpedoes against the *Yorktown* considerably earlier than they did against the *Lexington*."

Captain Perlman described three "phases" of the action. The second began about 1120 and consisted of a coordinated enemy torpedo plane and dive-bomber attack on the *Yorktown*. The *Portland* fired on these planes with all bearing guns without any effect other than a possible element of disturbance. The third phase consisted of uncoordinated attacks by single dive-bombers from several directions. During this phase two planes diving either at the *Portland* or

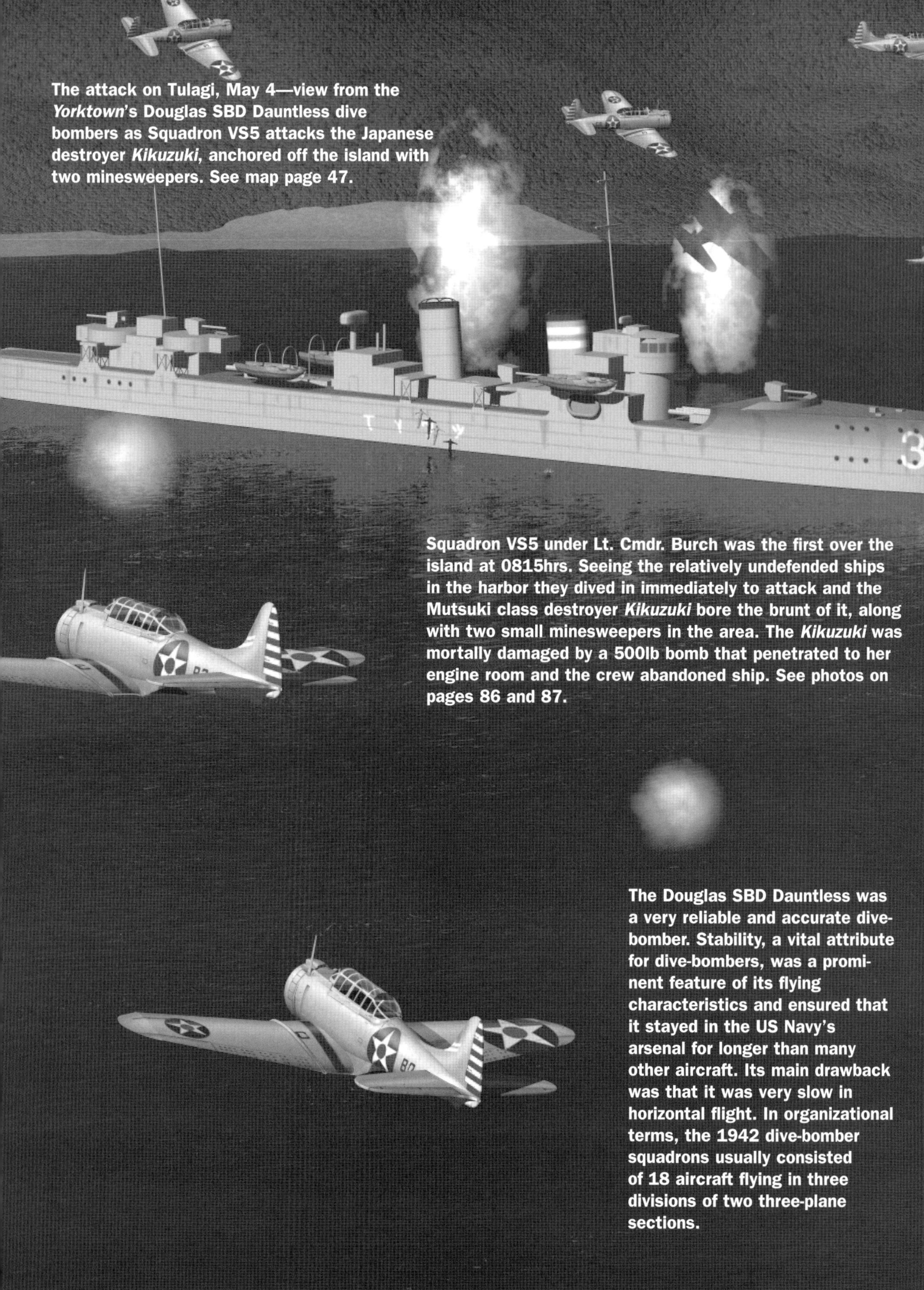

The attack on Tulagi, May 4—view from the *Yorktown*'s Douglas SBD Dauntless dive bombers as Squadron VS5 attacks the Japanese destroyer *Kikuzuki*, anchored off the island with two minesweepers. See map page 47.

Squadron VS5 under Lt. Cmdr. Burch was the first over the island at 0815hrs. Seeing the relatively undefended ships in the harbor they dived in immediately to attack and the Mutsuki class destroyer *Kikuzuki* bore the brunt of it, along with two small minesweepers in the area. The *Kikuzuki* was mortally damaged by a 500lb bomb that penetrated to her engine room and the crew abandoned ship. See photos on pages 86 and 87.

The Douglas SBD Dauntless was a very reliable and accurate dive-bomber. Stability, a vital attribute for dive-bombers, was a prominent feature of its flying characteristics and ensured that it stayed in the US Navy's arsenal for longer than many other aircraft. Its main drawback was that it was very slow in horizontal flight. In organizational terms, the 1942 dive-bomber squadrons usually consisted of 18 aircraft flying in three divisions of two three-plane sections.

It is normally claimed that two minesweepers were sunk by VS5 as well as the *Kikuzuki*. The minesweeper *Okinoshima* was certainly damaged. The second group, VT5 sank the minesweeper *Tama Maru* and two patrol ships.

the *Yorktown* were observed to turn away when engaged by one 1.1in. mount and four 20mm. guns. Both planes departed smoking. Two other planes, retiring on a course opposite to that of the cruiser at an altitude of 4,000ft, were fired on by one 5in. battery but escaped.
(*Naval Intelligence Combat Reports*)

The combat reports from the *Hamman* report that two aircraft were shot down during the action. The *Chester* reported three and the *Russell* two definites. So the anti-aircraft fire may have accounted for seven enemy planes, apart from those damaged by the *Yorktown* herself. The reports themselves indicate a degree of doubt. In terms of the *Lexington* group the *Minneapolis* claimed three shot down whilst the *New Orleans* did not claim any because she was about 4,300yds away from the *Lexington* and therefore was firing at extreme range. Capt. Good of the *New Orleans* stated "That the 5-inch guns were entirely too slow in train and elevation to effectively keep on fast moving dive-bombers or gliding torpedo planes," and that "the need for remote control of 1.1in. and 20mm. mounts is more apparent than ever." The only casualty aboard the *New Orleans* occurred among the crew of 1.1in. mount on the fantail, which was continuously wet from spray and occasional green seas. At one point, this gun was completely submerged, and the crew narrowly escaped being washed overboard. During the course of this one man received a broken nose. The Americans may have thought that their fire was not good enough but to the Japanese it was terrifying, as Capt. Shigekazu Shimazaki said after the battle, "We encountered a veritable wall of anti-aircraft fire. The aircraft carriers and their escorts darkened the sky with their tracer bullets, shells and shrapnel. It seemed impossible that we could survive such a stream of anti-aircraft gunfire."

Of the destroyers, the *Phelps* claimed one aircraft, the *Dewey* three and the *Morris* two, although it is entirely possible that claims were made from multiple ships for the same aircraft. Totaling these claims gives a figure of 13 aircraft shot down by anti-aircraft fire out of a total of 43 lost that, 33 of which to enemy fire.

The fighters that were involved in the combat over the *Lexington* were really involved in several complex and convoluted air combats that were typical of this battle but require to much explanation to go into detail here. Nevertheless, a brief summary will be attempted. Initially after the dive-bombing attack of Takahashi there were several dogfights between the defending Wildcats and Dauntlesses and the Zeros supporting the Japanese attack. The Americans had their Combat Air

USS *Lexington* from *Yorktown*, whose SBDs and F4Fs are preparing to take off. This photograph was taken early on the 8th.

Repulse of the Japanese air attack on Admiral Crace's Task Force 44 on May 7. The aircraft are "Nell" bombers (Mitsubishi G3Ms) from Rabaul (see pages 50–51)—the same type of aircraft that sank HMS *Repulse* and *Renown* on December 10, 1941. Task Force 44 is proceeding in a lozenge formation: 1. destroyer USS *Perkins*; 2. destroyer USS *Farragut*; 3. cruiser RAN *Australia;* 4. destroyer USS *Walke*; 5. cruiser RAN *Hobart*; 6. cruiser USS *Chicago*.

The torpedo attack on TF17, 1118–1121hrs, May 8, by Nakajima B5M Kates carrying torpedoes. During the attack *Lexington*'s port side is hit twice (note torpedo runs at lower level).

1. DD-349 USS *Dewey*.
2. DD-417 USS *Morris*.
3. CA-36 USS *Minneapolis*.
4. CV-2 *Lexington*.
5. CA-32 USS *New Orleans*.
6. DD-411 USS *Anderson*.
7. DD-360 USS *Phelps*.
8. CA-27 USS *Chester*.
9. DD-355 USS *Aylwin*.
10. CA-34 USS *Astoria* .
11. CV-5 *Yorktown*.
12. DD-414 USS *Russell*.
13. CA-33 USS *Portland*.
14. DD-412 USS *Hammann*.

Patrol in place and had an anti-torpedo plane patrol prepared for that eventuality. The Americans then set upon the returning bombers and fighters. These combats ranged from low-level attacks to the north of the task force to encounters at medium and high altitudes as well. This included aircraft from the fighter groups and a large number (probably as many as 15) of the bombers from the *Lexington*. Because the sky was thick with fighters and bombers it was obviously difficult to tell friend from foe and unfortunate pilots such as Lt. R Hale, who tried to land back on board the *Lexington* after he had been shot up by the Japanese, were lost to friendly fire. American gunners attacked his aircraft when he tried to land and the crew was killed. The aerial combat was vicious and confused, and it is incredible that the Dauntless pilots attempted to engage the Zeros from the *Shokaku* on equal terms. Hata and Izawa claim that Lt. Hoashi and nine fighters shot down 30 aircraft.

The *Zuikaku* group of fighters under Lt. Yuzo was also taking on the Americans under Lt. Cmdr. J. H. Flatley. There were four Americans and nine (some historians say ten) Japanese and at this point it seems that Flatley was flying at about 10,000ft. His division was at the rear of the Task Force and was apparently unoccupied. This is interesting as it highlights the fact that the fighter direction officer was overwhelmed by the amount of activity in the area and therefore on the radar. This would explain the difficulty found by the air controllers, whose screens were full of contacts not all of who could be identified. Not all the American aircraft had some form of IFF (Identification Friend or Foe) equipment and therefore in the middle of a fast moving battle such as this it would be almost impossible to tell which side they were on.

LEFT AND BELOW: *Lexington* and her destroyer escorts during the battle.

BELOW LEFT: Toward dusk on May 8 Lexington's crew abandons ship. In the smoke on port side a destroyer helps to take off the crew. At 1800hrs USS *Phelps* torpedoed the wreck and *Lexington* sank. Just over 200 men died during the fight, but 2,735 officers and men were saved.

MAIN PHOTO: ***Lexington*** **enduring a dive-bomber attack around noon, May 8.**

OPPOSITE, ABOVE: AA fire downed this attacker, but ...

OPPOSITE, BELOW: ... another takes its place. ***Lexington*** **was attacked by nearly 70 aircraft from** ***Shokaku*** **and** ***Zuikaku*** **on May 8.**

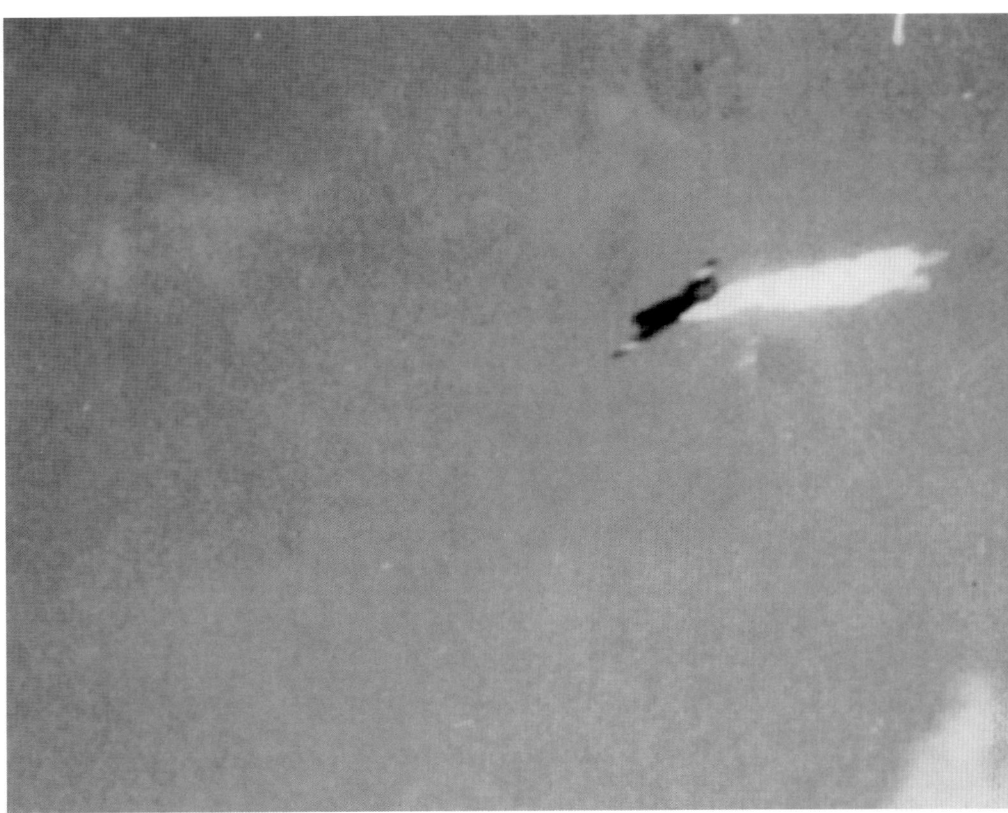

ABOVE: The flightdeck of USS *Lexington* at 1500hrs on May 8. Fires burning below decks cause the smoke to rise. At the front are F4F.3 Wildcats; further back SBD Scout bombers and TBD.1 torpedo bombers.

LEFT: *Lexington*'s anti-aircraft gunners did their best but still could not stop torpedo and bomb hits.

OPPOSITE, ABOVE: Japanese aircraft in the sky above *Lexington*.

OPPOSITE, BELOW: *Lexington* lists and burns after the attack.

Aftermath

The Japanese did not invade Port Moresby, Inoue delayed the advance through the Jomard Passage for a further 48 hours, by which time the main battle had taken place. The *Shokaku* was ordered back to Truk in the Caroline Islands for repairs. In fact she had been severely damaged by American attacks and it was not until she was halfway home and many of her plates began to loosen that the crew began to realize the serious extent of the damage. In the event it would take far longer to repair her than any one had foreseen. Takagi was ordered to return to Truk on May 8 and Operation MO was again postponed until July 3. This decision did not remain in place very long as soon as Adm. Yamamoto got to hear of it and ordered the ships to change course. He countermanded Inoue's order and Takagi was sent south again to look for the elusive Allies. By this time Crace's force had long departed southward. Takagi's force carried out the order at 0200hrs on May 9 and began to zigzag in search of the Allies. They were joined by Goto's force the following day. It was all in vain and no sign of Allied shipping could be found. Yamamoto must have realized the moment had passed as he confirmed a further order of May 11 seeking a general withdrawal and the striking force once again headed back to Truk. Inoue had been particularly concerned when the Tulagi group was attacked on May 10 by the American submarine *S42* and Shiwa's ship, the *Okinoshima*, was sunk. Inoue immediately cancelled operations until it could be proved that U.S. submarines were not a significant threat. The final straw came with the arrival of the *Enterprise* and *Hornet* after Nimitz sent them to the area. They were spotted by the Japanese east of the Solomon Islands and added a new and powerful dimension to the American naval force in the region. On top of the submarine attack the Japanese sought to withdraw to their bases.

What of the Americans? On May 11 they had already decided to split into two groups: the cruisers headed for Nouméa on New Caledonia while the *Yorktown* and her escort headed for Tongatabu in the Tonga Islands for replenishment and repairs. The trials and tribulations of the crew of the *Neosho* as she tried to stay afloat were horrendous. She did not sink after her attack but her rudder was jammed and she was unable to steer and so drifted on the sea currents. For four or so days the hundred odd men on board had put out her fires and hoped that search planes sent out to look for them would detect them.

In fact search planes had been sent out but eventually it was the destroyer *Henley* that was specifically ordered to find the tanker by Admiral Leary. On May 11 a Catalina flying boat did spot the ship and directed the destroyer onto her. After removing the crew the ship was torpedoed and the search continued until May 12 for other survivors. No more were found and the ship left the area and sailed to Brisbane, Australia. Unfortunately they had missed survivors through looking in the wrong place. On May 14 the destroyer *Helm* discovered four men in one of *Neosho*'s rafts that had been on the open ocean for seven days. The two extra carriers, the *Enterprise* and the *Hornet*, that Nimitz had sent to the Coral Sea arrived were recalled immediately to take part in the Battle of Midway.

Above Right: Following the Battle of the Coral Sea, the British supply ship *Merkur*, with destroyers, cruisers and auxiliary vessels, enters Nouméa Harbor, New Caledonia.

Right: An SBD takes off from *Enterprise*, May 12. Note the F4F "dud" with folded wings at left.

Left and Far Left: ***Kikuzuki*, a Mutsuki-class destroyer, was sunk by aircraft from *Yorktown* on May 4 during the Japanese assault on Tulagi. Later in the war, during mid-1943, the *Kikuzuki* was salvaged by the U.S. Navy for intelligence purposes. Subsequently she was moved to Purvis Bay where she remains to this day.**

Below: ***Yorktown* returns to Pearl Harbor after the battle. Amazingly, the refit she is about to undergo (she will enter drydock on May 27) will take place quickly enough—within three days—to allow CV-5 to be able to take part in the battle of Midway on June 4–5. This helped even the odds, as otherwise only *Hornet* and *Enterprise* would have had to face *Akagi*, *Hiryu*, *Kaga* and *Soryu*. *Yorktown* would not survive Midway, but the battle would be won.**

These photographs show USS *Lexington* burning, survivors gathering on the flightdeck, and clambering aboard a rescuing destroyer on May 8. The name Lexington did not die with CV-2. Essex-class carrier CV-16 USS *Cabot* was renamed *Lexington* and went on to survive a torpedoing off Kwajalein in December 1943 and a kamikaze attack in 1944.

Analysis

Historians love to get into the technical minutiae about the differences between equipment and the relative benefits and disadvantages derived from it. In a battle such as this where neither side had any previous experience it can be particulary relevant. Though time and again it is clear that the morale and experience of individual sailors and airmen can be critical to the outcome of a battle. At the Battle of the Coral Sea the Americans had the advantage of radar and the identification friend-or-foe device (or Zed Baker homing unit), whilst the Japanese had a greater proportion of fighters and bombers. The Japanese also had more battle experience and their morale was high. But the Americans appeared to have learned quickly from their mistakes and were more flexible. The Japanese worked to very complicated and intricate plans and once the Americans did not do what was expected of them they were nonplussed, whereas the Americans were more able to adapt and respond to the changing situation. The old maxim that any military plan only survives until first contact with the enemy is absolutely true. The main offensive weapon of both sides in this battle was the aircraft. We have already seen that Japanese fighters were more maneuverable and faster and that their dive-bombers were of higher quality. Yet the Japanese fighter pilots did not decimate the Americans, as one would expect considering the supposed inferiority of their aircraft. It has to be said that American aircraft were robust and reliable and could take a great deal of punishment, a decided factor in their sustainability during this battle. The Japanese aircraft also appeared too vulnerable to direct hits from anti-aircraft fire.

There are a number of key moments that deserve analysis here:

Did Admiral Hara's lack of fighter cover for the dusk attack on the May 7 reduce his fighting capacity? The failure of Admiral Hara to provide fighter cover for his aircraft on the dusk attack of May 7 meant that he wasted an opportunity to destroy American carriers when with fighter cover it may well have been possible. The loss of nine planes may not seem like much out of the possible number available but each time a failure like this occurred the numbers were whittled down, not to mention the vast quantities of fuel and ammunition wasted and this attack does come across as something of a gamble. However, both sides could be accused of gambling and the attack on the *Shoho* and the attacks on the *Neosho* and *Sims* were both wasted efforts when one considers what the ultimate prize could have been.

The confusion between Fitch and Fletcher when refueling between May 1 and 4 has been pointed out as a mistake that cost the Americans the element of surprise. Both Fletcher and Fitch have been accused of not keeping communication channels open during the refueling session on May 4. Fitch took much longer than Fletcher and the Americans lost a day because Fletcher thought Fitch was refueling when in fact he had finished on the 3 May. This had a direct effect on Fletcher's response to the attack on Tulagi forcing him to use the *Yorktown* independently. Had he had the support of the *Lexington* as well and waited for the opportune moment then it may well have been that the surprise experienced by the Japanese at the Tulagi attack would have been replicated by the whole Japanese Fleet.

The lack of air cover for the *Lexington* on May 8 and the poor fighter direction has also been considered as an American failing and there were vocal minority who blamed

LEFT: Japanese aircrew losses at the battles of the Coral Sea and Midway deprived them of some of their most experienced aviators. Losses that were to haunt the Imperial Japanese Navy for the remainder of the war.

it for the loss of the ship. In the report produced by U.S. Naval Intelligence on the battle much is made of the fighter direction during May 8 and Fighter Direction Officer is roundly criticized for not having planned for such an eventuality and allowing the event to happen. As has been seen the planes were low on fuel and that was one of the reasons why the Combat Air Patrol could not be vectored out to the attacking Japanese bombers—they were forced to stay near their mother ship.

This was a battle that was entirely new. Commanders can be forgiven for reacting in any way. The benefit of hindsight shows us that mistakes were made but in reality this takes in little account of the stress that commanders were under, failures in communication and the general fog of war. Tactically the Japanese destroyed a large American carrier and damaged another one. This did not actually affect the ability of the United States to wage naval war, so strategically they could live with the outcome. The Japanese lost an escort carrier and many aircraft. More importantly they lost many experienced pilots and sailors. The more their elite formations were broken up or diluted, the easier it became for the U.S. forces to grind them down.

Many commentators identify this battle as inconclusive. It is the opinion of this author that it was not so. The Japanese losses—of ships and, more importantly, experienced men—and the experience and expertise gained by the U.S. forces, provided, I believe, the first major United States' victory of the Pacific War.

Summary of Japanese losses

Ships sunk	Date
1 carrier—*Shoho*	May 7
1 light cruiser	May 7
2 destroyers	May 4
1 cargo ship or transport	May 4
4 gunboats	May 4
Ships damaged	**Date**
1 carrier—*Shokaku*	May 8
1 aircraft tender	May 4
Aircraft destroyed	**Date**
33 fighters	May 7 and 8
3 four-engined patrol bombers	May 5, 7, and 8
5 floatplanes	May 4
16 dive-bombers	May 7 and 8
17 torpedo planes	May 7 and 8
30 planes aboard *Shoho*	

Summary of U.S. losses

Ships sunk	Date
1 carrier—*Lexington*	May 8
1 oiler—*Neosho*	May 7
1 destroyer—*Sims*	May 7
Ships damaged:	**Date**
1 carrier—*Yorktown*	May 8
Aircraft destroyed:	**Date**
15 *Lexington* planes in combat	May 7 and 8
35 *Lexington* planes with ship	May 8
16 *Yorktown* planes in combat	May 4, 7, and 8

Personnel losses were estimated at 543; the enemy's at anywhere from 2,000 to 5,000.

References

Bibliography

Books

Belote, James H., and Belote, William M., *Titans of the Seas: The Development and Operations of Japanese and American Carrier Task Forces During World War II.* New York: Harper & Row, 1975.
A useful description of the design, deployment and operational history of carrier task forces, one of the most important naval developments of World War II.

Coffey, Thomas M., *Imperial Tragedy: Japan in World War II, the First Days and the Last.* New York: World Pub. Co. 1970.
As the title suggests, this book concentrates on the very early events of the war, predominately Pearl Harbor, and the final days. It is particularly good on the Japanese perspective.

Costello, John, *The Pacific War.* New York: Rawson, Wade, 1981.
A very good single-volume history of the entire war in the Pacific.

Cressman, Robert, *That Gallant Ship: USS Yorktown (CV-5).* Missoula, Mont.: Pictorial Histories Pub. Co. 1985.
Covers the history of the *Yorktown* through the early battles of the Pacific War to her demise at the Battle of Midway.

Dull, Paul S., *A Battle History of The Imperial Japanese Navy 1941–1945.* Annapolis: Naval Institute Press, 1978.
An interesting book composed with the use of previously unknown Japanese documents.

Dunnigan, J. F., and Nofi, A. A., *Victory at Sea, World War Two in the Pacific.* New York: William Morrow and Co., 1995.
This book has so much information on all aspects of

the war in the Pacific that it is difficult to be objective about it. Many of the facts and figures used to illustrate logistic requirements and supplies come from here and I would recommend it to anyone who requires a complete overview of the war backed up by significant data.

Hata, Ikuhiko, and Izawa, Yasuho, *Japanese Naval Aces and Fighter Units in World War II*. Annapolis: Naval Institute Press, 1989.
An insight into the stories of Japanese aviators and their units. The claims of kills are somewhat exaggerated but this book represents a very welcome Japanese point of view and is full of interesting insights into the Japanese naval air arm.

Howarth, Stephen, *Morning Glory, A History of The Imperial Japanese Navy*. London: Hamish Hamilton, 1983.
A general history of the Imperial Japanese Navy from its inception to its defeat.

Johnson, Stanley, *Queen of the Flat Tops—The USS Lexington and the Coral Sea Battle*. New York: Doubleday, 1979.
Contains many quotations from the men who were there and newspaper reports that were written at the time.

Lindley, John M. *Carrier Victory: The Air War in the Pacific*. New York: Dutton, 1951.
A Well illustrated, though somewhat dated, account of World War II in the Pacific.

Lundstrom, John B. *The First South Pacific Campaign: Pacific Fleet Strategy, December 1941–June 1942*. Annapolis: Naval Institute Press, 1976
Covers the early campaigns of the war from January 42–June 1942. it is particularly good on strategy.

Lundstrom, John B. *The first team. Pacific naval air combat from Pearl Harbor to Midway*. Annapolis: Naval Institute Press, 1976.
An excellent, detailed view of American naval aviation exploits in the Pacific. The detail is astounding and although it concentrates mainly on the aircraft it gives a brilliant insight into the way in which aircraft were handled during the early phases of the conflict. Just about the best combat reference of American naval aircraft activities in the early part of the war.

Millot, Bernard, *The Battle of the Coral Sea*. Sea Battles in Close Up, No. 12. Annapolis: Naval Institute Press, 1974.
A comprehensive account of the battle with the emphasis on the air encounters.

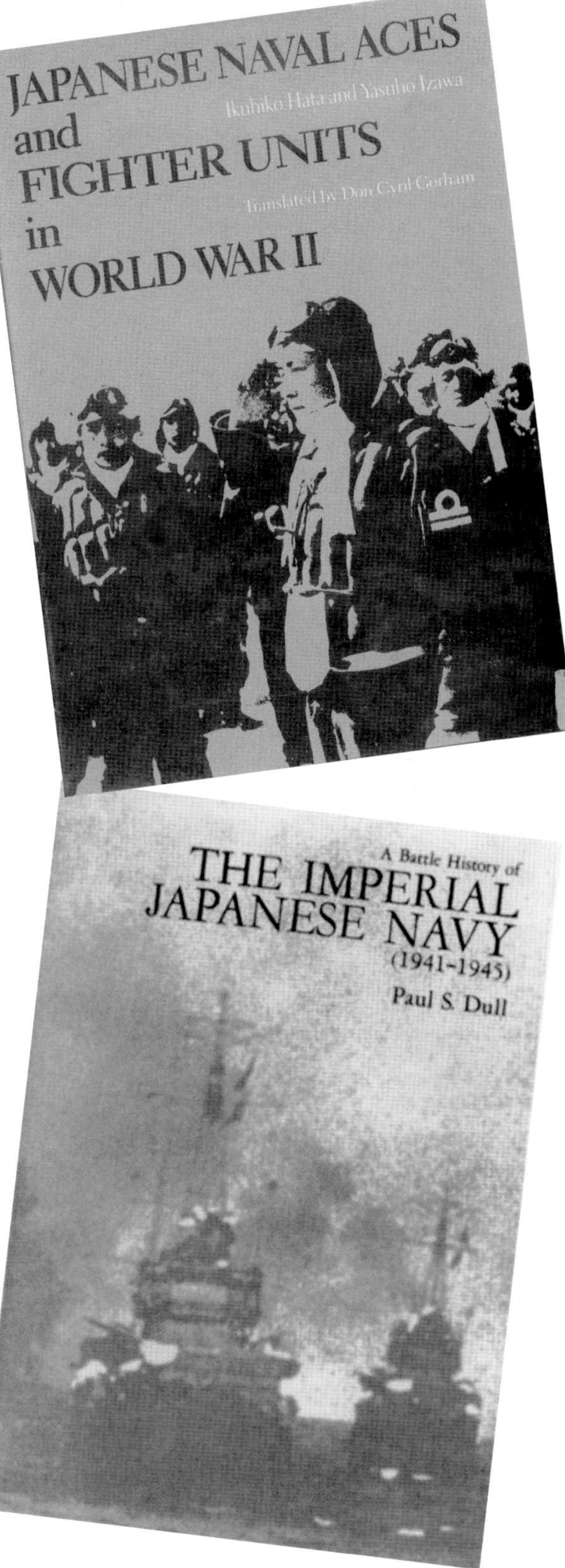

Morison, Samuel, *History of United States Naval Operations in World War II.* Boston: Little Brown and Co., 1947–62.
XV volumes.
The official history of the U.S. Navy and very readable. A starting point for those interested in the Pacific War.

Naval Intelligence Combat Reports. Navy Department, Office of Naval Intelligence: Washington, D.C. 1943.
Probably the best primary source of information with detailed comments of officers and ratings during the battle. It was written in 1943 after all the information had been assimilated and not only gives comments but also analysis of the shortcomings of the U.S. Navy. If there were a Japanese version of this document it would make interesting reading.

Smith, Peter C., *Impact! The Dive Bomber Pilots speak.* New York: William Kimber and Co., 1981.
This general title covers the dive-bomber pilots from all the combatant countries of World War II and has some very good first-hand accounts of the Pacific War.

Spector, Ronald H., *Eagle against the Sun.* New York: Free Press, 1984.
Spector's gargantuan work on the Japanese American war has covered all aspects of the political and military spectrum.

Tillman, Barret, *The Dauntless dive-bomber of WW2.* Annapolis: Naval Institute Press, 1976.
A very good analysis of this aircraft with insight into how it was used and all its variants.

The Battle of the Coral Sea Conference Proceedings 1992. Australian National Maritime Museum.
A rare and unusual perspective from several contributors but especially the Japanese contribution, which gives an interesting military perspective as to why the Japanese may have thought the Coral Sea was a failure.

The Japanese Navy in World War II. With an introduction and commentary by Raymond G. O'Connor. Annapolis: U.S. Naval Institute, 1969.
An anthology of articles by former officers of the Imperial Japanese Navy and Air Defense Force, originally published in the U.S. Naval Institute *Proceedings.*

Van der Vat, Dan. *The Pacific Campaign: World War II, the U.S.–Japanese Naval War, 1941–1945.* New York: Simon & Schuster, 1991.
Although limited by being only 400 pages long this is a good single-volume account of the war in the Pacific and a useful starting point.

Magazines

Warship Journal

This long-established journal contains many excellent articles on the navies of both sides. Of particular interest are:

Itani, Jiro, Legerer, Hans, and Takahara, Tomoko Rehm, "Anti-aircraft Gunnery in the Imperial Japanese Navy"

Friedman, Norman, "The 5-inch 38-calibre gun"

Websites

There are many websites relating to the Battle of the Coral Sea but they are often general or concentrate on the whole Pacific War. The Naval Historical Center, http://www.history.navy.mil/index.html, is probably the best and is more of an online museum giving accounts, photographs and biographies with the facility to contact them if further information is required. The following are also of interest:

http://navalhistory.flixco.info/—A naval history of World War II, with detailed coverage of ships, weapons and technical data.

http://www.bluejackets.com—A great site dedicated to the U.S. Navy with all sorts of information from technical descriptions to people.

http://www.combinedfleet.com—Has a really good section on the Japanese Navy although some parts are incomplete. It also has some very nice images of IJN ships.

http://home.vicnet.net.au/~gcasey/welcome.html—Coral Sea references from the point of view of Gavan Casey, including some good references for Australian ships and some firsthand accounts.

http://www.gunplot.net—Another Australian site with its own unique perspective.

http://www.warship.get.net.pl/—A more general Polish site dealing with warship history. It has excellent sections dealing with the vessels used in the Pacific War.

INDEX